Education and Justice

A VIEW FROM THE BACK OF THE BUS

Education and Justice

A VIEW FROM THE BACK OF THE BUS

EDMUND W. GORDON

FOREWORD BY LINDA-DARLING HAMMOND

Teachers College, Columbia University
New York and London

For Johanna S., Jessica G., Christopher W., Edmund T., and Susan G. Gordon.

Published by Teachers College Press, 1234 Amsterdam Avenue, New York, NY 10027

Library of Congress Cataloging-in-Publication Data

Gordon, Edmund W.
  Education and justice : a view from the back of the bus / Edmund W. Gordon.
    p.   cm.
  Includes bibliographical references (p.) and index.
    ISBN 0-8077-3845-X (cloth.)—ISBN 0-8077-3844-1 (paper)   1. Educational equalization—United States.   2. Social justice—United States.   3. Socially handicapped—Education—United States.   4. Minorities—Education—United States.   5. Multicultural education—United States.   6. Critical pedagogy—United States.   I. Title.
  LC213.2G65   1999
  379.2'6'0973—dc21   98-52531

ISBN 0-8077-3844-1 (paper)
ISBN 0-8077-3845-X (cloth)

Printed on acid-free paper
Manufactured in the United States of America

06   05   04   03   02   01   00   99   8   7   6   5   4   3   2   1

Contents

Foreword

Edmund Gordon is one of the few people alive who could bring together—with passion and precision—such wide-ranging concerns as the
nature of teaching and learning; the social and educational determinants
of academic achievement; the influences of culture and context on both
learning and achievement; and the problems and possibilities of performance testing and other educational reforms to illuminate the educational demands posed by a quest for social justice in a democratic society.
With the scope of a Dewey or a DuBois, Gordon marshals evidence from
cognitive and developmental psychology, anthropology, sociology, and
educational research to illustrate how schools can educate all children
well and to explain clearly and compellingly why it is increasingly important that they learn to do so.

Most academics are both informed and limited by the disciplines in
which they have been trained; it is sometimes said that when one has a
well-developed hammer, every problem looks like a nail. This characteristic of much social science often makes it difficult for us to approach
complex problems in productive ways that take into account the many
sources of overdetermined situations and the many dimensions that require attention for their solution. The cultural contexts in which we learn
and develop can also tend to limit our understanding of other perspectives and our visions of the possible, resulting in the "communicentric
bias" Gordon describes as constraining knowledge. Ed Gordon crosses
these disciplinary and cultural boundaries in ways that make seemingly
intractable problems understandable, and that provide new insights into
issues that have generally been the source of much heat but little light.
In his extensive corpus of work, Gordon has used the tools of psychology
to probe deeply into the nature of learning—and the ways in which it is
influenced by culture, dispositions, social and school settings, and individual attributes. But he does not stop there. He also explores research
on how social contexts influence learning and behavior; how these con-

texts are differentially constructed within various communities and school organizations; how income, opportunities, and beliefs shape what is perceived and what is learned; and how teaching makes a difference to learning and achievement. With an easy command of research methodology that is matched by a capacity to integrate and communicate, Gordon makes sense of ideas that are often posed as simplistic dichotomies: nature and nurture as determinants of ability, rigor and relevance as determinants of curriculum, content and processes as foundations for instruction.

This deep, integrative understanding of learning, teaching, and schooling is particularly important in transforming the contentious and often ill-informed dialogue about race and education in U.S. society. With a quiet mastery of facts and methods, Gordon debunks the myths of inferiority resuscitated in *The Bell Curve*'s arguments and cogently describes what does in fact matter for learning—and what can in fact be done to ensure academic success for students of color as well as those traditionally better served by American schools. In the process we are treated to an elegant discussion of the rationale for and means of attaining education that is strengthened by teacher professionalism tied to deeper knowledge of learners, learning, and teaching; greater personalization within redesigned school organizations that can care for individual learners; pedagogies and performance assessments that take account of diversity in learning approaches and experiential contexts; and considerations of culture as essential to learning—as the life's breath of all human endeavor—rather than at odds with it.

The importance of understanding the learner's frame of reference as a means for constructing productive forms of education is a central theme in this book, inspired of both a scholar's respect for knowledge from cognitive research and a humanist's respect for the importance of each individual's path to understanding. The path of understanding that Gordon constructs for the reader is made compelling by his respect for the knowledge of others—the understandings that young children bring with them to all of their encounters with the world as much as those of the research community that provides his professional foundation and the basis for the arguments he carefully pursues. His deep concern for developing understanding as the primary goal of education is equally rooted in cognitive psychology and political theory—and nurtured by a passion for democracy and justice. "Liberation," he asserts, "is a value worthy of science." To the benefit of all of us, this important work advances both.

Linda Darling-Hammond

INTRODUCTION

Education and Social Justice

Education is, perhaps, the quintessential human enterprise. Unlike other forms of animal life that train their younger members to recognize signs and signals and to execute the techniques by which they adapt to environments and communicate with each other, human beings educate each other. That is, we teach each other to learn how to learn. Of even greater importance, we teach each other how to think—how to use signs and symbols; how to develop and use techniques and technologies; how to generate and apply concepts, numbers, and information in other forms to address problems and situations that are real, as well as those that are abstract, even those that are only imagined. Human beings, as animals capable of transforming conceptual as well as material phenomena, use education deliberately to enable the development of human intellective competence—the developed ability and disposition to use knowledge, technique, and mental processes to engage and solve quotidian as well as novel problems, adaptively and efficiently. Humans do, of course, use training to transfer knowledge and skill from more experienced learners to novice learners. However, what is unique to education as a human developmental enterprise is the intentional involvement of learners in such intellectual processes as:

1. Engagement in the discovery of phenomena and the real and imagined relationships between them;
2. Engagement in the recognition and generation of the meanings of things, that is, making sense of one's experiences and the experiences of others;
3. Engagement in the construction of knowledge, and in its critical understanding and appreciation;
4. Engagement in the adaptation, application, and internalization of knowledge, values, and techniques.

Education so conceived—unlike training, which is done for and to others—is a process in which persons are enabled to engage. In its essence, it is a process learners must experience for themselves. We who teach can only guide and mediate those experiences.

Education, then, is both a social and a very personal process. To the extent that it is initiated, guided, and mediated by others, the process is necessarily social. To the extent that education cannot be fully experienced without the complicity and engagement of the learner, it is a very personal phenomenon. If the process is one that requires social interaction and engagement by teaching and learning persons, then the social context must be one that enables and supports such human transactions. Thus the reciprocal social and personal nature of the process makes the social context in which pedagogy is experienced potentially as important to the achievement of the purposes of education as are the processes of the teaching and learning transactions.

There may be some educational context/process relationships that are so symbiotic as to defy separation. It appears that education and social justice are so symbiotically related. In modern societies the achievement of universally effective education may not be possible in the absence of contexts in which social justice is valued and practiced. Similarly, the achievement of social justice may not be possible in the absence of the achievement of universally effective education.

The failure to achieve universally effective education in our society is known to be a correlate of our failure to achieve social justice. By almost any measure, there continue to be serious differences between the level and quality of educational achievement for children coming from rich or from poor families and from ethnic-majority or from some ethnic-minority group families. Low-status ethnic-minority groups continue to be overrepresented in the low achievement groups in our schools and are correspondingly underrepresented in high academic achievement groups. Most disturbing is the fact that non-Asian minority-group students from middle-class families are grossly underrepresented, in proportion to the number of such students, in the high-achievement student pool. This suggests that poor academic achievement among low-status groups may be a castelike phenomenon—relatively independent of family income and class status. If you are Black, high income and social position may not lift your children as high in achievement as similar status does for White children. The sometimes camouflaged absence of social justice is evidenced by differentials in such intergenerational influences on development as conditions of life, income and especially wealth, participation in the political and social intercourse of the society, quality of the institutions to which members have access, quality of health and health care, sustained employment that is capable of supporting one's family, and sense of belonging to—membership in—the social order.

We have tended to think of social justice as a value that we are morally committed to pursue for the underprivileged, for ethnic minorities, or for any low-status group. However, in this book, I argue that the absence of justice is more than a moral problem. It is a plague on the houses of all of us. It is incompatible with the purposes of education. It is a threat to the economic and political stability of the society. With respect to education, I argue that full engagement in the pedagogical process and optimal educational outcomes are impossible without it. I assert that once the issue of human diversity is permitted to enter the calculus of human affairs (and it must), the question of social justice becomes critical. I argue that education, then, is emerging as a unique and essential human endeavor; that concern for social justice is a necessary condition for education; and that our nation cannot continue to function as a democracy in the absence of social justice. Toward the end of this book, I argue further that social justice is a necessary condition for the production of the knowledge and understanding by which pedagogical theory, policy, and practice are informed.

Several issues concerning the relationship between education and social justice lend support to the positions advanced above. We begin with the moral and philosophical issues related to the construct of social justice. In *A Theory of Justice*, Rawls (1971) has developed a conceptual framework for the examination and explication of a system of justice in which a concern for fairness as an expression of equitable treatment is a central feature. His effort at explication of such a theory rests on two principles of justice. The first is:

> Each person is to have an equal right to the most extensive total system of equal basic liberties compatible with a similar system of liberty for all. (p. 302)

His second principle holds that

> social and economic inequalities are to be arranged so that they both (a) are to the greatest benefit to the least advantaged, consistent with the just savings principle [reasonable reserve for future generations], and (b) attached to offices and positions open to all under conditions of fair equality and opportunity. (p. 302)

Rawls's principles rest on the dual notions that justice requires not only equality in the treatment of all members of the society but also the protection of the least advantaged members of the society. It is the concern for equal treatment that has dominated much of our nation's efforts toward the achievement of democracy. Through constitutional provisions, court decisions, legislative actions, and administrative mandates we have affirmed the nation's official commitment to equal access and equal justice. Although we recognize that these goals have not been achieved, and debate continues as to how best to achieve them, there is almost no open debate as to the validity of the commitment to equality as opposed to equity as a national value. Most of us seem to agree that *equality* requires sameness, but *equity* requires that treatments be appropriate *and* sufficient to the characteristics and needs of those treated. In the pursuit of a just society, our nation has tended to hold equal treatment as its criterion. Yet for educational equity to be served, treatment must be specific to one's functional characteristics and sufficient to the realities of one's condition. To address the problems of appropriateness and sufficiency, we seek to go beyond the status labels that apply to individuals and groups and examine their functional characteristics, which, in concert with their status, may facilitate or interfere with the success of their school experience. Rawls's concern for the protection of the least favored has not gained wide acceptance as a guiding principle of justice in our society, yet it may be that with respect to equalizing educational opportunity, it is the sensitive protection of those least advantaged by its context and processes that may be at the heart of this problem of social justice.

Foundational to concern with justice and pedagogy is a concern for the human resource capital available to the society and its members for investment in education (see Bourdieu, 1986; Coleman & Hoffer, 1987; Miller, 1995). While such resource capital is in good supply in the United States, there are critical problems in the distribution of these resources and access to them by most low-status persons. In the absence of access to essential human resource capital, there well may be limits to what any within-school educational reform can achieve. Among the varieties of human resource capital that form the basis for teaching and learning one must consider:

- *Health capital*—physical developmental integrity, health, and nutritional condition
- *Financial capital*—income and wealth, family, community and societal economic resources available for education
- *Human capital*—social competence, tacit knowledge and other education-derived abilities as personal or family assets
- *Social capital*—social-network relationships, social norms, cultural styles and values
- *Polity capital*—societal membership, social concern, public commitment, political economy

- *Personal capital*—disposition, attitudes, aspirations, efficacy, sense of power
- *Institutional capital*—quality of and access to educating and socializing institutions
- *Pedagogical capital*—supports for appropriate educational treatment in family, school, and community

In addition to the issues related to the critical role played by human resource capital in both education and social justice, other issues addressed in this book as instrumental to the achievement of the ends of education and social justice are fourfold.

First, with regard to the political economy of education, I address the many ways in which economics and politics intersect to influence access to, quality of, and progress in education. This dimension of the problem, often addressed in my work, is consistently neglected by most scholars of education. Bowles and Gintis (1976), Pliven and Cloward (1993), and Sexton (1964) are notable exceptions. Yet the correlations between educational achievement on the one hand and income, wealth, and power on the other are common knowledge among members of the education profession.

Second, I assert that the issues of class, culture, ethnicity, gender, and other social divisions to which students are assigned make attention to the social psychology of teaching and learning an important source of pedagogical influence. As important as is the need for improvements in the technical aspects of pedagogy, it may be the attitudes toward some students as "others" or as different that is most problematic. Throughout this book attention is called to the processual and relational dimensions of pedagogical practice and children's development.

Third, as we struggle to play catch-up in the education of low-status persons, the rest of the world is racing forward with rapid change. The contexts for and the processes of education are changing. Increasingly, we recognize the critical role that academic achievement plays in one's life chances. The processes of education are shifting emphasis from content transfer and mastery to the use of academic content to foster the development of intellective competence. As epistemologies change and become more fluid, the processes of education are becoming more accommodative and generative. The children that I worry about most could be left behind by these changing contexts and epistemologies, if their education is too much informed by old conceptions of compensatory and remedial education.

Finally, the comprehensive conjoining of education and social justice may require a broader and more integrated knowledge base than is typically encircled in support of education. Fortunately, in recent years the relevance for pedagogy of several of the behavioral and social sciences has become more obvious. In my own efforts at understanding the relationship of cultural differences to education, I have begun to try to make more explicit notions and postulates from these disciplines that seem to have something to say that is of importance to education. I refer to these as the sciences of pedagogical praxis. This book ends with a discussion of culture and the sciences of pedagogy as a new and changing knowledge base on which to continue the struggle to improve the pursuit of education and social justice.

Collected here to form this book are 11 essays, written over a period of several years, all of which reflect my lifetime commitment to efforts at improving the effectiveness of education and advancing the practice of democracy. The chapters may be read as autonomous essays but are best understood as the reflections on education and social justice of a humanist, psychologist, and educator. In Part I, I seek to pose the problems of diversity, equity, and educational excellence within their sociopolitical contexts. The title for Part I reflects the perspective of an African American who has spent most of his life in racially integrated sections of the society, but who has never completely lost the sense that he is representing those who have been relegated to the back of the bus. One's position does not change the issues as much as it changes the perspective. In Part II, I try to engage these problems from the perspective of their collective challenges and our approaches to meeting those challenges through (1) more adaptive approaches to teaching and learning; (2) more ecological sensitive approaches to behavior change; and (3) more equitable systems of educational assessment. Part III reflects my continuing concern with the state of the knowledge base for pedagogy and its professional practice. The chapters in Part III give special attention to culture and the problems posed by cultural hegemony. As is true of so much of my experience at representing the interests of low-status persons in education, although some of these interests are specialized, most speak to the generic problems of education and democracy. Low-status persons may need more able and dedicated teachers, but all people need able and committed teachers. Children with special needs may need more adaptive curriculums and teaching strategies, but the diversity in the broad range of characteristics that we find in the general population demands adaptability, diversity, and plurality in the available opportunities to learn.

In the writing of many of these chapters I have been assisted by my students. Where their contributions have been substantial, I have listed them as second authors. In the adaptation of these essays for publication in this volume I have been assisted by Maitrayee Bhattacharyya, Leah

Cohen, Christine Juhl, Aundra Saa Meroë, and Nkechi Obiora. All of my intellectual work reflects the influence of my wife, Dr. Susan G. Gordon, who is the cogenitor, not only of our children, but also of so many of our ideas. The many others who have contributed to this work will go un-named but are not without my sincere thanks. One does not live an effective life without the help of others.

EWG
Pomona, New York

PART I

A View from the Back of the Bus

As an African American, one of the problems I experienced while coming to prominence as a scholar during the early years of the 1960s civil rights movement was that of confusion concerning invitations to participate in the discourse of the academy. I could not easily determine whether the invitations were the result of interest in my substantive contributions to the discussion or the result of interest in my participation as a Black person. It was easier when it was clear that I had expertise that was relevant to the issues being discussed. At one such meeting, the topic was "beginning reading instruction." I knew that reading instruction was not one of my areas of special competence, so I added a subtitle to my presentation—"A View from the Back of the Bus." My reference was to the public transportation practice of requiring that Black folks sit in the back of the bus. Not only was it not entirely clear that I would have been expected to be at that conference except for purposes of minority participation; I was also scheduled to be the last speaker. In all fairness to my very decent friends who invited me to participate, I should add that the meeting concerned early reading instruction for disadvantaged students. I was, no doubt, invited because of my reputation as a good synthesizer and for my expertise on the education of low-status persons. But the subtitle did attract the attention of the group!

In this first part of *Education and Social Justice,* I have opened with a group of essays that contextualize the problems posed for education in a democratic society when diversity in human characteristics, in life conditions, and in access to pedagogically relevant resources is factored into the equation. In Chapter 1 a wide variety of factors that impact access to and achievement in educational opportunity situations are discussed. These factors include access to educational services and academic learning experiences of high quality; racism, classism, and ethnic isolation; economic resources; health and nutrition; socialization experiences and others. Discussions of these factors are quite prominent in my contributions to the periodical literature, where they initially were used to describe the deficiencies in the target population, but have come to be used to describe differences and to inform implications for intervention.

Chapter 2 is devoted to the old "nature versus nurture" controversy. This futile debate is discussed in the context of possible relationships between the social divisions (class, ethnicity, gender, etc.) to which persons are assigned and the qualities of intelligence in the members of such divisions. Rather than the "either nature or nurture" debate, an interactionist perspective is presented. Within this perspective the question is transformed into a problem in adaptive pedagogy where the task is to determine and provide the teaching and learning experiences that are both appropriate and sufficient to achieve the specified standard. One of my friends and mentors put it so well: "The improvement of education and other environments is really the only means available to a civilized society for the improvement of the lot and fate of man" (Bloom, 1969, p. 421).

So much of our attention in the concern with environments and nurture has been focused on artifacts—material things—that we sometimes forget that artifacts and symbolic representations of things have their objective and subjective meanings. In Chapter 3, I have addressed cultural dissonance as a risk factor in the development of students. Here we are concerned with the matches and mismatches between the cultures with which persons identify and those that have achieved hegemony in the social order to which one must adjust. It is possible that too much attention has been given to the objective characteristics of these cultures. While these are important to consider, the various attributions that individuals assign to these characteristics may be critical.

The final essay in this part is an essay review of *A Common Destiny* (Jaynes & Williams, 1989), the sequel to *An American Dilemma* (Myrdal, 1944). In this essay, my co-authors and I take another look at a variety of the factors that influence the development and status of African Americans.

CHAPTER I

Educating the Poor in the United States

In the 1960s we believed that more money, extra effort, and improved technology would solve the problems of educating the minority poor. We have spent more money. At the peak of activity, over $2 billion per year was allocated to the education of poor children by the federal government alone. We have garnered more effort. At least half the school districts of the nation have initiated programs of some sort directed at the education of the poor. At the peak of activity, 550,000 children were exposed to Head Start, and another 3.5 million were reached by the programs funded under Title I of the Elementary and Secondary Education Act of 1964. In addition, better than half of the colleges and universities have developed special programs to train teachers for disadvantaged children. We have also developed more guidance programs. Most of them have simply meant more guidance services rather than different guidance services, yet some have tried to make the guidance process more meaningful for the target population. Some programs have effectively used peer tutoring with gains reported for the tutors as well as for those tutored.

We have considerably more access to educational technology. Teaching machines, programmed materials, audiovisual aids, multisensory materials, and computer-assisted instruction are available in classrooms across the nation. We have made progress in developing cultural and ethnic pluralism in educational materials, so that teachers can now use materials that are indigenous to the specific minority cultures of their students. We have seen the introduction of Ethnic Studies and a renewed concern for vocational education and career development.

PROBLEMS OF ASSESSMENT

All of these innovations are major shifts in the delivery of educational services that have resulted from the use of more money, more effort, and

Adapted from a paper presented at the conference on Educating the Children of the Poor, held in Chicago, April 1974.

more technology. Yet despite more in all these areas, national assessments of impact have proven discouraging. Why has productivity not matched expectation? One explanation is that we are unable to assess the real impact of these programs on pupil achievement. In evaluative research, there are three levels of concern. First, research can be designed to discover whether a particular intervention program helps achieve a specific goal. Second, research can compare programs to determine which is more or less effective. Third, evaluative research can seek relationships between the specific aspects of intervention programs and subsequent changes in behavior. This final form of research is explanatory as well as evaluative.

Most evaluative research has been directed at the first two levels, ignoring the third. Yet only by answering questions on this third level can we begin to specify treatments that relate to known characteristics of the children to be served. Unfortunately, evaluative research of this quality has seldom been applied to the education of the poor.

In all levels of research, it is difficult to isolate variables with the necessary degree of precision and to discover the effects of specific treatments on targeted behaviors. One particular problem involves the method for selecting subjects. Even though "control" groups are closely matched with experimental groups, the control group is often different from the experimental group in crucial aspects. In addition, researchers must take into account the "radiation effect." Even if the two groups are initially "comparable," the effects on the experiment subjects are radiated onto their families and acquaintances. Eventually, the control subjects are also contaminated if there is any contact, direct or indirect, between these groups. Finally, in the evaluation of education for the poor, interferences such as teachers' expectations (i.e., the "Pygmalion effect") or generalized student reactions (i.e., the "Hawthorne effect") have usually not been identified or controlled; consequently, the real effects of various programs cannot be determined from these studies.

Still other problems in the evaluative research design can confuse, distort, or limit the initial data as well as subsequent findings. For example, most evaluations of compensatory education studies depend on static and quantitative measures that neglect the qualitative analysis of behavior or process. This static approach leads investigators to look for generic indicators of pupil characteristics and global or categorical indicators of treatment characteristics. Often this approach is combined with the researcher's tendency to see differences between minority and majority groups as deficits to be overcome rather than as assets to be developed. In such cases, there is little opportunity to study the dynamic processes by which success or failure may be more adequately understood. Even more serious is the apparent disregard of the probability that individual pupils respond differently to the same treatments.

Finally, researchers tend to focus on univariable input and output data, despite the existence of complex relationships between dependent and independent variables. When studied, these relationships are treated as constants. The evidence, however, indicates that a variable that is dependent in one context may be independent in another. Even more confusing is the possibility that a variable may be concurrently dependent and independent. These narrow approaches are often accompanied by an inadequate appraisal of program variables that pays little or no attention to the fact that interventions are uneven. Control of treatments in large-scale studies is almost nonexistent.

Those of us who can still be optimistic about the current status of our interventions in the education of the poor can argue that the relatively modest payoff is less a reflection of inadequate or inappropriate interventions, and more an indication of our inability to adequately measure the positive impact that must be there.

RAISING THE ISSUES

This leads us to raise the possibility that we have been insufficiently sensitive to the nature of the problems with which we are dealing. For this reason, a review of the ways in which the problems may be conceptualized is necessary in order to determine the logical relationships that exist between these and available treatments. There are, then, several issues related to the education of poor and minority populations that deserve our attention.

Problems of Educability

Prior to the late 19th century, little attention was given to the problems of educability. Since educational opportunity had been largely limited to eligible members of the aristocracy, the definition of educability had not emerged as an issue. The Reformation and the Industrial Revolution, however, produced a need for education in broader segments of the population. To be sure that education was provided to those most likely to benefit, instruments were designed to measure intelligence.

The emergence of IQ tests, however, led to false assurance about our ability to measure intelligence and to predict achievement from test scores. Concern with intelligence measurement and achievement prediction has dominated 20th-century selection procedures. Although this represents a shift from an aristocratic to a meritocratic basis for social stratification, lately most instruments developed to measure intelligence have been challenged because they no longer serve the purposes of education. American society is increasingly concerned with the development of all its people. Consequently, prediction of achievement has become less important than description of conditions that will encourage development of adequate functioning. In other words, as the need to democratize educational opportunity has increased, we have begun to broaden the definition of educability. Once narrowly defined, educability is increasingly viewed as a universal human characteristic. The issue of who is educable has become a function of whom society wants to educate, rather than who is most likely to benefit from the opportunity to learn.

Educational practices have also influenced the concept of educability. Traditionally, education provides services to learners and leaves the responsibility for learning with the student. If the learner did not learn, we questioned the quality of the learner, not the quality of the educational intervention. Although recently there has been some movement toward shared responsibility, we continue to place the blame for educational failure primarily on the learner in spite of Bruner's (1966) proposal that almost anything can be taught to anyone if the learning experience is appropriately designed. This facet of educability was demonstrated forcefully in animal psychology by K. S. Lashley's (1963) experiment with mice. Lashley challenged the assumption that mice have nervous systems that are incapable of discriminating between geometric figures. By modifying the conditions under which these discriminations are learned, Lashley was able to demonstrate form discrimination in his mice. Although it is not safe to make broad leaps from animal research to human applications, this concern for determining the learning experience design necessary to ensure mastery deserves attention in human learning.

Analysis of Learning Situations

For example, more careful analysis of learning behavior, the learning environment, and the task to be mastered may help us determine a more appropriate and productive combination of these factors. Such investigations may lead us to discover that educability results from the quality of these combinations. This conclusion certainly implies a shift in the responsibility for learning—or failure to learn—from the student alone to the participants in an interactive process.

Perhaps we originally placed responsibility on the student because our system of educational evaluation is biased in favor of a quantitative rather than a qualitative functioning. An emphasis on measurable quantities of ability loads the dice in favor of the teacher. On the other hand, if we seek to assess quality of learning we must examine more carefully the delicate balance of interactions among learning behavior, learning environments—including quality of teaching, and learning task demands.

I am making a plea for the qualitative analysis of these aspects of educational experience in our schools. The data from this analytic approach will be more helpful to teachers and others responsible for curricular and educational experiences design than scores or diagnostic categories generated from quantitative analysis alone. Our lack of progress in education in general, and compensatory education in particular, may be due to the fact that we have drawn the patterns for organizing learning experiences too narrowly. Instead, we need to expand the ways in which we conceptualize and assemble learning experiences. We can do this in two ways: First, we can proceed randomly, by thinking of as many variations as we can imagine in curriculum organization; second, we can take identifiable patterns of learner characteristics and then design learning experiences that match those patterns. It follows from this that the use of better analyses of the characteristics of learners to prescribe instructional experiences might well result in the delivery of more effective educational services to all children—including the poor and racial or ethnic minorities.

Most current work in individualized instruction matches mastery of the learning task to the rate of student learning. There has been some work matching pupil interest with specific learning materials and tasks. Other research has investigated the relation between learner personality and teacher personality. Of course, none of these combinations is adequate alone. We need to make designs for learning that are sensitive to such variables as rate of learning, cognitive style, interest, and temperament; in other words, a wide range of learner characteristics must be considered. These are all involved in the learning experience, and there are probably quite different distributions of characteristics among individuals and groups. We need greater sensitivity to this whole profile of functional levels and qualities if the appropriate match is to be made. Education of poor children and racial and ethnic minorities would be greatly improved if the approach to individually prescribed instruction were broadened to include these dimensions.

Education and psychology have given some attention to the characteristics of learners, particularly as these predict achievement—or failure. Unfortunately, comparable attention has not been given to the conditions in which learning and development occur. Yet environmental conditions (the ecology of learning and development) are generally as important in determining the quality of function as characteristics of the learner. This is clearly seen in urban minority poor populations, which often suffer a relatively poor match between their indigenous experiences and what happens at school. Such populations also experience a relatively high incidence of subtle to severe developmental defects, which may form social handicaps. The capacity of these populations to do well results as much from available supports as it does from the individual and group characteristics—strengths or weakness—that are brought to the schools. If a student enters an experience with a possible disability, but his family and community circumstances are rich enough to provide him with ways of circumventing or compensating, then the disability may become relatively unimportant. But if the environment is lacking in support, the disability is doubly difficult to overcome.

Importance of Home Environment

One body of research that speaks to this issue was developed by Herbert Birch in Aberdeen, Scotland, where he examined the relationship between health and school achievement for an entire population of 10-year-old school children (Birch & Gussow, 1970). Birch found that youngsters with comparable intelligence and similar levels of health impairment showed varying degrees of school success. A better indicator of success or failure in school seemed to be the degree to which the youngsters' home environments provided support for school learning in the presence of disabilities. If the home provided ways of circumventing the difficulty, achievement tended to be better. In contrast, youngsters with the same degree of impairment from homes that were not supportive showed much lower functional levels.

In a pilot study conducted to meet course requirements, one of my graduate students, Hershel Gruenwald (1963), investigated reading achievement in young adults with mild retardation. He found low correlations between the quality of reading achievement and mental age or Bender Gestalt test scores. He found higher correlations between reading achievement and the fact of having been reared in homes in which there had been a high degree of support for the mastery of reading. In those cases where there had not been support, reading achievement was low even in the presence of higher mental age or better Bender Gestalt scores.

Both of these studies suggest that given the same degree of intrinsic resources for learning or development, the quality of environmental supports for mastery of a learning task may become a deciding element. Perhaps we may infer that achievement is related to the quality of support for mastery available. Thus, environmental support may be as potent a force for learning as are the indigenous characteristics of the learner.

Additional data supporting this assertion are available in work by James Coleman, who found relatively low correlations between quality of schooling and achievement (Coleman et al., 1966). In other words, characteristics of individual schools do not account for the variations in achievement among American public school children. Yet, when Coleman looked at the data for poor and minority children, he found that the quality of schooling made a great difference in their achievement. For society at large, quality of schooling was a relatively unimportant correlate of achievement; yet for poor and minority children, quality of schooling—teacher characteristics, kinds of materials available, amount of teacher training, money spent on schooling—was more strongly associated with achievement. When support for academic learning was not a part of the natural environment, the relatively modest support supplied by the school did make a difference.

These findings suggest that the crucial factors responsible for differences between achievement levels, intelligence test scores, and the like are not to be found solely in the characteristics of disadvantaged children. The extent to which a child's environment supports mastery of school learning tasks is also a crucial factor.

Importance of Nutrition and Health

In close relation to the problem of ecological support for learning are life conditions such as nutrition and health. Many of the behaviors and conditions encountered in children from economically disadvantaged backgrounds are either induced or nurtured by conditions of poverty. The existence of a continuum of reproductive errors and developmental defects influenced by level of income is substantiated by research such as the excellent studies by Pasamanick and Knobloch (1958) of health status and school adjustment for low-income African-American children in Baltimore; by Lashof (1965) of health status and services on Chicago's South Side; and by Birch (1966) of the health status of children from indigent families in the Caribbean area. Such studies indicate that the incidence of reproductive error or defect is greatest in the population for which medical, nutritional, and child care are poorest.

These studies also point clearly to the following facts about low-income families:

1. Nutritional resources for the mother-to-be, the pregnant mother and fetus, and the newborn are inadequate.

2. Medical care—prenatal, obstetrical, and postnatal—is generally poor.
3. The incidence of subtle to more severe neurological defects in children is relatively high.
4. Case finding is hit or miss, so children are not only handicapped by the disorder but there is not official awareness that the condition exists.
5. Family resources and sophistication do not provide the remedial or compensatory supports that can make the difference between disabled and competent function.

These health-related conditions have important implications for school and general social adjustment. Impaired health or organic dysfunction influences school attendance, learning efficiency, developmental rate, and personality development. Pasamanick and Knobloch (1958) attribute a substantial portion of the behavior disorders among disadvantaged youngsters to a high incidence of subtle neurologic disorders. Other writers relate a variety of specific learning disabilities to mild or severe neurologic abnormalities. Clearly, in our society, adequacy of health status and health care is influenced by adequacy of income. The obvious conclusion is that poverty leads directly to health problems and indirectly to general developmental problems.

Although it seems clear that conditions of life greatly influence the quality of development and function, questions remain about the hereditary limits of development. When the problems of compensatory education are discussed in the context of the nature/nurture controversy, confusion, if not distortion, often results.

Plasticity of Intellect

The plasticity of intellect is a critical issue reflected in the nature/nurture controversy, which is basically unresolved despite a great deal of research (see Chapter 2 for further discussion of this matter). Building on Binet's early concern with the trainability of the intellect and Montessori's efforts to modify intellectual function in children with subnormal performance levels, investigators have worked with children of all mental capacities. These studies have produced mixed findings, yielding no definitive conclusions.

Educators need not debate the question of the origins and plasticity of intellectual potential. Instead, we should shift our attention to more aggressively attempting to influence the quality of function. With this line of thought we can take the position that all human beings, except about

5% who are truly mentally defective, have potential for adequate functioning. Further, we can surmise that it is possible to develop conditions that will enable all people to achieve adequate levels of functioning. Within this frame, the task is not to change the potential, but to improve the quality of function so that the potential can be expressed.

Importance of Affect

Zigler (1966) is one researcher who has attempted to account for changes in the quality of intellectual function on the basis of changes in the affective state (motivation, task involvement, and so forth). By manipulating the conditions under which his subjects were examined, Zigler achieved a significant shift in quality of function (20-point IQ gain) with mildly retarded subjects. He also determined that there were no major changes in the basic cognitive process, but that the subjects responded differently depending on the quality of their task involvement and affective responses. Zigler emphasized the conditions that lead to optimal intellectual functioning, rather than a change in basic cognitive processes, which is usually connoted by "potential."

Zigler (1966) also argues that too much attention has been given to interventions directed at changing basic cognitive processes, since these processes are likely to be either so fixed or so recalcitrant that they will not respond to most kinds of intervention. Instead, he suggests that the affective domain may be considerably more plastic and malleable. This means that cognitive function may be more susceptible to change by affective rather than cognitive intervention. For example, I may move to a qualitatively higher level of intellectual functioning because I am motivated to apply whatever skill and potential I have to the task. On the other hand, efforts intended to teach me how to change my basic cognitive process may have no effect because those processes are too fixed or because my energies are not sufficiently directed at the task. If the social interaction provides motivation to become involved and the aspiration level is high enough, the affective process may induce changes in the cognitive process.

Unfortunately, our tendency has been to separate the affective and cognitive domains from each other. Yet we cannot separate the two, whether for study, for emphasis, or for instructional purposes. They are so integrally related that it makes no sense to talk about one independent of the other. If we analyze affective function, it is difficult to have anything more than mere sensations unless we also understand the experience in cognitive terms. For example, although lower animals develop habitual affinities for each other, they do not develop love. Animals such as humans, however, develop love for each other because the feeling of love requires symbolic mediation. In order to generate love feelings for you, I must also generate ideas about you. The two are inseparable.

Nonetheless, in the field of compensatory education, we have tended to treat the two as if they were separate. In some programs, the primary emphasis is on affective development; however, most programs put the primary emphasis on the cognitive. Both types lack sufficient understanding of the varied interactions between the two domains. The early experiences that many of us had with preschool programs provide one illustration of our misunderstanding about the affective and cognitive domains. Some of the first teachers involved in one particular program worked out of a kind of personal concern or missionary zeal. They approached their youngsters with a great deal of compassion, empathy, and support, because they believed that poor children needed this kind of intervention. When money became available for preschool work, people were hired in part because they needed jobs; such teachers approached their work a bit more systematically. In one project with which I was associated, conflict developed between "old-timers" and "newcomers." The old-timers felt that the newcomers were racists, hostile to the children, and too demanding. The newcomers described the old-timers as "coddling." When we looked at the effectiveness of these two groups, we found that the children in the classes managed by the more recently employed teachers were ahead of the others. It is quite possible that we were hiring a better quality of teacher, yet it was also very obvious that these new teachers made more demands on the youngsters than the older teachers did. In this instance, the performance demand apparently had a positive affective as well as a cognitive effect. The effect was stronger than that produced by reduced performance demands and surplus affection or support.

Two things may have happened to the students of the older teachers. First, they may not have been sufficiently challenged by the situation. Second, they may have been sophisticated enough to sense that the excessive "love" showed less "respect" for them than the more demanding situation. An alternative explanation may be that because of the demands placed on them, the children accomplished more things. Through this, they began to perceive themselves as competent people and experienced a corresponding improvement in self-concept. In the "loving" situation, the children perceived themselves primarily as dependent persons. Actually, these speculations are less important than the demonstrated interplay between affective and cognitive domains that is seldom understood and presented in sophisticated applications of educational interventions.

The separation of affective from cognitive functions makes little sense in any educational setting, but it is particularly senseless in the education of socially disadvantaged children. The social context in which education occurs is often alien for poor and minority students. Consequently, such students are less likely to be attracted, motivated, or involved in the learning situation than more privileged children, for whom school has a more obvious relationship to what is happening in the rest of their lives. In schools, the learning difficulties of disadvantaged children are most prominent so the tendency has been to focus very sharply on cognitive development. Such efforts are invariably defeated before they begin, because they move directly to a factor that is not only one of the major needs of the youngster, but also a major source of frustration. Furthermore, if we assume that progress in the learning situation is related to student involvement and that such involvement requires some degree of identification with the school's values and purposes, then again, these youngsters are at a significant disadvantage since both the content of the school experience and the purpose of schooling may be different for them than for youngsters from the majority culture.

William Labov (1972) has done one of the best studies of the relationship between learning and identification with the material being studied. In his work on the sociology of language, Labov demonstrated a major difference in task involvement and quality of function when black students were taught in their indigenous dialect. His work and that of William Stewart (1972), among others, indicate that young black pupils who show retarded levels of academic and intellectual function in standard English proceed, in their own dialect, to deal with and to solve social and technical problems that would otherwise be thought beyond their grasp. Moreover, when examined in their own dialect, many young people whose language skills in standard English are judged to be grossly inadequate show a richness and complexity of language that can be associated only with average or better intellectual capacity.

In another context, the early efforts to modify curricular materials so that they more adequately reflect the variety of ethnic and cultural backgrounds represented in our public schools showed poor results as long as they concentrated on elements of form, such as skin color, hair texture, and other physical characteristics. However, as these efforts became more sophisticated, the content as well as the form captured elements of the indigenous culture, and exposure to these new materials improved the effectiveness of learning. In both of these instances, it appears that where the materials to be dealt with are problems to be solved, or vehicles to be utilized, they enable the pupils to build on strengths, rather than having them struggle only with their weaknesses. This often results in an improvement in the quality of function.

Importance of Shared Purposes

A more difficult problem arises in the incompatible purposes of schooling as seen by the dominant society and the target population. The anthropologist Anthony Wallace (1961) argues that the purposes of education are closely tied to the purposes of society and that these purposes vary in relation to the stage or phase through which the society is passing. He identifies the social phases as conservative, reactionary, and revolutionary, and he classifies the purposes of education depending on whether they are being focused on the development of skills, the development of intellect, or the development of morality. He argues that in the revolutionary phase of a society, the greatest emphasis is placed on moral development, second on intellectual development, and third on skills. These priorities are related to the purposes of the revolution in that a revolution needs people who are concerned with human rights and humanistic concerns. Also, revolutionaries want to sharpen the intellectual function of the masses because support for the revolution is stimulated by this kind of awareness. Only after these two priorities are satisfied can the revolutionary phase switch its attention to skill development. In contrast, societies in the conservative phase give top priority to skill development because skills are needed to maintain the society. Moral development is next in importance, but now it takes the form of socialization and answers to questions like "What does society expect of me?" "How do I behave?" or "How do I get along in society?" Intellectual development is given least attention because there is a reduced need for the development of the intellect in a society that is trying to maintain the status quo. In fact, intellectuality may be discouraged since a conservative society frequently cannot tolerate "free thinking." According to Wallace, intellectual development is neglected or even discouraged in both conservative and reactionary societies. Finally, in reactionary states, moral development is moved back to high priority, but now it takes the form of a concern for law and order or "What does the state expect?" The emphasis is on correct behavior and behavioral control rather than on value examination or humanistic goals. Of course, concern is given to skills because skills are needed, as in the conservative society, to maintain the existing order.

In the context of this theory, the United States and most of the industrialized countries of the West cannot be considered revolutionary. This nation has not been a revolutionary society for more than 100 years. For most of that period it has been conservative, though lately it has been thought of as reactionary. Yet poor people and minorities soon realize that what they need is not maintenance of the status quo but radical change. Our schools are primarily focused on the concerns of the conservative to reactionary society; yet the people who are not making it in that system are primarily concerned with radical change or revolution. The purposes of schooling are incongruous for them and for the society at large. Poor minority children coming into the school need ways to radically change things. At the same time, the school is operated by a society that intends to maintain the status quo. As one solution, Ivan Illich (1971) talks about "deschooling society." He sees the school as reactionary, force-restricting, distorting, containing, and confining rather than liberatory and empowering. The relevance for compensatory education is that schools may not be able to deliver the thing that is most essential to the development of the target population. Schools may be reasonably proficient at developing skills, yet they have never been good at developing intellect or morality in humanistic and expansive frames of reference.

Thus, the overall purpose of the school is not consistent with the basic needs of disadvantaged people. This incongruence is more difficult to reconcile than the incongruence between language and the cultural emphasis of materials, both of which can be and have been modified. The incongruence of purpose requires change in the society, a change external to the school, which is not likely to come shortly. The capacity to feel good about an experience, to identify with it, and to assign a high value to it is directly related to the purposes that one attributes to the experience. This conflict of purpose in schooling not only limits what the school can do, but defeats most efforts to help the youngster identify with or become enthusiastic about the experience.

A counter-illustration of the point is found in the work of the Black Panthers in the early 1960s. The Black Panthers, along with the Black Muslims, were probably more successful in rehabilitating and educating young-adult and late-adolescent Blacks than any other movement in this country. Both groups talked about things that had a high degree of congruence with the values and the purposes of these young people. This high degree of congruence helped turn around youngsters who had been arrested for criminal behavior and juvenile delinquency, were unemployed, and so forth. Many of these fellows went back to the schools or into responsible work situations. The capacity to attract, hold, and involve is too often lacking in the schools, even though this is a crucial element in effective education.

Control of Decision-Making

Another important issue that arises from this concern with the social purpose of schooling is control of school policy and accountability for the educational process. As more and more poor and disadvantaged children fail to learn or achieve the standards set by society, there is increasing concern about who should control curriculum development and change. In addition, we must ask who should be held responsible for correction of the barriers stacked against the development of poor and minority students. The democratic tradition of this nation presupposes that citizens will actively participate in political decision-making. Yet political and administrative momentum often leads to increased centralization of power, varying degrees of representation rather than participation, and the alienation of citizens from decisions that affect their lives. A small body of research suggests that as people become more involved in making decisions related to the enterprise in which they're involved, their productivity in that situation increases. Participation in decision-making is greatly influenced by organizational size—the smaller the group, the higher the degree of involvement. An example from industrial psychology may prove helpful. The Acton Society Trust studies (1953) revealed that interest in the affairs of the organization and knowledge of the names of administrators decreased as the size of the organization increased. Voting on work-unit issues also suffered, as did subscription to professional periodicals, output, and punctuality.

In addition, decision-making and participation are crucially influenced by how meaningful and efficacious the interaction proves to be. Again a study from industrial psychology illustrates the point. To examine ways of effecting production changes in an industrial firm, Coch and French (1948) created three different work groups. In the first group, changes were introduced by management decision and the members of this group in no way influenced the changes in the production process. In a second group, the "partial-participation" group, changes were made by representatives selected by the group. In the third group, characterized as "total participation," all members were involved directly in making decisions about changes. Coch and French found that the production of the first group dropped after the changes were introduced and the workers became hostile toward management. The partial-participation cohort, however, continued to produce satisfactorily after a momentary drop in production, and the total-participation group quickly exceeded its pre-change rate of production and remained satisfied with the job. This study was replicated in a Norwegian factory by French, Israel, and As (1960). There, the investigators found that the extent of workers' participation in decision-making had little relevance to production. These findings suggest the need to distinguish between token and legitimate participation. They imply that participants must feel that their participation is meaningful and related to the immediate tasks.

These two factors—size of organization and legitimacy of participation—both have applications in the education of the disadvantaged. The rise of metropolitan school systems has widened the gulf between decision makers and those affected by decisions until many school systems are simply too large to sensitively administer to the needs of their clients. Many of the minority-group members feel they have little access to power in educational and other social-political institutions. Since they have found that the public school is ineffective in fulfilling their needs, they have become unwilling, and at times hostile, participants in schooling.

The importance of actively involving individuals in decisions that affect them is demonstrated in several areas. For example, research indicates that when parents of schoolchildren are involved in the process of education, their children are more likely to achieve. This heightened achievement may result from a closer correspondence between the school and the home. It may also be caused by changes in the attitudes of teachers who feel more accountable when the parents of their students are visible in the schools and concerned about their children's progress. Increased participation may also enable children to achieve better, because they have an enhanced sense of control when they see their parents actively exert influence or engage in decision-making in the school. Moreover, the heightened sense of community integrity and ethnic group self-esteem that results from parent and community groups' influencing educational changes in turn solidifies the children's sense of their own worth. Presumably, one of the things going for middle-class children in their community is their social class. This perception inspires a feeling that "I am important," "my people are important," "the school is an instrument of my concern." Involvement and productivity are greater because privileged children view the school as something over which they have power. In contrast, lower-class children perceive schooling as something that controls and influences them, their family, and their community.

Importance of Social-class Mix

Much also has been made of desegregation and ethnic mix in its relation to increased achievement of disadvantaged children. The data seem to indicate that such achievement is more a matter of social-class mix. A number of studies have examined the possible relationship of integration (along racial or status-group lines) and achievement. The overall results seem to demonstrate that when children from lower status groups are a minority in the school, the lower status groups tend not to improve their level of achievement.

Although these observations are generally supported by mass data compiled from large-scale populations, there is a need for caution in drawing similar conclusions for smaller populations and individual cases. Studies of minority-group performance under experimental conditions of ethnic mix indicate that assigned status and perceived conditions of comparison (that is, the subject's awareness of the norms against which data will be evaluated) result in a varied pattern of performance on the part of the lower status group subjects. For example, Katz (1967) has reservations about the effects of ethnic mix. His studies suggest that the results of ethnic mix are not unidirectional. For some it accelerates achievement, yet for others it depresses performance. Thus, it may be dangerous to generalize that across-the-board economic and social class integration will automatically result in positive improvement for the lower status group.

The Relevance of Schooling

Finally, I must mention another issue of overriding importance. Some critics have asserted that schools make little difference and are not effective in changing the life chances of the pupils who pass through them. For example, Christopher Jencks's *Inequality* (1972) concludes that the process of schooling has little effect on the way in which income is distributed in the society. Jencks argues that if society is really concerned with the equalization of income or economic status, it must go about it directly instead of by manipulating marginal institutions such as schools. The data of the several studies that Jencks and his associates reanalyzed used intelligence and achievement test scores as primary indicators of competence. None of these studies was concerned with happiness or social usefulness as outcome dimensions. Jencks acknowledges some of the limitations of intelligence and achievement testing, but he dismisses the affective domain with a four-page chapter in which he concedes that he knows little about this area and has neglected it in his reanalysis. There are several problems here. Jencks ignores what schooling can do to develop people, and concentrates on what schooling can do to increase and equalize economic status. This is only one of the possible outcomes of schooling. In our changing society, it may rapidly become one of the least important outcomes.

Let us, however, examine the Jencks (1972) position from another perspective. Schooling serves different purposes for different segments of the population. If a person comes from a population whose social and political position places him outside the line of opportunity, then schooling versus no schooling is a relatively unimportant issue. With or without the benefits of schooling, opportunity is unavailable. However, if the person comes from a population subset that places him in the line of opportunity, the fact of schooling becomes important but the quality of school is relatively unimportant. If I come from a segment of the population from which civil servants are likely to be selected and schooling is viewed as a credential necessary to appointment, then having that credential is very important. Yet if I come from an excluded subgroup, that credential is still necessary but not sufficient. In other words, schooling in relation to social position is important whereas schooling in the wrong social position becomes relatively unimportant. Since schooling as a credential has more to do with entry than it has to do with progress in the job, quality of schooling appears superfluous. The evidence for this can be found in the relationship between schooling and upward mobility for different segments of the population. Some members of the minority population do make it along the same route as the majority, but simply having equal credentials does not ensure it for them.

Another line of evidence is to be found in the work of Ivan Berg (1971), who has studied the relationship between entry requirements for work and job requirements. Berg concluded that entry requirements are consistently higher than job requirements. In addition, entry requirements are used not to determine who is qualified to do the job, but to select "desired" people from the society. Given that fact, school provides a credentialing function that is essential and necessary, but not sufficient. In the process of work establishment there are other factors such as culture, social background, economics, politics, social class, and social caste that may have more weight than schooling.

Thus, Jencks (1972) is actually correct in concluding that schooling is not the route to the equalization of income. We equalize income, if that is our goal, by redistributing income, by eliminating exploitation of wealth-producing labor, and by making it impossible to hoard capital. True schooling has little relation to economic sufficiency despite the fact that compensatory education and education in general have been sold to the public as vehicles for upward mobility. This objection, however, does not mean that there are not good reasons to make schooling equally available and optimally effective for all people. If the object of schooling is humanistic development, then there is an important relationship between the effectiveness of schooling and general social competence. To the extent that one can better understand and communicate, then to that extent one is a more effective member of society. In other words, we should upgrade schooling for reasons other than economic sufficiency. For that pursuit we should move out of the school and into the political economic arena to talk about the way in which the distribution of power and resources must be changed.

CONCLUSION

Education is not an antidote to poverty. Furthermore, the school is immoral when it continues to hold that as its goal. Education is concerned with the total development of people and their preparation for the multiple roles that make up their lives. Schools are one of the resources by which society prepares and develops its members. When other societal resources are unequally distributed, quality of schooling becomes even more important. When the society produces subpopulations less well prepared to benefit from the standard offerings of the school, we have the additional responsibility for broadening, expanding, and enriching the offerings of the schools, not as our first line of defense against poverty, but as protection against the effects of an unjust society, which, if they go uncorrected, systematically erode the human resources of that society.

CHAPTER 2

Human Social Divisions and Human Intelligence: Putting Them in Their Place

More than 25 years ago, in *Science and the Concept of Race*, under the leadership of Margaret Mead, a group of writers addressed the relation between human social divisions such as class, ethnicity, and gender and the genetic origins and limits of intelligent behavior (Mead, Dobzhansky, Tobach, & Light, 1968). That volume elicited nothing like the public attention that had just been given to Arthur Jensen's (1967) allegations of a genetic basis for differences in the measured intelligence of Blacks and Whites or the recent hoopla surrounding *The Bell Curve* (Herrnstein & Murray, 1994).* *The Encyclopedia of Human Intelligence* (Sternberg, 1994), published just before *The Bell Curve*, and the classic work of Stephen J. Gould (1981), which appeared more than a decade earlier, are just two among many writings that help to clarify our knowledge of the nature and origins of intelligence and the various attempts at its measurement. The scholarship of *The Bell Curve* is not up to the standard of any of these works. Even the quality of its authors' sources is questionable, since as many as 20% of their extensive references are to reports of investigators who have been supported by the Pioneer Fund, well known for its patronage of research that endorses the genetic origins of racial differences in intelligence.

A POLITICAL POLEMIC

Why, then, has *The Bell Curve*, so poor in quality and so problematic in its treatment of the issues, been the focus of such wide attention? Clearly, it is not interest in the underlying scientific questions that determines the manner in which our society addresses this issue. The more likely answer

Adapted with permission from The American Orthopsychiatric Association. Copyright © 1995 by The American Orthopsychiatric Association. *Readings: A Journal of Reviews and Commentary in Mental Health, 10*(1), 7–13.
*This chapter comprises a discussion of *The Bell Curve* (Herrnstein & Murray, 1994). All references to this title and these authors are to this work.

can be found in *The Bell Curve*'s justification of privilege and selfishness, a message that powerful segments of our populace want to hear. Just as in the mid-sixties we began to feel the White backlash in response to the civil rights movement, in the mid-nineties the middle class and the would-be middle class—those on the top rungs of the lower class—began to flex their political muscles in defense of their declining sense of security. *The Bell Curve* is not part of a debate about science or the manner in which science can inform public policy decisions. It is not simply another effort at asserting the alleged genetic superiority of Whites over Blacks or rich over poor. This is a book about membership in the social order and the rights of members to share in the resources of the society.

Too often we are inclined to confuse the manner in which social orders are organized and controlled with the purpose for which they exist. A society is organized to serve the needs of its members. However, it is not unusual for people of financial and political privilege to structure the social order for the protection of their own special positions, and to present these maneuvers as serving the advancement and stability of the society. Such strategies are often rationalized as appropriate to a society's protection of the rights of its members. Thus membership in the social order is of crucial importance, even if one is not a privileged member.

This is the essence of the political problem raised by *The Bell Curve*. We could live with its distortion of scientific knowledge, especially since the misrepresentations of Charles Murray and the late Richard Herrnstein are so opaque and their misinterpretations so unoriginal. It is their implicit designation of some members of the society as *nonmembers*, or as being entitled to membership only on the sufferance of their social superiors, that truly qualifies Murray for the *New York Times Magazine*'s designation of him as the nation's "most dangerous conservative" (DeParle, 1994).

This is a time of worldwide economic, political, and social transition. Things are changing and those of us who are well positioned fear that things may get worse for us, almost as much as do those for whom fortunes have already turned sour. Consider for a moment that computers and machines have largely replaced human hands in the production of commodities. In those industries where human labor continues to be required, jobs have been exported in the search for docile and low-cost labor. Although service industries are replacing manufacturing industries, income from service jobs is insufficient to provide the level of support to which many families in the United States have become accustomed. Thus, the Fordist conception of economic development (many people employed to produce low-cost products that they can, in turn, purchase), which flourished for most of this century and produced a large population of relatively affluent citizens, is no longer operable. Instead, we have a weakened economy in which wealth is increasingly concentrated in the top 10% of the population while the poverty of the bottom third deepens. But it is among those in the middle, some 60% of the population, that anxiety is highest, as the downsizing of commerce and industry and truncated economic growth portend realistic doubts about the economy's capacity to support their standard of living.

It is in times like these that people begin to look for scapegoats. It is in conditions such as these that books like *The Bell Curve* are produced, promoted, and widely discussed. And it is in a climate such as this that those of us who would be informed and who believe in a democratic and humane society must read books like this one with care and foreboding.

Herrnstein and Murray appear to be the epitome of intelligent scholars, individuals with the capacity to manipulate numbers and ideas so as to represent (or misrepresent) reality. In *The Bell Curve*, they use their intelligence and the symbols of the academy to attack our national sense of polity—the recognition of our society as an organized political unit of all our peoples, with collective responsibility one for the other—by exacerbating the awareness of difference and transforming it to mean "inferiority" or "otherness." At a time when resources are said to be shrinking, they would have us reduce the number of community members who are entitled to a share. They define superior and inferior groups based on differences in the manifestation of intelligent behavior that they claim to be genetically determined (read "natural" or "God-given"). They assert that these less able people are inherently locked into their lower status and that little can be done to change it. But these authors apparently want to be perceived as humane, as well as intelligent; they advance the case for charitable inclusion as a substitute for the *right* of inclusion in the society.

At bottom, this work by Herrnstein and Murray is a polemic in support of selfishness. It makes a case for circling the wagons so as to protect the "threatened" resources of the privileged few. We who have enjoyed some degree of affluence in the past several years now see it menaced by the need to share what we have with growing masses of people who have not. If we can justifiably exclude these have-nots as inferior and undeserving of society's protection, there will be more left for us (read "pay less in taxes") and we can feel more secure.

Some of us are old enough to remember that this is the road taken by Germany earlier in this century. At that time of economic stress and sociopolitical change, cultural and religious minorities were isolated, declared inferior, and otherwise scapegoated in the name of national progress. Jews and Gypsies were simply declared inferior peoples and nonmembers of the German social order. Here, at the end of the century, Herrnstein and Murray urge that we recognize that people are separated by levels of developed ability, which they refer to as intelligence. Recall that some 50 years ago, at about the same time as Jewish people were suffering the Holocaust in Germany, individuals in the United States with IQs of 75 and higher could be absorbed in the general population and function as productive members of the social order. If the cognitive demands of our current technologically advanced society require that we exclude or disenfranchise those with IQs under 100, who among us will have to be excluded in 2025? It could be anyone whose developed abilities are not at IQ levels of 150, or some other number that future scholars will designate. It could be you. And, except for an increasingly select few among us, it almost certainly will be your children.

REVIEWING THE FLAWED SCHOLARSHIP

The Bell Curve's packaging and girth announced it as a book of major importance. In addition to its 552 text pages, it contains appendices, notes, an extensive bibliography, and an index that account for another 293 pages. It even includes an excellent discussion of statistics and their use for those of us whose quantitative abilities are less well developed. Yet the authors do not seem to expect all 845 pages to be perused. Early on, readers are encouraged to use the abstracts provided for all but two of the book's 16 chapters. One might conclude that the book's message is quite short and its bulk purely for show. Indeed, its message is short but not nearly as simple as the authors' advice to readers might suggest. There is considerable information and some disinformation, and the two are so intermingled and sometimes incompletely developed as to make careful and critical reading essential to avoid being misled.

The 12 chapters in the first two parts of the book present evidence of a relationship between measured intelligence and a host of social indicators of status or polity. The message is that low IQ is associated with low socioeconomic status, low educational achievement, low occupational status, low income, low-level family functioning, high crime and welfare dependency, and low levels of civility and citizenship. These chapters are also used to alert readers to the "emergence of a new cognitive elite." They sound legitimate cautions concerning the growing gap between the competencies of this elite group and the undereducated (they imply unintelligent) masses. The authors also use these chapters to argue the case for a high degree of genetic influence on the quality of measured intellect, independent of ethnic group membership. In fact, the data used for this section of the book are limited to the test scores and achievements of persons thought to be European American.

It is in the third part of their book that Herrnstein and Murray introduce questions concerning the relation between ethnicity and cognitive ability. They present data indicating that Blacks score about 15 points lower than Whites on most standardized tests of intelligence. There is little controversy among scholars concerning the existence of this gap; most of the debate is about its causes. The authors maintain that genetic differences, in this instance between Blacks and Whites, are an important factor. They also show that Chinese and Japanese score somewhat higher than do European Americans on these tests, and that test scores of high-income Spanish-speaking people are close to those of European Americans (not mentioning that high-income Spanish-speaking people tend to be White).

The patterns in these scores and the persistence of the gap between high-status and low-status populations reassure Herrnstein and Murray of the accuracy of their earlier assertion that the basis of differences in intellective behavior is genetic and that, further, cognitive differences between ethnic or racial groups can be similarly accounted for. This section of the book contains no new information; it concludes with discussions of the contribution of demographic changes to the lowering of intelligence in the United States, and of the authors' view of the relation between low cognitive ability and several indicators of social pathology.

Important issues lie buried in this section of *The Bell Curve*, and they should not be clouded by Herrnstein and Murray's polemical and racist treatment. The Black–White gap is critically important. The high proportion of socially dysfunctional and violent behavior in some low-status populations cannot be ignored. The disastrous state of the political economy for Blacks and other low-income groups, the very pessimistic outlook for improved national economic development, the low likelihood for many of obtaining adequate income from employment, and the absence of meaningful participation by members of many low-status groups in the political affairs of the nation are problems that threaten the future stability of our democracy.

In their final section, the authors turn to issues of public policy, beginning with a view of the potential for raising cognitive ability that is confusingly pessimistic since they are quick to dismiss the very interventions in which they seem to sense possibilities for success. They demean the impact of Head Start and other programs that most educators agree have been moderately effective and insufficiently implemented. Although they concede that improvements in nutrition and other conditions of life could affect cognitive development, they do not seem to regard such efforts as feasible or even worth trying.

Herrnstein and Murray maintain that the nation's educational resources are being wasted on students of low ability while those with high IQs are being neglected. They argue that public education should focus on the enhancement of talent in our most able students instead of on the educational development of the masses of disadvantaged. That these goals are not mutually exclusive does not seem to be part of the authors' considerations. They are pessimistic, as well, about issues of access to higher education and the workplace, institutions that they see as having been weakened by efforts at democratization. Although they are forceful in advancing these assertions of failure, they offer few data to support conclusions that many would challenge. Efforts to better life chances through education and employment may not have been universally successful, but certainly the United States has made tremendous progress in these areas. Herrnstein and Murray, believing that genetic limitations render such efforts futile, would have us give up before we have really tried.

The authors' concluding chapter, "A Place for Everyone," is characteristically odd. Having told us that at least a third of the population is hopelessly inferior and that efforts at improving its competence will prove fruitless, they end with a kind of sermonette on humane consideration and compassion, appealing here to "what makes America special" and defining that specialness by telling us that the United States

> contains one of the friendliest, most eager to oblige, neighborly peoples in all the world [and that as] a by-product of this generosity and civic mindedness, America has had a genius for making valued places, for people of all kinds of abilities, given only that they played by a few basic rules. (p. 550)

What is especially odd here is not only that Herrnstein and Murray's view of U.S. history is so different from mine and that of many other people I know, but that these two, who fit so well their own criteria for membership in the intellectual elite, should assert in apparent good faith that this increasingly competitive society will spontaneously embrace and make a place for its "inferior" nonmembers. This chapter appears to run counter to the spirit of their book, as well as to the experience and knowledge of vast numbers of this nation's citizens. But its optimistic tone may be part of its purpose: to justify the assignment of "otherness" and "inferiority" to parts of the population by asserting benevolent concern for their humane treatment.

Even these benevolent concerns are problematic. Although the authors seek to support them by an extensive literature review, their policy recommendations are less a product of the pseudoscholarship that precedes them than they are a reflection of the authors' values and world views. While I think that a responsible publisher should have turned down this reactionary tract, Herrnstein and Murray were certainly within their rights to have submitted it for publication. However, scholars do not have a right to use scientific information in so profoundly biased a way as to mislead readers deliberately and to misinform public policy by substituting personal opinion for scientifically informed judgment.

These are intelligent authors, and the inherent problem of their book is not a function of their lack of understanding of the science or the issues, but of their intention to deliver a political message that they feel is appropriate to the current *zeitgeist*. Their scholarship is flawed by their uneven use of research studies, their misinterpretation of issues, their failure to represent more recent conceptions of the theoretical constructs utilized, and their contradictory treatment of data on social interventions. These matters have been addressed in detail in other reviews of *The Bell Curve*.

EXAMINING THE ISSUES

The balance of this chapter will focus on several issues that I find especially troubling about the book. The first has to do with the use of human social divisions like class, race, and ethnicity as indicators of group membership. Not only is there debate concerning the meaning of these categories; there are also problems concerning their application. To use social divisions in biological and genetic research is to assume that biological characteristics adhere to social designations. Since both the validity of such divisions and the reliability of assignment to them are questionable, such assumptions appear to have no foundation in the sciences of behavior and the resulting inferences must be viewed as flawed.

Although scholars continue to debate definitions of race, there is some consensus as to what the construct references. Almost all contemporary definitions of race include physical characteristics; *Webster's 3rd New International Dictionary* (1966, p. 1870), for instance, defines race as "any of the different varieties of mankind distinguished by form of hair, color of skin and eyes, stature, [and] bodily proportions." Most modern anthropologists recognize three primary human groups, the so-called races: Caucasoid, Mongoloid, and Negroid; within each of these major human divisions, various subdivisions (sometimes also, although incorrectly, called races) are recognized. Biologists, according to *Webster's*, use race to refer to "a population that differs from others in the relative frequency of some gene or gene pool patterns."

Many scholars, including biologists, disagree not only on the definition of race but on the existence, validity, and reliability of the construct and its use. Shuey (1966) and Fried (1968) have asserted that geographic and typological divisions have been used to categorize humanity into discrete racial groups, but rarely, if ever, has a truly scientific notion of race been made explicit, defined, or employed. Furthermore, scientists have neither isolated gene pool patterns that are specific to certain subpopulations (races, so-called), nor determined the factors responsible for race-specific morphological evolutions.

Meaningful classifications of individuals are made even more difficult because of the social and political nature of race designations. According to Fried (1968), individuals are both self- and other-identified and may be assigned to different races by different individuals and in different contexts. Thus self-identification and identification by others may vary from situation to situation and can be in error or simply misrepresented. Some researchers would like to think they have controlled for such factors, but, in Fried's words, "correct racial typing becomes more and more difficult and demands full-scale attempts to control the genealogical histories of all subjects" (p. 128). However, efforts to control genealogical histories are fraught with unresolved problems and have been ill-conceived. For example, in several of the southern states in the United States, racial designation has been based on the discernible percentage of Black "blood" or heritage. The criterion, which has varied from 1:1 to 1:64 "Black blood," has often been influenced by public records, collective memory, or inspection of physiognomy. Inevitably, the effort to detect proportions of blood attributable to one or the other race was not itself informative. Hence, even where investigators are aware of the problems of classification by race and try to deal with them, precise and valid classifications are seldom, if ever, achieved.

The problem of reliably identifying biological subgroups of human beings is intractable. Appiah (1992), reminding us that relatively few physical traits are unique to "racial" groups, called attention to the fact that, apart from the visible morphological characteristics by which broad racial assignments have been made, there are

> few genetic characteristics to be found in the population of England that are not found in similar proportions in Zaire or China, and few too (though more) that are found in Zaire but not in similar proportions in China and England. (p. 35)

Others (Glass & Li, 1953; Hiernaux, 1975; Maurant, 1983) have called attention to the heterogeneous genetic characteristics of the so-called races. Rose and Kamin (1984) suggested that the differences within so-called races are more significant than the differences between them. Nonetheless, race designations have been arbitrarily assigned based almost solely on a few physical differences such as skin color, hair curl, and eye-fold, which are probably only small morphological adaptations to different physical environments. If the colloquial designation of a group as a race is thus not a function of significant biological or genetic differences, it is clearly a function of society's perception that differences exist and its determination that such differences are important.

Second, the interchangeable use of the terms *genetic determination* and *heritability* to refer to the origins of traits and complex behavior is problematic, since the science of heredity does not support the assumptions of the heritability of such complex forms of human behavior as intelligence. It can be said that intelligence is both inherited *and* the result of environmental encounters, but to attribute the construct to either one or the other is erroneous, as is the assignment of percentages of origin to genes or environments in the absence of known and specified interactions. In their use of these terms in *The Bell Curve,* it is not always clear that Herrnstein and Murray have avoided such errors. It is certainly the case that their public policy recommendations do not reflect a sophisticated understanding of the differences between heritability estimates and genetic determinants of human characteristics.

According to Hirsch (1969), a genome, the unit that contains one's genetic makeup, is a mosaic of information; development is the expression of one of many possible alternative phenotypes. Hirsch's description makes clear that the characteristics of any offspring are the product of the arrangement of genetic components derived from the parents, including both the similar and dissimilar features expressed in the development of siblings. Siblings make readily observable a small portion of the variety of ways in which inherited components can be rearranged, and they also reflect the variety of expression that can be observed in similar environmental circumstances.

Just as each gene has a range of possible phenotypic expression (behavior, traits, and so forth), each phenotype has a range, or norm, of reaction for a given genotype. Thus the limits of heredity are plastic at every stage of expression, including genotype and phenotype and their integrated expression in the behavior of individuals. Variability may change over the life span. Individuals with similar genotypes can thrive in a variety of environments. Conversely, because expression of the genotype depends on environmental influences, individuals with different genetic makeups may express similar phenotypes in similar environmental circumstances. The specific outcome (phenotype) within the range of possible reactions is not predictable a priori from genetic information alone.

Individual variability in expression means that heredity is not a simple translation of genetic material into physical outcomes. Fuller and Thompson (1960) cautioned that heritability is a characteristic associated with populations and not with the traits in question; thus, heritability measures are estimates of the proportion of variance in trait expression within a population and do not predict the likelihood that an individual within a given gene pool will display a particular trait.

Many complex forms of behavior, such as intelligence, depend on the presence of multiple genes, and the expression of those genes depends on multiple levels of interactions with the environment. This intricate sequence of interactions suggests that differences in phenotypes for complex behavior cannot and should not be thought of in terms of abstract trait expressions. Traits represent distributions of realized phenotypes, among alternative expressions, but distributions represent trait expression within a population at a given time; these can be expected to change as genetic and environmental factors within the gene pool change (Plomin, Defries, & Fulkner, 1988).

Baumrind (1991) cautioned that the proportion of genetic variation between individuals in a population tells nothing about how or why individuals differ in development. Nor does it suggest how to nurture that development, or how genes and environments interact. Heritability estimates cannot measure the potential impact alterations in the environment will have on development of a given genotype, nor are they indices of the efficacy of targeted interventions (environmental manipulations) designed to alter trait expression positively. In essence, heritablity measures are a kind of census taking. A proper census can estimate the number of people living in a given area and percentages falling into various categories (gender, ethnicity, occupation, socioeconomic status, and so forth) within that locale at a specific time. However, the census does not usually tell how the persons surveyed came to be there, when they arrived, or how long they plan to stay; it helps to identify general trends, but not individual behavior.

Third, the concept of intelligence utilized in *The Bell Curve* is archaic and does not do justice to emergent views that reflect a more dynamic, multifaceted, modifiable, and context-specific construct than does the traditional notion (Gardner, 1983; Sternberg, 1994). Modern cognitive scientists take a more optimistic view of the possibilities for growth and change. When we limit the measurement of intelligence to those developed abilities that have traditionally been privileged in academic and technologically advanced settings, we neglect a wide range of highly valued human capabilities for adaptation that may have developed in other settings but could well be adapted to current needs and expectations.

Webster's New Collegiate Dictionary (1977, p. 600) defines *intelligence* as the "ability to learn or understand from experiences; the ability to acquire and retain knowledge; mental ability" and "the ability to respond quickly and successfully to a new situation, the use of the faculty of reason in solving problems." Intellectual behavior, then, refers to the cumulative capacity for processing and storing information, and for making adaptive responses to familiar and novel circumstances. When Cole, Gay, Glick, and Sharp (1971) concluded that all groups of human beings appear to represent in their developed abilities a wide range of intellective competencies, they were, no doubt, thinking of intelligence as the capacity to adapt to one's environment and to apply past experiences in dealing with both similar and novel environmental encounters.

Weinberg (1989), examining Mayr's (1982) division of intellective styles into "lumpers and splitters," identified the former with the notion of intelligence as a

> general unified capacity for acquiring knowledge, reasoning, and solving problems that is demonstrated in different ways (navigating a course without a compass, memorizing the Koran, or programming a computer). (p. 103)

Although Weinberg's "different ways" connotes some diversity, there is a narrowness in the lumperian approach that refers not only to an overall summative ability but to its manifestation in abstract reasoning and recall. In contrast, the "splitters" seek to isolate (at least for study) different types of intellectual ability. Gardner (1983), for example, has posited linguistic, spatial, and other types of intelligence, the assessment of at least some of which seems to call for heterogeneous indicators.

Because this variety of manifestations of intellectual behavior is largely ignored, many forms of response and coping are not recognized as "intelligent," and intelligence readily becomes synonymous with the privileged practices of the dominant culture. The particular form that cognitive abilities or bodies of knowledge come to possess is dependent on the experiences of individuals within their environments. Whether the focus is on practical problem solving, logical reasoning, abstract symbolization, or social judgment, if the frames of reference by which criteria are drawn are too narrow, evaluation of any one or all of these categories of intellectual function is likely to be flawed.

The adaptive or "intelligent" status assigned to a particular form of behavior should be determined with reference to its current and historical contexts. Failure to judge behavior by its adaptive functions at numerous levels of expression and in particular environmental contexts appears to be a common problem in prevailing notions of human intelligence. This holds true for the unitary notion of intelligence employed in much of the psychological research, which fails to deal with the construct as genuinely complex—a composite of dispositions, aptitudes, and developed or developing abilities and achievements (Anastasi, 1980).

This brings us to the growing division between the worlds of the cognitive elites and the cognitive have-nots, which, while real, is not necessary. Whether one believes that intellectual abilities are developed or inherited, in a society where the number of people with less ability is increasing faster than the number with more, we have no choice but to foster the development of intellect in all people, and to engage seriously the task of applying what we know about the development of individual abilities. Given the changing demographics in the United States, even if intellectual ability *were* constrained by genetics, prudent policy would favor testing the limits of deliberate and directed development of intelligence and intellectual achievement in all their diverse expressions. The broad range of possible reactions of genetic material to environmental interactions suggests that human societies have only begun to explore the possibilities for developing human competencies that fall at varying points along a wide distribution of developed ability.

Finally, even if Herrnstein and Murray's interpretations of the science were accurate, their policy judgments are needlessly negative and sometimes pejorative. As Gardner (1994) has asserted, their data can equally well support more humane and interventionist policy solutions. For example, a national response to the persistent gap between Blacks and Whites on most tests of intelligence could aim at ensuring more nearly equal life circumstances and opportunities between the two groups or the maintenance and reinforcement of interventions that have shown promise. Early intervention is a case in point. Studies of the long-term effects of Head Start indicate that the life chances of children exposed to programs of high quality are significantly better than those of children who have not had the benefit of such intervention. However, even if the immediate benefits of Head Start are found to fade over time, it is at least as sensible to conclude that the program needs to be prolonged (e.g., Project Follow Through) as to conclude that Head Start itself is not effective.

What if, despite Herrnstein and Murray's flawed treatment of the issues, their assertion of a genetic basis for developed abilities in different social divisions of human subjects turned out to be true? What policy implications would flow from differences in the biological underpinnings of adaptive abilities? From all that we currently know, such possibilities are quite remote. Still, before dismissing the questions as heretical, consider how often these days we hear of new findings identifying a genetic basis for specific human conditions.

I, for one, do not choose to be placed in the position of rejecting the scientifically established facts of genetics. It is my considered opinion that groups that share the same gene pool and similar environmental interactions are likely to share patterns of behavioral adaptation. I believe that certain patterns of mental functioning may adhere to members of specific groups of human beings who share common life conditions. I do not believe that mental functioning is immutable, even if it were proved to be in some ways predetermined. However, I am unable to embrace the notion that ethnicity and class are appropriate indicators of group membership for purposes of studying intelligence. I am dubious about the manner in which we go about assigning persons to these specific social divisions, and about our tendency to make generalizations concerning their characteristics and experiences.

But let us return to the questions just posed. What if differences in the measured developed abilities (call it intelligence if you must) of groups of human subjects were definitively determined to be of *genetic* origin? What is a humane and democratic society to do? Alas, the questions are not new and their answer remains the same. It was some 25 years ago that Benjamin Bloom (1969), having to address these very same issues, concluded: "The improvement of education and other environments is really the only means available to a civilized society for the improvement of the lot and fate of man" (p. 421).

CHAPTER 3

Cultural Dissonance as a Risk Factor in the Development of Students

WITH CONSTANCE YOWELL

In human social organization, when one's characteristics are at variance in significant ways from the modal characteristics of the social group that has achieved hegemony, one is likely to find little correspondence between the developmental supports provided by the dominant group and the developmental needs of the persons whose characteristics are different. This is a function of the operation of a principle of social economy whereby social orders design and allocate resources in accordance with the modal or otherwise valued characteristics of the social order. Thus, we have schools, public facilities, media, and so on, that are designed and allocated to fit the needs of persons whose vision and hearing are intact rather than to serve the needs of persons with sensory impairments. Consequently, persons with disabilities in these sensory modalities are at risk of developmental and educational failure, not necessarily as a function of the impairments, but because the society is not organized to adequately support the developmental needs of persons whose characteristics are at variance with those that are modal.

Following this line of reasoning, the identification of a population as being at risk of failure is always situational and relative. In its early usage, "at-risk" status was used to refer to persons with identifiable sensory, physical, or intellectual disabilities that were likely to result in their failure to benefit from the normal range of developmental resources generally available. Their risk of failure was related to the goals or objectives the society expected most children to achieve even in the absence of specialized resources, and to the implicit recognition that without such resources expected achievement was unlikely. It was in the latter half of the current century that we began to think of persons as being at-risk of

Adapted with permission of Teachers College Press. Copyright © 1994 by Teachers College, Columbia University. In R. J. Rossi (Ed.), *Schools and Students at Risk* (pp. 51–69).

failure to achieve an adequate education because of their social circumstances—that is, their ethnicity, culture, language, or economic status.

This shift in emphasis from one class of indicators to another may be a reflection of a decline in the relative number of persons with mental, physical, and sensory disabilities; the society's enhanced capacity to address the problems of these groups; an increase in the numbers of persons whose social status places them at a disadvantage in the society; and the increasing recognition of the society's lack of success in meeting the developmental needs of this newly recognized group.

In the identification of populations of children at risk of failure to adequately develop or be educated, it is important that both the old and the new categories of persons be included. It is also important that we recognize the special at-risk status of persons who are doubly or triply at risk; that is, those who fall into two or three of the at-risk categories. An example of such a person is a language-minority group member who is female, hard of hearing, and African-American. For the purposes of our discussions, however, these will be treated as extreme cases, and the more common patterns of at-risk status will be our focus. Traditionally, at-risk status has referenced the characteristics of the persons so designated. Typical of this approach is Rosehan's (1967) list of attributes of at-risk students.

1. They commonly come from broken homes.
2. They are nonverbal and concrete-minded.
3. They are physically less healthy than their middle-class peers.
4. They lack stable identification figures or role models.
5. They lack stable community ties because of their constant migration.
6. They are often handicapped by their color, which provides them with a negative self-image.
7. They are handicapped in the expression and comprehension of language.
8. They tend to be extroverted rather than introverted. (p. 39)

However, it may be useful to utilize a more dynamic conception of the construct. We hold that at-risk status refers not simply to the characteristics of persons, but to an interaction between the traits of such persons and the context in which they live their lives. Being at risk of failure may be an iatrogenic condition; that is, it may be more appropriately conceptualized as a condition or circumstance brought on by the failure or incapacity of the developmental environment to support the needs of the developing person. Consider the fact that all persons who show some of the above characteristics identified with being at risk do not appear at risk in their interactions in many contexts. All persons for whom English is a second language or who claim African-American identity or who have a physical disability do not flounder. In fact, some such persons have relatively uneventful courses of development and achieve quite adequately. In our work (e.g., Gordon & Song, 1992), we have found that many such persons develop in environments that have been specially structured to ensure that appropriate supports are available and that incapacitating barriers are eliminated or circumvented. We conclude that at-risk status is a function of the inappropriateness of developmental environments to the needs of the person and that a focus on these deficient environments may be more productive than a focus on the characteristics of the persons. We can, then, define at-risk as referring to a category of persons whose personal characteristics, conditions of life, and situational circumstances, in interactions with each other, make it likely that their development and/ or education will be less than optimal.

To better understand the interactions between these characteristics and life situations, it is important to make still another distinction— between the status and functional characteristics of persons (Gordon & Shipman, 1979). Status characteristics like ethnicity, gender, class, and language generally define one's status in the social order. Status is likely to influence one's access to resources, the nature of one's opportunities and rewards, and what is expected, as well as the character and quality of society's investment in one's development. Functional characteristics refer to the "hows" of behavior and generally to the ways in which persons function. Functional characteristics, often culturally determined, include belief systems, cognitive style, dispositions, language systems, mores, skills, and technologies (i.e., ways of doing things). Obviously there are interactions and overlap between status and functional characteristics, but either set of traits can facilitate or frustrate development and education by virtue of its primary characteristics. However, there are secondary characteristics that adhere to each category that may be of greater consequence for development than is the influence of status on the distribution of resources or the influence of function on the organization of behavior. We refer to the personal identification and attribution processes that derive from one's status as well as from one's way of functioning. Both help to define one's concept of self and the manner in which one identifies oneself. Ultimately, even though status and functional characteristics may be the developmental antecedents of identity, it may be identity that provides the energy behind behavioral adaptation. How then do human characteristics in interaction with social circumstances influence the development of identity, and what is the relationship between sources of one's identity and one's being at risk of developmental and educational failure to thrive? We submit that culture is the context and the ubiquitous vehicle.

CULTURE AND HUMAN DEVELOPMENT

Psychologists and anthropologists such as Cole et al. (1971) have concluded that regardless of cultural, ethnic, gender, or class differences among human groups, there are no corresponding differences in cognitive and affective processes. Rather, it is held that the basic processes of mentation in the human species—for example, association, recall, perception, inference, discrimination, and so forth—are common and it is prior experiences, situations, and meanings that form the context for the development and expression of these processes. Because experiences, situation, and meanings are culturally determined, the quality of the development of a process, the conditions under which it is expressed, and even our ability to recognize its manifestations are dependent on cultural phenomena that are often mediated through ethnic, gender, or class identity.

Our conception of risk factors offers an example of the importance of discussing the culturally embedded nature of human experience and meaning. In the past, we have framed our conception of at-risk status or vulnerability in terms of risk factors, such as gender, demographic status, social and intellectual resources, genetic history, mobility patterns, and negative or traumatic life events. What we have not accounted for in this conception of at-risk status is the fact that over half of the individuals who may experience the most severe stressors do not report psychological or social dysfunction (Waxman, de Felix, Anderson, & Baptiste, 1992). Gordon, Rollock, and Miller (1990) have suggested that threats to the integrity of behavioral development and adaptation may exist along a continuum, with the degree of threat better defined by existential meaning than by "reality" factors; the individual's reaction to the threat may depend on the actual perception or the connotation that is permitted by the context in which the phenomenon is experienced.

Culture Defined

It is becoming clear, then, that culture is a construct with a wide variety of definitions and conceptions. Authors have often sought to distinguish between material and nonmaterial aspects of culture. Belief systems, attitudes, and attributions are examples of nonmaterial culture, while tools, skills, and artifacts serve as examples of material culture. We hold, however, that at its core, culture is responsible for all human behavior. That is, when we speak of culture, we are speaking of both the cause and the product of human affect and cognition.

Both Geertz (1973) and Tylor (1958) have provided us with widely accepted indices and definitions for culture. In his perception of culture, Tylor included "knowledge, beliefs, art, morals, law, custom, and any other capabilities and habits acquired by man as a member of society" (p. 1), while Geertz (1973) viewed culture as a "historically transmitted pattern of meanings embodied in symbolic form by means of which men communicate, perpetuate, and develop their knowledge about and attitudes toward life" (p. 89). We see, then, an effort to discuss culture in terms of objects or tools as well as language and shared conceptual schemata. In joining these perceptions of culture, we can derive five fundamental dimensions of the construct.

1. The judgmental or normative dimension is a reflection of society's standards and values, which often provide the constraints within which thought is facilitated.
2. The cognitive dimension consists of categories of mentation (such as social perceptions, conceptions, attribution, and connotations) that are often expressed through language.
3. The affective dimension refers to the emotional structure of a social unit and its common feelings, sources of motivation, and so on.
4. The skill dimension relates to those special capabilities the members of a culture develop in order to meet the demands of their social and techno-economic environment (Ogbu, 1978).
5. The technological dimension refers not only to different or more highly developed technological practices, but more importantly to the impact of the different information inherent in these practices on cognitive and affective behaviors.

These dimensions serve to emphasize those characteristics by which a culture may be identified or by which the culture of a group may be characterized. It is in this descriptive definition of culture that we begin to see the reference points for one's social or group identity, as well as the experiences that provide a context for one's conception of his or her own (as well as others') patterns of behavior.

Function of Culture

The function of culture in human activity, however, does not end with its role as a descriptive concept. In addition to providing the referents for group identity, culture also provides the stimuli and the consequences of human behavioral patterns. Thus, culture also serves as an explanatory construct. As mentioned earlier, when we discuss cultural information in terms of description, we are articulating the status phenomenon of culture, and in general are both referring to the social identity of individuals (Goffman, 1963)—the group to which I belong—and describing the effect of this identity on an individual's access to resources. When we seek to explain behavior, however, and discuss the influence of one's personal identity—the group to which I feel that I belong—we begin to wonder how particular language and belief systems, specific objects and tools, not to mention technological advances, influence or enable the behavior of individuals. When we examine ways of thinking—such as linear and sequential thought, tendency to generate abstractions, field dependence and independence, connotations and taxonomies as well as allowable metaphors—we are becoming aware of culture as a vehicle for cognition. Ultimately, culture provides the constraints within which mentation and affect are enabled.

Furthermore, culture serves as a mediator for learning in two fundamental respects. According to Vygotsky's (1978) notions of cognitive development, learning occurs within social interaction—that is, in contrast to the Piagetian conception of self-constructed knowledge. Vygotsky argued that the development of higher psychological functions is rooted in children's primary social interactions. Learning, based on the cultural-historical theory, consists of three fundamental activities: transmission of knowledge and cognitive skills, cultivation of cognitive abilities, and the encouragement of these cognitive abilities. According to this conception, knowledge in one's culture is socially transmitted by adults and capable peers to children. The adult or capable peer, in joint activity, serves as a role model or expert tutor on a task that allows for cognitive processes to be demonstrated and then practiced and learned. New cognitive abilities emerge as the adult works with the child on tasks that may have originally been too demanding for the child. As the pair work in collaboration, with the adult providing encouragement as well as appropriate feedback, the child gradually begins to take on the responsibility of the task. While initiating the activity within the child's "zone of proximal development," the adult in time begins to remove support as the child becomes more competent at the task. It is in this form of social scaffolding that we see the mechanism for growth and development in cognitive functioning.

We cannot overstate the importance of an individual's group and personal identity in the social interaction that constitutes the learning process. A secondary human characteristic to status and functional characteristics, one's sense of self—mediated by culture—provides the fuel for the social interaction inherent in learning behavior. Not only does human cognition develop through cultural encounters, but it is also through these same social interactions that we begin to recognize and identify our identity. Culture provides the reference points that allow me not only to recognize myself in terms of my gender, class, and ethnicity, but also to acknowledge that I am separate from others. It is this complex sense of self that I bring to the classroom, that must in turn be met and integrated into the dynamic culture of the learning environment in order for optimal development to occur. This interaction between self and the learning environment is dialectical in nature: Not only will the learning process enable me to grow and change in fundamental ways, but my development will clearly have an impact on the culture of the learning environment.

Mechanism for Culture

We have discussed in detail the impact of culture on what one does and how one does it. Similarly, we have also addressed the manner in which culture frames as well as enables one's feelings and thoughts concerning what one does. This question arises, however: By what mechanism does culture serve as the vehicle and context for human activity? This question can be answered across several levels of understanding—biological, psychological, and social. We will begin at the cellular level and work our way up to the arena of social institutions.

Work in the field of cell assemblies and synaptogenesis provides new perspectives on the interrelationships between neural activity, experience, and behavior. Specifically, Hebb (1949) discussed a model for understanding the relationship between brain function and experience. Neural cells differentiate and, based on experience, associate with each other in a manner that forms "cell assemblies." While a single cell may associate with several assemblies, under appropriate stimulation specific assemblies are activated. It is possible to argue, then, that it is culture that provides the stimuli and the context through which experience actively shapes the organization of brain cells. Further, with respect to reinforcement, it is certainly culture that serves to give meaning to the overt expressions of behavioral products of these cell assemblies—meanings and reinforcements, which in turn allow the behavioral products to become established patterns of behavior activity.

In addition to the association or differentiation patterns of cells, the density of synaptic connections is also fundamentally determined by experiences during the late prenatal and early postnatal periods of development. During the process of synaptogenesis, synaptic connections are first overproduced, followed by a later period of selective degeneration.

Greenough, Black, and Wallace (1987) have theorized that experience, in its role as activator of neural activity, is responsible both for the organization of synapses and for the selection of which of these synapses will degenerate.

Greenough et al. (1987) further advanced a theory of experience-expectant and experience-dependent processes to account for the relationship between synaptic connections and experience. Briefly, the experience-expectant theory hypothesizes that relevant or normal experience results in normal neural activity that in turn maintains typical synaptic connections. Conversely, an absence of experience or atypical experience may lead to irregular synaptic connections. In Greenough's second theory, the experience-dependent hypothesis states that specific neural activity, which results in the formation of synapses, is caused by new information processing on the part of the organism.

It is clear, then, that on the biological level we see a dynamic interaction between the environment and human development. This is also true for the interaction between social institutions and human behavioral patterns. Sociocultural context is mediated through institutional structures as well as personal interaction. This sociocultural context, in the form of family, religious institutions, schools, and the like, provides the stimuli (values, norms, skills, and technological devices) that serve to organize cognitive and affective behavior in much the same way that experience shapes synaptic connections. It should be understood, however, that the relationship between culture and social institutions is a reciprocal one. The relations between education and culture serve to exemplify the dialectical nature of change. Our educational system exists as a broader social context. Over the course of time, our society has moved to embrace the concept of education for all citizens. In turn, however, this educated citizenry is now capable of creating tremendous change within our culture.

On the micro level, the sociocultural context is mediated through personal social interactions. It is here, in teaching interactions that take the form of social scaffolding, that learners develop a system of structures and affective cognitive skills that are congruent with the values, beliefs, and conventions of their sociocultural group. The interaction between learner and significant other is premised on reciprocity. While it provides the learner with the opportunity to develop personal attributions, dispositions, and motivations to behave in essentially appropriate ways, the growth of the learner creates new demands on the tutor.

Ultimately, it is the social institution that may come to replace or function in parallel with the significant other, as both a source of reinforcement and a vehicle for the normative dimension of culture. It is through the processes of assimilation, accommodation, and adaptation of schemata that cultural transmission occurs. Schematization represents the mechanism by which conceptual structures come to represent cognitive, conative, and affective components of phenomena experienced. In accommodation, then, the acquisition and replication of stimulus/response/situation triads is related to existing schemata, while in adaptation the existing schemata or emerging conceptual frames are adapted to the demands of currently perceived or changing conditions.

Cultural Conflict

It is in the relationship between social institutions and the learner that high degrees of dissonance can result in failure to learn or a distortion of the learning process. In a society with tremendous cultural diversity and a culturally hegemonic educational system, dissonance between what is learned in personal interaction with the significant other may come into conflict with demands and expectations of the social institution. Precision of language offers an example of such dissonance. It is not uncommon in some cultures for individuals to use signal words to represent deeper meanings rather than the elaborated language we have come to associate with the academy. In some groups, numbers and time are evoked in the form of estimation rather than the precise calculations and specific references used in high-technology-dominated cultures. In an educational system that allows only for the precision of exact calculation—that is, a system that does not appreciate the potential for cultural differences in the ways that people use numbers—this demand for exactness may place a child at risk of failure to thrive in the school setting.

It should be understood that while some cultures may place a greater emphasis on technological development than other cultures, the notion of a "culturally deprived" people is a misnomer. The challenge for education thus becomes the enabling of bridging between cultures and of the learning of multiple cultures, and the appreciation of multiple ways of viewing things in all students.

It is the failure or inability of the school to bridge between conflicting cultures that renders schooling a risk-inducing phenomenon for many students. Since learning is such a personal achievement, it is critically dependent on the learner's engagement in the process. When the learning process comes to be associated with that which is "not me," that which is alien to me, learning task engagement is interfered with. E. T. Gordon (1992) has described what he calls "resistant culture" to refer to the sometimes elaborate systems of belief and behavior adopted by African-American males to insulate themselves from the demands of acculturation and socialization experiences that they consider alien or hostile to their interests. Some of these adaptations serve prosocial ends. Others are clearly antisocial. In both instances, however, they represent defense mechanisms for the youth and barriers to intervention. Given the ineptitude of much that we do for these youth and the actual destructiveness of some of our actions, these adaptations cannot be rejected. Rather they must be understood and taken into account as intervention plans are developed. In the absence of such respect, alienation and resistance in the face of cultural conflict must be expected.

It is these instances of cultural conflict that are so challenging and frustrating in the design of educational services for children who are at risk. Educators who are sensitive to the diversity of at-risk children should be respectful of their indigenous orientations and values, but these are sometimes at odds with the goals toward which education is directed. If it were simply a matter of cultural taste, the choices would be simpler, even if the implementation might not be. However, in some circumstances, what we are dealing with are resistant cultural values that are politically functional but developmentally dysfunctional. Decisions concerning the quality of educational pursuits and the choice of more challenging courses are examples. For some time now we have taken the position that the educator has a professional responsibility to make these hard choices for the student, when the student's risk status renders him or her incapable of making an informed decision. In such cases, the final criterion must be increasing options for the student. If the professionally made choice reduces future alternatives for the student, we feel that it is probably not in his or her best interest. If it increases alternatives for choice, we feel that the professional has the responsibility to act.

IMPLICATIONS FOR EDUCATIONAL REFORM

Several implications for educational reform flow from this way of thinking about at-risk status. Among these are

1. limitations of reform of school governance;
2. limitations of efforts at accountability and standards;
3. social justice and distributional equity;
4. adaptability and complementarity; and
5. diversity, pluralism, contextualism, and perspectivism.

Limitations of Reform of School Governance

Most of the action on the school reform front has been directed at changes in the organizational structure and governance of schools. In a number of school systems across the nation, efforts are under way to increase teacher participation in decisions concerning what happens in schools. This notion rests on the logical conclusion that people are likely to work more effectively when they are pursuing goals and actions of their own choosing—when they feel some sense of ownership of the programs and projects in which they are engaged. The basic idea is consistent with related developments in the industrial sector and is thought to partially explain the reported differences between the productivity of autocratic and democratic management styles.

In what was perhaps the largest effort to apply this concept, the public school system of Chicago at one time directed most of its reform efforts at the decentralization of governance and site-based management. The funds from a court decree were used (1) to provide staff development in decision-making and management in schools implementing site-based management, and (2) to provide modest support for curriculum enrichment. However, available achievement data do not yet suggest that the goal required by the decree, a 50% reduction in academic underachievement, was reached (Gordon, 1991).

Site-based management seems to have become the current panacea for much that is considered wrong with schooling, despite the finding that such efforts have done more for teacher morale than for student achievement (Collins & Hanson, 1991). Most advocates for this approach to school reform argue that real change cannot occur without support from staff, and site-based management is the supposed route to such involvement and support. But active participation in the decision-making and management of schools requires more than authorization to participate. It requires know-how, resources, and societal commitment—none of which is in adequate supply. With respect to know-how, until we strengthen the pedagogical and substantive competence of our teaching force, their involvement in decision-making and school improvement is likely to have limited impact. In addition, if the primary goal of many of our efforts at school reform is to reduce the incidence of school failure among those students who present very diverse characteristics to the school and who are currently served poorly by our schools, the current reforms in school governance hardly seem to be the treatment of choice.

Limitations of Efforts at Accountability and Standards

Many of the states and certainly the federal government have staked their hopes for school reform and the improvement of education for children at risk of failure on the imposition of higher standards of academic achievement and some attempts at establishing systems by which schools can be held accountable for their productivity. Now there is no question that the standards by which we judge academic achievement and to which we consistently fail to hold schools accountable are too low. They compare poorly with the standards achieved in other technologically advanced countries. However, it can be argued that our standards and achievement are low not simply because our sights are too low but because our practices of and provisions for education are inappropriate to the requirements of educational excellence. Among the most prominent efforts at goals and standards-setting are the president's National Goals for Education, the efforts of several states in setting higher standards, the discipline-based standards work, and the (nongovernment) New Standards Project. All have begun by devoting prime attention to the achievement outcomes of schooling. While the National Goals and state standards would be measured by new educational achievement tests, the New Standards Project proposes a new system of educational assessment. The latter is headed in the right direction with respect to assessment, but all of these efforts give woefully little attention to the importance of educational inputs, commonly referred to as "opportunity to learn."

One cannot argue with the substance of the national education goals, for each iterates a rational expectation of what will be required for meaningful, satisfying, and responsible participation in the social order. The values reflected in such goals send a powerful message to school systems across the country concerning what the nation expects from its schools. However, a very negative message is sent by the promulgation of such goals in the absence of the resources, know-how, and national commitment to ensure that schools and students are enabled to meet these goals. Nothing in the national effort speaks to the desperate need for staff development and the improvement of the quality of the labor force in schools. In that effort there is no attention given to the states' responsibility for ensuring that schools have the capacities to deliver the educational services necessary to the achievement of such goals. Nowhere is there any recognition of the things that must happen outside of schools to enable schools and students to reach these goals. Without attention to these extra-school forces, it is folly to expect that the national effort will address questions of responsibility for ensuring that these enabling conditions will prevail.

In the New York City Chancellor's Commission on Minimum Standards (Gordon, 1986), the case was made for the importance of symmetry in the pursuit of school accountability. After identifying achievement-level targets as standards, the report proposed that standards also be set for professional practice and for institutional capacity. New York City, other school districts, the federal government, and the New Standards Project have yet to seriously engage standards for practice and capacity. Yet if we are to expect that children at risk of failure and other children as well will experience great improvements in their academic performance, it is more likely to come from holding to higher standards those of us who manage their education and guide their learning. Darling-Hammond (1992) has begun the iteration of an approach to such standards of practice and capacity. The problem is that it is relatively easy to arrive at agreement on what students should know and know how to do, while it is very difficult to agree on what the educational inputs should be to achieve these aims without becoming overly prescriptive or—what is more problematic politically—without facing questions concerning entitlements and the fixing of responsibility for costs. If the field can ever agree on a set of standards for professional practice and school capability, do we then have a basis for asking the courts to hold schools or states responsible for making them available, especially to children at risk of school failure?

Social Justice and Distributional Equity

As we turn to the actual distribution of educational resources, we encounter different kinds of problems. In their now classic report, Coleman and colleagues (1966) challenged the society to separate school achievement from such social origins as class and race. The nation responded with several efforts directed at the equalization of educational opportunity. Enlightened as these efforts were and despite considerable expenditure of money and effort, educational achievement has continued to adhere to the social divisions by which status in our society is allocated. One of the reasons this problem is so recalcitrant is the confusion of distributional equality (ensuring that all have equal access to the educational resources of the society) and distributional equity, which requires that resources be distributed in proportion to need. Persons who need more educational resources cannot be said to have been treated with equity on receiving an equal share, when what is needed is a share equal to their need. What is required here is a more appropriate conception of justice. Rawls (1971) has advanced a theory of justice that holds acceptable an unequal distribution of resources that favors the weakest members of society. Our concern for resource distribution sufficient to the needs of persons most at risk of failure is in keeping with Rawls's theory of social justice. In the presence of students with widely diverse learning characteristics and conditions of life, standardized educational treatments may be dysfunctional (Gordon & Shipman, 1979). We may not be meeting the needs of student A when we provide for her the same educational treatment that we provide for student B, just as we do not provide for medical patients with different needs when we dispense the same medical treatments to them. Where there are groups of students known to present themselves at school without the acknowledged prerequisites for optimal learning, social justice requires that they be treated differently in order to serve their needs. We had begun to honor this notion in the court decision in *Lau v. Nichols* (1974), which required that where there were concentrations of non-English-speaking students, schools must provide some instruction in the students' first language. In such cases, the school's adaptation was to the language characteristics of the students. Readers are no doubt aware of the growing efforts to limit or eliminate such accommodations for those students who either demonstrate limited English proficiency or are English language learners. The courts have not yet extended this concept to include learning styles, cultural referents, temperament, temporal factors, or health/nutritional conditions. Yet if the needs of students who are at risk are to be adequately (and equitably) served, schools must find ways to adapt to the full range of characteristics that place students at risk. Without such adaptation, the values implicit in our conceptions of social justice and equity are not served.

Adaptability and Complementarity

If we recognize that children come to our schools with varying degrees of readiness for academic learning and differential patterns of support for educational pursuits, it is necessary that schools be adaptable to these different characteristics and circumstances as educators guide students toward the goals of schooling. When we add the fact that students have been differentially acculturated and socialized, giving them quite different cultural schemata, cultural styles, and related attitudes and dispositions, schools have the added task of developing the capacity to complement much of what students bring to school in bridging from where these children are to where they will need to go in the process of gaining a sound, basic education and becoming effective adult members of society. In the service of adaptation, both our students and our schools must give and take as we try to reconcile differences between the worlds of home and school. In the service of complementarity, the focus is on conserving the respective strengths of both students and schools as we construct connections between the two. Complementarity assumes that beneath the surface differences that exist between groups and institutions, the basic human needs and goals are quite similar, and when made explicit, can be brought into facilitatory and supportive relationships with one another. For example, we point to the investigation of the acquisition of higher-order thinking skills and strategies by inner-city high school students. After considerable effort at teaching such skills, with little success at getting students to transfer what they had learned in the laboratory to regular academic tasks, we discovered that many of these young people already knew and used some of these skills (e.g., "executive strategies") in their daily lives. However, these students were typically unaware of their applicability to academic problems and, consequently, did not use them in school settings. In addition, then, to teaching new skills and strategies, we turned to making the utility and application of such skills explicit. We bridged the two problem-solving situations and made explicit the applicability of these strategies, which they had learned and did apply in the indigenous situation, to the alien situation. Success in using something they already knew from an "old" setting, to solve problems in a new setting, proved to be easier than learning what appeared to be new skills that were to be applied in a new (academic) setting.

For years, good teachers have attempted to adapt learning experiences to the characteristics and circumstances of learners. Bloom's (1968) mastery learning, for example, does not simply require more time on task for those who require it, but introduces variations in methods of presentation to counteract boredom and more fully engage students. Even some of our misguided efforts at ability grouping are based on the idea that different teaching strategies and pace are useful in the teaching of students who differ. Although the aptitude-treatment-interaction paradigm has failed to find support in much of the extant research, even Cronbach and Snow (1977) still find the paradigm appealing. It may well be that Messick (1976) is correct in suggesting that the problem with the absence of supportive research findings is related to the fact that many of us have been counting the score before we learned to play the game. Cronbach and Snow provide an excellent critique of the technical problems in much of this research (see also Chapter 6). However, the prevailing conception of the relationships in the paradigm may be misconceived. It may not be the direct interaction between learner characteristics and learning treatments that produces learning outcomes, but that learner characteristics interact with learning treatments to produce learner behaviors (time on task, task engagement, energy deployment, etc.) and that it is these learner behaviors that account for learning outcomes.

Without appropriate learner behaviors, achievement is not likely to occur even in the presence of an appropriate match between learner characteristics and learning treatments.

Diversity, Pluralism, Contextualism, and Perspectivism

Concern with the cultural backgrounds out of which learners come forces us to give attention in education to such philosophical constructs as diversity, pluralism, contextualism, and perspectivism. Each of these notions has its conventional meaning, but in education each has special significance. Attention to diversity requires that differences that adhere to individuals and groups be factored into the design and delivery of teaching and learning transactions. We have discussed some of these implications above under adaptability and complementarity. Attention to diversity in schools is often reflected in the individualization or at least the customizing of education relative to individuals' idiosyncratic characteristics.

Pluralism, which is often used as if it were synonymous with diversity, actually refers to the increasing demand that learners develop multiple competencies, some of which will apply generally while others will be more applicable to idiosyncratic settings. All of us find ourselves increasingly in situations where we must meet other than indigenous standards. Thus it is required that we become multilingual, multicultural, multiskilled, and capable of functioning in multiple environments and settings. So, while education is influenced by and must be responsive to the differences with which learners enter the educational system, the exit characteristics of its students must reflect the pluralistic demands of the society in which they live.

In a similar manner, education must be sensitive to variations in the contexts from which students come and in which schooling occurs. Here, values and belief systems provide important examples. Engagement in schooling and effectiveness of learning seem to proceed best when there is congruence between the home context and the school context, when the values of the community are not contradicted by the values of the school. Concern for parent involvement in the school is often misplaced on actual presence or participation in school activities. However, we are increasingly persuaded that the critical variable is not participation, but the absence of dissonance between home and school. Where there is support for common values, participation on the part of parents may be a by-product. Nevertheless, while participation is desirable, it is neither necessary nor sufficient, whereas contextual complimentarily, or congruence, is both.

Context refers to environment, surrounds, conditions, situations, and circumstances; context specificity, however, cannot be permitted to preclude the school's attention to perspective. In our concern for perspective we recognize that diverse characteristics and contexts are associated with differences in world views. People who live their lives differently are likely to have different perspectives on things. However, it is dysfunctional for education if students are not able to see the world from the perspectives of persons and peoples who differ from themselves. Cultural variation in populations is associated with people with different characteristics, who come from different contexts, and who may have different perspectives. These differences may place them at risk of school failure if education does not function effectively to build on these differences to enable pluralistic competencies and the capacity for multiperspectivist thought and problem solving. Especially for children who are at risk of failure by virtue of their differences from those children schools find it easy to serve, respectful concern for diversity, pluralism, context, and perspective must be at the heart of educational planning and service.

CONCLUSION

In the current debates around improving education and opportunities for at-risk students, related dimensions of the problem such as multicultural education, educational equity for students who are at risk of failure, and approaches to school reform are most often treated as separate issues. Unless the several components are viewed and treated conjointly, as if they are all parts of a single problem, we continue this separation at the risk of continued educational failure. For those who are other than members of the hegemonic culture—that is, for those whose cultural identity or experience is alien to that of the dominant culture—such identity can be experienced as a risk factor. This recognition of cultural dissonance as a risk factor has implications for what we do in our efforts to achieve a higher degree of social justice in and through education.

Sensitivity to the facts of cultural dissonance should reshape the school reform agenda. The focus on change in school governance alone is an insufficient resource and could lead to reforms that are largely irrelevant to the quality of education received by children who are at risk. In addition, the current emphasis on accountability and outcome standards based on educational achievement test data is questionable education policy, especially in the absence of bilateral symmetry in the concern for standards (concern for quality of school and staff inputs that is equal to concern that has been expressed for achievement outcomes) and in the absence of a social contract that guarantees that students are enabled to meet the new standards. Neither the focus on governance alone nor the emphasis on student achievement standards will realize desired outcomes for students who are at risk of failure. Both areas of reform will have to be coupled with a commitment to educational standards. With respect to the concern for equity, we argue that social justice requires that educational resources not be equal but be sufficient to the needs that students bring to the schools. This will in some instances require different and unequal resource allocations. In response to the facts of cultural dissonance, that is, cultural diversity under conditions of cultural hegemony, we argue for the creative application of pedagogical principles and practices that reflect and respect adaptability, complementarity, context sensitivity, human diversity, and social pluralism. Cultural dissonance places students at risk of educational failure. If education is to be made more effective for such students, efforts at the improvement and reform of education must address this risk factor.

CHAPTER 4

Common Destinies—Continuing Dilemmas

WITH AUNDRA SAA MEROË

I must again in candor say to you members of this Commission—it is a kind of Alice in Wonderland—with the same moving pictures reshown over and over again, the same analysis, the same recommendations, and the same inaction.
— Kenneth Clark's reflections on the 1968 Report of the National Advisory Committee on Civil Disorders (Kerner, 1968)

The publication of *A Common Destiny* (Jaynes & Williams, 1989),* the product of a committee appointed by the National Research Council to study the current status of Blacks in American society, was welcome but frustrating. Jaynes and Williams compiled a valuable body of data that forms an important information resource concerning the current status of African Americans in the United States. Like one of its predecessors, *An American Dilemma* (Myrdal, 1944), the book serves the dual purpose of informing with respect to the status of Black U.S. nationals and reminding White U.S. nationals of one of the continuing unsolved dilemmas in this democratic nation. Embedded in the Jaynes and Williams work is an often-ignored dilemma for social science scholars.

AFRICAN AMERICANS IN THE UNITED STATES

Two highly competent scholars were chosen to conduct this study—a scholar of European-American background who was a party to the initiation of the idea of this new study and an African-American scholar who appears to have been selected not only for his accomplishments, but also in response to questions raised concerning the appropriateness of such a

---

Adapted with permission of Cambridge University Press. Copyright © 1991 by Cambridge University Press. *Psychological Science*, 2(1), 23–30.
*This chapter comprises a discussion of *A Common Destiny* (Jaynes & Williams, 1989). All references to this title and to these authors are to this work.

study's being conducted without African-American representation in its directorate. Robin Williams, the European-American scholar, was designated committee chairperson and Gerald Jaynes, the African-American scholar, was designated study director. Their report was published with Jaynes, a professor of economics at Yale University, and Williams, a professor of sociology at Cornell, as editors, assisted by a host of other scholars.

The historical scope of *A Common Destiny* extends from the 1940s to the 1980s and explains as its goal the desire to describe and analyze various components of Black American life, including family, health care, education, judicial system, employment/economics, politics, and Black culture. *A Common Destiny* gives a historical analysis of the United States as a whole, specifying the ways in which Black people are affected by national trends. Jaynes and Williams express the hope that their appraisal of the situation of African Americans will serve as a catalyst for serious discussion and social policy reforms. From the beginning of the report, they emphasize the interdependent and dialectical relationship of all American ethnic groups and urge people of all skin colors and classes to consider the present hardships of Black Americans as a warning to all of America for the future.

The major findings of the study tell us that the status of Black Americans has risen in comparison with the 1940s (due for the most part to their own political agitation, and a long period of national economic growth) but is still alarmingly low in comparison with the status of the average White American. It is a disappointment to find that while for the slowly growing Black middle class, living conditions have almost caught up with those of the White middle class, for the working class or the rapidly expanding poverty-stricken Black community, many of the conditions documented earlier in DuBois' *The Philadelphia Negro* (1899), Myrdal's *An American Dilemma* (1944), and Drake and Cayton's *Black Metropolis* (1945) have remained the same or have become worse. *A Common Destiny* describes the major issues of African Americans today as the desire for equal opportunity and access to housing, education, employment, political power, and the actual benefit of these privileges enjoyed by White America. It lists four major events since the 1940s that have affected the lives of Black and White Americans: industrialization and the subsequent mass migration of Blacks from the rural South to the urban North; the civil rights movement of the 1950s and 1960s; the economic growth of America from the 1940s to the early 1970s; and the following stagnation of the American economy after 1970.

As a result of northern migration, the civil rights campaign, and subsequent government concessions such as the creation of special agencies and the 30-year stretch of economic prosperity, many Black Americans were able to practice middle-class life-styles, enjoying the pursuit of academic, political, and economic advancement. Nonetheless, the faltering economy, most noticeable between the 1970s and the 1990s, disproportionately affected the majority of Blacks—who did not make great progress because they had so little leverage originally. This situation was compounded by the persistence of (1) racist discrimination, however subtle and indirect; (2) most Blacks' lack of access to social networks necessary for attaining certain academic and employment opportunities; (3) residential ghettoization, both economic and ethnic, breeding poverty, crime, and despair; and (4) a dearth of role models to influence the positive socialization of Black youth.

Some highlights of *A Common Destiny* illustrate the interrelatedness and progressive and regressive causal effects that the areas of politics, education, economics, the judicial system, and Black family life have on each other. The National Research Council's discussion of Black political activism and the resulting civil rights legislation give insights into the potential political efficacy of African America as well as its frailty in the face of national racist sentiment. The gains and setbacks of Black political power are mirrored by African-American progress in education and economic stability. Even though legislation awarded Black people greater access to education and equal opportunity employment, the subtle reorganization of school systems and labor unions helped to keep Black progress to a disproportionately low level.

The decreased hiring of Black teachers in integrated schools, the neglect and/or abandonment of schools in areas heavily populated by Black people, the busing of Black children out of their communities into hostile environments, and the resegregating, "tracking," of Black children into special education classes and White children into honors classes have not prevented some Black children from academic success. Yet these practices have promoted underachievement among the majority of this group. Equal opportunity employment has shown similar effects, in which Black people had better chances of working in racially integrated environments but repeatedly encountered limited access to prospects for promotion or the benefits of organized labor unions during the zenith of their political influence. *A Common Destiny* describes how Black women tend to fare better than their Black male counterparts in terms of employment, yet families comprised of single Black mothers and their children predominate in the third of the Black American population that lives below the poverty level.

In addition to lacking the educational qualifications or the social network resources to find adequate employment, many Black men are not working because they are either in jail or are victims of violent crime. The National Research Council maintains that racism in the judicial system has decreased; however, the economic resources of an individual often determine the outcome of a court hearing. For many Black people who are poor, this form of classist discrimination in the courts does little to improve their already disenfranchised relationship to the judicial system and law enforcement.

In line with the conservative Republican regime of the 1980s, popular media representations of African-American family life often featured the curiously indolent and devious "welfare queen" as head of the household. *A Common Destiny* provides a more accurate analysis of the situations faced by low-income families and single-parent homes in the United States, and some reasons for such negative media depictions. We are given data to show that Black and White families are both experiencing higher rates of divorce resulting in single-parent families. Too many of these families live at or below the poverty line. In the case of Black women, the scarcity of economically secure Black men along with the inability of these women to support their families independently has made it easy for the media to advance the myth of the Black woman with throngs of children, who prefers to be on welfare.

Even though many Black families are headed by a mother and a father and have adequate living wages, in the poorer sections of the Black community, the issue of health care is a serious problem because quality health care is so expensive, and the services provided by Medicaid and Medicare tend to be insufficient and impersonal. As a result, many Black people do not have a regular health-service provider or preventive health care. They receive their primary care via major hospital emergency rooms only when their health is at serious risk from dangers such as inadequate diet, lack of prenatal care, substance abuse, hygienic neglect, and unprotected sexual practices.

DILEMMAS WITHIN *A COMMON DESTINY*

A Common Destiny is frustrating for several reasons: first, because there are dimensions of the status and the conditions of Black people that are not addressed; second, because the information is reported in the "objective," almost sterile tradition of the "scientific" community, which leaves this treatment of one of the nation's most recalcitrant problems devoid of passion and any sense of urgency; and third, because this nation and especially the victims of racial oppression simply cannot afford to have a group of its most talented scholars devote 2 years to reviewing and organizing information without also analyzing it more critically and contemplating solutions.

Some early critics of this study might have predicted this frustration. Aside from debates concerning which scholars should have been involved when the study was proposed, questions were raised concerning the wisdom of a study limited to the analysis and review of existing data. Some of us thought that another study of status without a concurrent study of process would provide too limited an understanding of existing conditions and possible solutions. For example, the education of African Americans simply cannot be understood in the absence of an analysis of the educational processes to which Black people are exposed at school and at home. The Coleman et al. report, *The Equality of Educational Opportunity* (1966), made that error 25 years ago.

It is not surprising that Jaynes and Williams should stumble on aspects of the paradoxical circumstances that adhere to this study. Quite apart from the issues chosen for investigation, for which these editors and their sponsors must assume responsibility, there is serious debate within the social sciences with respect to the problems of objectivity and subjectivity and the question of the scientist's responsibility for anticipating the consequences of, as well as providing solutions for, the problems embedded in one's findings. With respect to this debate, we hold that within the social sciences, objectivity is a misleading assertion and that knowledge production can be a crucial component to emancipatory endeavors (see also Chapter 11). We believe that the politically transformative (liberating) potential of the social sciences lies in raising explanatory questions relative to collected substantive and contextual data, critical analysis relevant to these issues, and interpretation of the manner in which findings serve differential interests, as well as inform theory, policy, and practice. Especially with respect to questions concerning oppressed groups, to treat them as if they were a mere scientific curiosity is a travesty of social and intellectual responsibility. We are aware that this view is, no doubt, not popular. Some would argue that it is a mistaken view. For example, the distinguished scholar John Hope Franklin takes pride in his lifetime commitment to objective historiography despite his equal commitment to the struggle for equality for African Americans. Franklin would assert that he reports the facts of history in his scholarship and fights for civil rights in the political arena. But we do not think that Franklin writes without passion (see *From Slavery to Freedom,* 1967). Neither are his public policy statements without passion and projected solutions (see the monograph *Visions of a Better Way: A Black Appraisal of Public Schooling,* Lightfoot & Franklin, 1989). However, as much as we are indebted to and respect Franklin, we feel even greater respect for DuBois (1899), whose brilliant analyses never hid his passion or perspective and who consistently used his scholarship and wisdom to inform theory and practice.

We believe, with DuBois (1899), that we who are academically prepared and economically advantaged, and especially those of us who are Black, and all who are committed to justice must not succumb to narrow academic self-satisfaction as our brothers and sisters struggle for day-to-day survival. We cannot afford to serve primarily aesthetic purposes (knowledge for knowledge's sake) with the intellectual tolls that our ancestors sacrificed their lives to enable some of us to obtain. We are all struggling to survive the many manifestations of racist, sexist, and classist oppression. And for the present, an invitation to debate is not sufficient—while Black babies die of malnutrition and drug and alcohol poisoning; while Black children do not have the opportunity to receive the same quality of education from which we have benefited; and while Black adults are overtaken by the suicidal behavior of substance abuse, Black-on-Black violence, ill health, unemployment, crime, despair, and defeat.

A component of liberatory scholarship is "methodological rigor" (Gordon, 1985). Certainly this term applies to ardent efforts to produce and use efficient research tools, materials, and methodologies. However, this "rigor" also involves critical analysis. We have spoken briefly about the transformative potential of critical analysis of knowledge production. Rigorous intellectual initiative is inextricable in this process. Liberatory scholarship seeks to break not only the chains of oppression, but also the shackles of mediocrity. Critical analysis implores scholars to move forward in light of what they already know.

CRITIQUE

Of course, one book cannot eradicate all mutations of oppression, but there are certain concerns that might have been addressed by the National Research Council's Committee in light of the fact that its members were privy to such a profusion of information. In the case of Blacks' participation in society in general and the economy in particular, a deeper analysis of the absence of a substantial Black American capital base or of the control of accumulated wealth is an obvious omission. The fragility and marginality of the Black middle class cries out for a more enlightening analysis. Included in this analysis, educated speculation concerning the debilitating effect of racial integration on the efficacy of African-American economic and political power could have enhanced our understanding of the political economy of the African-American experience. Similarly, an analysis of the role of Black workers in the pool of excess labor in the United States is critical to our understanding of the problems of Black unemployment. To better understand what appears to be stagnation in the economic and sociopolitical development of Black Americans, as well as the feminization of poverty, some analysis of the impact of the exportation of industrial jobs by national and multinational corporations—a loss of some 30 million jobs—to Third World countries is essential. Any discussion of the economic status of African Americans is inadequate if done outside the context of the deliberate redistribution of income and wealth to favor the richest members of the society. Given that at the time of the publication of *A Common Destiny* many African Americans were poor and in some way dependent on the welfare state, such an analysis might have at least framed the discussion in the context of the nation's shift from being a world credit source to becoming the largest debtor nation.

In the realm of Black American political activity, a discussion of the effects of routine assassination, literally or figuratively, of Black leaders or their co-optation into the dominant political power structure might have pointed to serious hindrances to Black political self-determinism. Also with respect to politics in the Black community, probably more important than the number of Blacks we have been able to elect is an analysis of the limitations on the power that can be exercised by persons in the positions to which they have been elected. Richard Hatcher (1973) has provided a brilliant analysis of how the modern office of the city mayor has been stripped of power. In addition, our attention might well have been called to the fact that with the emphasis on the struggle for civil rights, the protection of all citizens' civil liberties is threatened by increasing secrecy in government and reactionary conservatism in politics.

This preoccupation with civil rights, important as it has been, has influenced all life in the Black community, even in its scholarship and knowledge production. Neglected in *A Common Destiny* is the African-American intellectual community's preoccupation with cultural, literary, and theoretical protest in response to the community's perceived distortion of "the Black experience" in academic as well as popular media. This has entailed, among other things, the proliferation of defensive attempts to refute "ethnically offensive" interpretations and theories, to the neglect of the development of alternative or competing explanatory paradigms. Some of the best social science scholarship from this community is manifest in deconstructionist writings, with little attention given to constructionist theory development and empirical investigations. Meanwhile, too much attention continues to be given to the mindless accommodation and replication of canon-constrained theoretical models, many of which are thought to be dysfunctional to the better understanding of African-

American behavior and social organization. (For example, see Banks, McQuarter, & Hubbard, 1979; or Stanfield, 1985.) Not only do Jaynes and Williams give no attention to these epistemological issues; they also neglect to discuss related questions having to do with the narrow context and limited content of the traditional academic canon and its constraining influence on the production of knowledge as well as on education.

In their treatment of educational issues, attention could well have been given to the consequences of privileging skill development over intellectual development for African-American human resource conservation. The status of the education of Blacks in the United States cannot be fully understood in the absence of an appreciation of how this value choice in the total society, but especially in the African-American community, influences such factors as resources and resource allocation, reward structures, socialization practices, allocation of learner time and effort, instructional behavior, and subsequent educational and vocational opportunities. Such a discussion could well have contributed to a better understanding of the Black/White differentials in academic achievement and thus provided an alternative to the rather futile debate concerning race-related heritability of levels of intelligence.

We are well aware that there is a plethora of questions that need to be addressed and that the concerns raised above reflect our own political and intellectual biases. Nonetheless, the recognition that so many crucial considerations exist, when speaking of the future of the Black American community, emphasizes the need for a commitment to more comprehensive and critical knowledge production and synthesis from the level of the individual scholar to the academic conglomerate.

For those of us who are not well versed in the perilous conditions of Black America, the publication of *A Common Destiny* was welcome. For those of us who are formal and lay scholars of these situations as a result of our lived experience, this book was greatly appreciated for its careful documentation of the status of a long-oppressed people. At the same time, this technically excellent work leaves one with the feeling of a well-articulated millstone around the neck of hope for the future. Reality can oftentimes be the best medicine, yet it seems as though dissatisfied Black folks have swallowed their fill of the reality of past and present social, political, and economic oppression. What is desperately needed is explanation and direction.

The plea of DuBois (1899) to Black people who have been privileged with economic success, exceptional talent, or education to give of their wealth of resources to the less-fortunate members of their community was not a hokey notion of some foolish visionary. Those of us living or planning to live out our careers in intimate proximity to the academy must never forget that not too far away, in the nearest Black ghetto, we can find people who have never seen the inside of a university, or worse yet, who are unable to make sense of the words in *A Common Destiny*. These people and their advocates do not need to be reminded of how bad, or good, things are for Blacks. They need to know how to make them better. The producers of works like *A Common Destiny* have a responsibility for somehow bridging this chasm at least at the level of program specification.

RELATED STUDIES

Jaynes and Williams suggest that *A Common Destiny* is likely to be analyzed in the company of previous social science documents concerning Black Americans. In this review we found it useful to make comparisons between *A Common Destiny* and four similar works. Like *The Philadelphia Negro* (DuBois, 1899), *An American Dilemma* (Myrdal, 1944), *Black Metropolis* (Drake & Cayton, 1945), and *The Report of the National Advisory Commission on Civil Disorders* (Kerner, 1968), *A Common Destiny* documents the many facets and styles of African-American life. The five books were extensive in their scrutiny of the issues facing Black Americans and the underlying social/political structures that frame these issues. Unfortunately, despite a time span of about nine decades, the five documents report many of the same problems plaguing the Black community, such as unemployment, family disruption, criminal violence, financial lack, poor health and health care, inadequate housing, and the psychological hardships produced by racial discrimination. In the context of the times in which the works were produced, some issues may have changed or demanded greater attention. In comparing the information presented in these five reports, the major change throughout the last century seems to have been the political advancement of Black people as a result of their heightened consciousness, intensified levels of protest, and the sensitivity of the United States to significant changes in world politics.

The intellectual moods of these five books were influenced by the political consciousness of the authors and the social sentiment existing during the time in which each book was written. *The Philadelphia Negro, An American Dilemma,* and *Black Metropolis* were pieces of work committed to rationality and the use of social science data to present the real experiences of a people. However, in each of these works, there is a certain passion that reflects the depth of feeling of the authors and the urgent need for action. *The Kerner Report* and *A Common Destiny* inform readers concerning some of the causes of the problems and how much further we need to go beyond the enforcement of civil rights. These five texts undertook the task of reporting on the status of African Americans and eloquently and rationally informing the agents of social change of their responsibility to engage the problems. However, it is not so much that these agents were unaware that many Black people were poor and unemployed and suffered under racial discrimination, but that they, and the society that supports them, were not taking the proper and efficient steps in order to rectify these problems. A weakness in all of these works is that they neglect to critically analyze the roots of the problem in the society's political economy rather than singularly in the society's compassion or morality.

Of the authors of the four related books previously mentioned, Myrdal (1944) perhaps is the model most closely followed by the editors of *A Common Destiny*. Myrdal sought to instruct White Americans with respect to the duality of their spirits and the hypocrisy of their ideals with a straightforward analysis of accumulated data that was objective and dispassionate. Myrdal exercised the prerogative to engage the conscience of White America; however, he neglected to address the potential for social and political transformation to be found in African Americans acting in their own, as well as their country's, interests.

The Report of the National Advisory Commission on Civil Disorders (Kerner, 1968) responded to the growing concern of White Americans for their protection from the riotous aftermath of three centuries of African-American oppression. Tom Wicker's introduction to the report responds to the criticism made that the report excluded the views of those deviating from the moderate European-American stance on the issue of racial equality. His explanation that the moderate position may be more acceptable to White Americans may be taken as an acknowledgment of bias. However, Wicker provides explanations for this position that validate the White status quo, thereby once again marginalizing the views of the disempowered.

One year after the publication of Myrdal's (1944) work, two Black social scientists, Drake and Cayton (1945), restored the political agenda for Black Americans with the publication of *Black Metropolis*. Drake and Cayton suggested post–World War II national policy reforms, but emphasized the need for consolidation of Black leadership, talent, and energies to create a massive political movement through which the integrity of the Black community and its agenda could be expressed. Drake and Cayton suggested that political leaders, scholars, and artists continue to express the African-American desire for freedom to the European-American community in ways that might make White people understand the destructive nature of their racism. They asked for a progressive political effort aimed at the destruction of segregation and discrimination. The inclusion of the concerns of Black folk in the post–World War II national agenda was suggested. Drake and Cayton thought that Black people needed to strengthen their ties to each other in terms of family, political alliances, and community in order to build a basis for a massive political movement of nonviolent protest. Some would argue that this work and the spirit it reflected helped to spark the nonviolent civil rights revolution that emerged in the years that followed.

Before any of the three texts just mentioned, in his *The Philadelphia Negro*, DuBois (1899) supplied a body of well-documented data along with suggestions for individual initiative, social policy reform, and political protest. DuBois (1899) made it clear to his White audience that the United States would always have a Black community despite the efforts of lynch mobs and the like. He tried to explain to the White community that it was in their best interest to give African Americans their democratic liberties to avoid the aftermath of racism, which would manifest itself in crime, hostility, and economic dependence on the government.

Even though White racism was seen as the main culprit in the hardships in the lives of Black people, DuBois (1899) told his community that while they did have every right to feel angry, the energy of their anger, pain, and resentment must be channeled in a positive way in order to uplift the race. He suggested defiant and dignified protest and conscientious cooperation between the privileged and the disadvantaged.

Even more than Gunnar Myrdal's *An American Dilemma* (1944), Jaynes and Williams's extensive analysis of the status of Black folk in the late 20th century meets a high standard of objectivity. Unlike the works by Drake and Cayton, DuBois, or even Kerner, it gives one the impression that the editors assume that the present period calls for dispassionate discourse to reach an otherwise preoccupied audience. One senses that Jaynes and Williams were so intent on being objective that passion and righteous indignation were screened from every page. It is as if they borrowed DuBois's (1899) commitment to scholarship without being influenced by his commitment to protest and prescription.

This lack of politicization of academic work may sometimes be attributed not so much to the scholars themselves as to the conservatism of the institutions and foundations that fund the production of knowledge. Jaynes and Williams may have been as much constrained by their assignment as by their style. In the charge to this committee on the status of Black Americans from the National Research Council, the investigators were asked to

> marshall descriptive data on the changing positions of Blacks in American society since 1940; draw from the wealth of existing research to describe

the cultural context, including an increasingly complex framework of laws, policies, and institutions within which the observed changes have occurred; and explore the consequences, anticipated and unanticipated, of public and private initiatives to ameliorate the position of Blacks in America. (p. x)

CONCLUSION

Jaynes and Williams and their collaborators have amassed a rich body of data concerning the status of African-American people in the late 20th century, but the report is the same news, with the same implicit recommendations, and it threatens to result in the same inaction. It is the objectivity, absence of explanation, neglect of prescription, and absence of passion that make this work so problematic. By most standards of good science and scholarship, Jaynes and Williams have done the job assigned and done it well.

But if one maintains, as we do, that science—especially social science—seldom is and perhaps cannot be objective, this pretense of objectivity can be a disservice to truth. If one believes that even the scholar cannot afford to be dispassionate about human oppression and the violation of human rights, the dispassionate review of the data descriptive of such conditions does violence to one's sense of what is moral. Our position is a minority one. Dispassion and objectivity are traditions long honored in the professed values of scholarship. We often wonder if the socially adapted human being who happens to be a scholar is truly capable of discarding his or her individual frame of reference when it comes to the study of a subject to which he or she has chosen to commit his or her life's work. This is a precarious situation because too many times "objectivity" has served as a mask for the political agenda of the status quo, thus marginalizing and labeling the concerns of less empowered groups as "special interests." The interest in objectivity and dispassionate study is in part a function of a conception of knowledge as truth and of the basic relationships between specific phenomena as universal. One seeks to be dispassionate and objective in order to reduce the likelihood that one's biases or prior conceptions will cloud the perception of the truth or the universal relationship.

However, it may be that this search for the universal and for the truth—rather than the truths—of the observed relationships may be dysfunctional to knowing and understanding. McGuire (1983, 1989) has reminded us that relationships between variables may be susceptible to the context in which the variables interact, leading to the possibility that one might seek to discover the relationships that adhere to differential contexts or the differential truths of the relationship between two variables in differing contexts. Attention must be drawn to the manner in which the perspectives that inform the investigator's work shape the question, the methodology, and, ultimately, the findings. Sullivan (1984) argues that it is impossible for the social scientist not to have feelings, ideas, or prior conceptions about the things one studies, and concludes that objectivity is not possible for social scientists. Mills (1959) asserts that human thought and feelings are important components of scientific work and suggests that knowledge production devoid of these human factors is problematic.

This lack of objectivity in social science is not necessarily detrimental, but it is the illusion of objectivity that leaves many human beings convinced that they have obtained an objective point of view in the singularity of their own minds. Our particular socialization to scholarship may make it impossible to come to unbiased conclusions. Our biases themselves may blind us to the multiple perspectives that must be understood before we can approach objectivity. At almost every decision point the investigator makes choices and those choices are based on the information and perspective of the investigator. The questions posed and the methodology by which these questions are pursued reflect the investigator's experience and point of view. When it comes to the interpretation of data, despite deliberate efforts to distance the investigator from the data, meanings tend to be constrained by the prior questions and the data generated to answer these questions. Thus, efforts to separate the message from the messenger may be futile. In these circumstances, some of us argue for the acknowledgment of bias on the part of the messenger. Such acknowledgment of personal bias can be dealt with explicitly or implicitly.

In the case of *A Common Destiny,* it is apparent and appreciated that the works of many scholars of different disciplines were incorporated into this book, and its contents reflect different points of view about many of the same topics. In terms of the efficacy and value of the use of "objectivity" or multiple disciplines in order to produce an "unbiased" piece of social scientific literature, Jaynes and Williams more than amply meet this criterion as they provide the academic and African-American communities with a fertile source of information. The material is flawlessly presented with the painstaking accuracy and attributional balance that will most likely place it as the premier academic resource covering to the Black American condition at the end of the 1980s.

As with most "objective" texts, the politically transformative potential of *A Common Destiny* may escape those who are reading in order to better understand and to find informed recommendations for effective change from some of America's leading social science scholars. Of course, the title of scholar, intellectual, doctor, or professor does not make a person responsible for the state of humanity. However, it does entail the responsibility to provide the conceptual leadership that enables the society to engage in self-corrective action. Some think that there is the further responsibility of the developed intellect to protect and enable the liberation of the weakest members of society (Guess, 1981; Rawls, 1971; Sullivan, 1984). Fay (1975) addresses the issue of knowledge and liberation in his definition of emancipation when he suggests that "a critical social theory is meant to inform and guide the activities of a class of dissatisfied actors—revealing how the irrationalities of social life which are causing the dissatisfaction can be eliminated by taking some specific action which the theory calls for" (pp. 97–98). Habermas (1972), speaking from the intellectual perspective of the Frankfurt School, identified three types of intellectual pursuits: prediction and control, as found in the analytical and empirical disciplines of the natural and social sciences; understanding, which is the focus of historical and hermeneutic disciplines; and emancipation, which is the goal of critical interpretation. *A Common Destiny* provides impressive examples of the use of prediction and control and certainly adequate levels of understanding of the status of the phenomenon under study. However, the function of emancipation is poorly served in *A Common Destiny.*

DuBois (1899), Myrdal (1944), Drake and Cayton (1945), the "Kerner Commission" (Kerner, 1968), and the National Research Council have all told us of how increasing levels and quality of education correlate positively with levels of political unrest, protest, and progress. Somehow this sociological phenomenon must be rediscovered among many members of the academic community. The mere act of monitoring the situation does little except to maintain it and contributes little to the fulfillment of the communal admonition that "each one should teach one" in the struggle for social "uplift."

On this issue, the cautious prose of *A Common Destiny* stands in contrast to the spirit of lived experience captured in the essay *Visions of a Better Way: A Black Appraisal of Public Schooling,* published by the Joint Center for Political Studies Press under the authorship of Lightfoot and Franklin (1989). As an example of notable Black scholars working together to combine intellectual and political pursuits, the Committee on Policy for Racial Justice has been able to produce academic work of a superior quality with the Joint Center for Political Studies Press that manifests a determined and strong Black American political agenda:

> The Committee meets periodically to review the conditions of Blacks in American society, to inform itself and others about progress and failures in

the struggle for racial equality, and to seek to chart a course that will advance the cause of justice for all. (p. vi)

The textual organization of *A Common Destiny* in some ways embodies the absence of progressive and proactive knowledge and conceptual production in the face of massive tasks of social, economic, and political transformation that lie ahead in the interest of racial, gender, and class equality in the United States. "Overview: Then and Now," a chapter at the beginning of the book, is effective in creating a historical framework within which the reader could place all of the information that is given in the body of the text. Jaynes and Williams make very good use of the device of the repetition of certain findings, in the same chapter or in different chapters, in order to illustrate the interrelatedness of all of the issues facing Black Americans. A major problem in the organization of the work is the absence of a much-needed final chapter that would give the reader some concrete and valuable input from the authors about the subject matter they have extensively explored. A comprehensive conclusion is desperately needed especially since Jaynes and Williams give some scanty proposals about policy reforms at the beginning of the book. To end the book with the "Children and Families" chapter, which is incidentally one of the most problematic aspects of Black American life, was simply too depressing to effectively inspire and facilitate political mobilization. The editors, as highly respected scholars of economics and sociology, might have been more generous with their wisdom and shared with the reader some of their insights and recommendations as tools for Black folks to use in order to determine their own futures. We assert the inseparability of serious scholarship, intellectual rigor, and social responsibility. Such a perspective need not be limited to the scientist who happens to belong to a minority group.

PART II

Toward Equity in Educational Achievement

More than 30 years ago, at the height of the enthusiasm for the "War on Poverty," I was so troubled by the mechanical and mindless approaches to the race to create new programs for the poor that I wrote an editorial for the *American Journal of Orthopsychiatry*. In that article I cautioned against the rush to embrace false answers to complex problems. I worried aloud that our interventions were insufficiently informed by available research and that in some instances the needed research had not yet been conducted. What I did not anticipate as clearly was the possibility that what we knew how to do, and many of the things we knew should be done, would not be done, or that they would not be done well enough or with sufficient quantity to achieve the desired ends. In Part II I have included four essays in which I address conceptual and practical issues relevant to interventions designed to make a difference in the lives of children with disadvantages. In Chapter 5, I set forth a vision of what education is about and the challenges facing pedagogy, if social justice and equity are to be achieved. In the three chapters that follow, I discuss: teaching and learning transactions in which adaptations to the characteristics of learners are the focus (Chapter 6); counseling, guidance, and other approaches to behavior change (Chapter 7); and some implications of a concern for equitable educational assessment (Chapter 8). These chapters reflect my continuing conviction that education involves teaching and learning that are appropriate to the learner, guidance and support for the academic and personal development of students, and assessment processes that are appropriate to the learner and to the standards toward the achievement of which learners' pedagogical experiences are directed. My 1965 editorial, which follows, provides a poignant introduction to these suggestions for intervention:*

All of us who identify with the scientific-humanitarian traditions that characterize the Orthopsychiatric Association must derive some sense of achievement from the growing attention being directed at problems of the disadvantaged. Our Association only recently has lost its uniqueness in devoting serious attention to the implications of cultural difference and/or disadvantaged status for service in the helping profes-

*Reprinted with permission of *American Journal of Orthopsychiatry.* Copyright © 1965 by American Orthopsychiatric Association. In Vol. 35(3), 445–448.

sions. Indeed, it appears that the Association, which for so long stood almost alone in advocating the application of concepts of differential psychology, public health, compensatory education and aggressive casework to mental health, social work and educational services, now has many companions. In addition, isolated and pilot programs which for years have struggled to stay alive suddenly now face the prospects of abundant support and massive replication. Private foundations and government stand ready as never before to pour money and human resources into work directed at the plight of the disadvantaged.

It is tempting to anticipate that the current outbreak of enthusiasm will produce results consistent with the quantity of time, energy, money and concern being expended. However, in dealing with problems for which solutions are based upon significant social and scientific advances, popularity and productivity do not necessarily go hand in hand. In the present situation there is grave danger that work with the unfortunate may, unfortunately, become a fad. This threat is so great that those truly committed to the long-range goal to significantly improve the life chances of disadvantaged populations need to adopt an attitude of restraint and considered action. It is not the quantity of effort that will solve the complex problems of disadvantaged populations, but rather "high quality" approaches—those that reflect scientific and social reality.

Having recently reviewed much of the research and most of the current programs concerned with the disadvantaged, I am impressed by the pitifully small though growing body of knowledge available as a guide to work in this area. The paucity of serious research attention to these problems has left us with little hard data, many impressions, and a few firm leads. Equally distressing, is the slight representation of even this research in the rapidly proliferating programs. Much of what is being done for and to the disadvantaged seems to be guided by the conviction that what is needed is more of those things we feel we know how to do. Despite the fact that much of our knowledge and techniques of behavioral change have proved to be of dubious value in our work with more advantaged populations, these same procedures and services now are being poured into the new programs. Although service to the disadvantaged has become popular, there remains a serious lack of basic research on the developmental needs of such children as well as on the applicability of specific techniques of behavioral change to their directed development.

It is not intended to suggest that the extension of known techniques to these previously neglected populations is entirely negative. Humanitarian concern calls for the use of all possible resources to relieve human suffering. However, there may be vast differences between what we feel we know how to do and that which must be done. To settle for what we "know" while we ignore new concepts and the exploration of new leads renders us less humanitarian, less scientific, and less professional. Unfortunately, our society has permitted us to place the burden of proof of the worth of our services on the beneficiaries of these services rather than on the professional worker or the system in which he or she functions. This has permitted us to ignore or rationalize our failures. If real progress is to be made, we as professionals must assume greater responsibility for the success of our work, recognizing that it is our role to better understand these problems and to design techniques and measures more appropriate to their solution. It must be clear to all of us that more counseling is not going to solve the problems of a population we have defined as nonverbal. Reading texts in Technicolor are not going to solve the reading problems of youngsters who we claim are deficient in symbolic representational skills. Reduced demand curricula and work study programs are not going to advance the conceptual development of youth whose conditions of life may have produced differential patterns of intellectual function so frequently interpreted as evidence of mental retardation rather than as challenges to improved teaching. Occupational information and aspirational exhortation are not going to provide motivation for youth who have yet to see obtainable employment opportunities, employed models with whom they can identify and accessible routes to achievement. Intensive psychotherapy is going to have little impact on an overburdened mother whose energies are consumed by the struggle to meet the minimum physical needs of herself and her children. Similarly, preschool programs that capture the form but not the content of some of the more advanced models are doomed to failure. Nor will good programs that are not followed by greatly strengthened primary, elementary, and secondary school programs likely to make a major difference in the lives of these children. Improved and expanded mental health services will mean little unless our nation comes to grips with the problems of economic, political and social opportunities for masses of disenfranchised and alienated persons.

To honor our traditional concern and for the sake of the disadvantaged, it is essential to recognize the limitations of the current effort. If the products of serious research were as well represented in this effort as the good intentions, the enthusiasm, the "bandwagon hopping," and the grant hunting, we could be more hopeful that meaningful solutions would be found to the problems of the disadvantaged. Unfortunately, some of us viewing the current efforts are left with a nagging suspicion that the net result of many of these programs will be to provide (for those who choose to interpret it so) empirical evidence of fundamental inferiority in these populations we are trying so hard to help. When, 5 or 10 years from now, the populations we now call disadvantaged are still at the bottom of the heap, those who only reluctantly acceded to the current attempts to help may revive their now dormant notions of inherent inferiority to explain why all the money and all the effort have failed to produce results. The more likely fact will be that we shall have failed to produce the desired results simply because we shall have failed to develop and apply the knowledge and the skill necessary to the task. Unless the issues are more sharply drawn, we may not even then recognize the nature of our incompetencies. In retrospect, we see that bleeding was an ineffective cure for the plague, not because the barber-surgeons did not know how to draw blood, but because they did not sufficiently understand the nature of the disease with which they were dealing.

To honor our commitments to science and professional service, we must understand the limitations of our knowledge and our practice. Much of what we do is based on the hopeful assumption that all human beings with normal neurological endowment can be developed for participation in the mainstream of our society. We believe this because we have seen many people from a great variety of backgrounds participate and because we want to believe it. But we do not yet have definite evidence to support our belief. We operate out of an egalitarian faith without knowing whether our goals are really achievable. Yet it must be our aim, not only as scientists and professional workers, but as humanitarians as well, to determine the potential of human beings for equality of achievement. If, in the light of our most sophisticated and subtle evaluations, we conclude that equality is not generally achievable, if in spite of the best we can do, it seems likely that some of our citizens will remain differentiated by their own biology, then we shall merely have answered a persistent question. We will still have no evidence that group differences per se imply any inability on the part of particular individuals to meet the demands of society. We will then be able to turn our energies to helping individuals meet those demands. And if, on the other hand, as we believe, true equality of opportunity and appropriate learning experiences will result in equality of achievement, then we must organize our professional services and our society such that no person is kept from achieving that potential by our indifference to his or her condition, by the inadequacy or inappropriateness of our services, or by the impediments society deliberately or accidentally places in his or her path. It is not an unhopeful paradox that the only way we shall ever know whether equality of human achievement is possible is through providing for all our citizens, privileged and underprivileged, the kind of service and society that assumes it is possible and makes adequate provision for the same. As we pursue the "Great Society" let us not be misled by the plethora of activity or companions in the cause.

CHAPTER 5

Equity and Social Justice in Educational Achievement

WITH CAROL BONILLA-BOWMAN

Throughout the United States, ordinary citizens, educators, political leaders, and employers are involved in a reevaluation of the public education enterprise. Various combinations of people and special-interest groups are involved in evaluating the present performance of our schools in light of new demands posed by the sweeping changes our society is undergoing in the process of preparation to meet the demands of the 21st century. Everywhere, we hear proposals for school reform. There is almost universal concern for moving the education enterprise toward standards of excellence for all participants, staff and students. Although the specific standards continue to be the subject of debate, there is little doubt that excellence is increasingly defined by reference to critical literacy, higher-order thinking, quantitative and scientific competence, and complex problem solving. In the pursuit of such educational standards, it is becoming more and more apparent that concentration on the cognitive components of human competence is insufficient. We now recognize that the affective domain is so critical a component of human competence that the language of attitudes, dispositions, and values is heard increasingly in the educational dialogue concerning the outcomes of education.

In this chapter, we are interested especially in the relationship between these radical changes in the expected outcomes of education and the problems posed by the society's commitment to equity in educational opportunities and achievement, despite wide diversity in its population and the fact of pluralism in the performance demands and values of the changing social order. In addressing these issues, attention is given to:

1. The purposes and goals of education in answer to the question, What is education about?
2. A discussion of educational equity and social justice.
3. An iteration of the conditions of effective education.

4. An analysis of several problems in the determination that equity in educational opportunity and achievement has, in fact, been achieved.

WHAT IS EDUCATION ABOUT?

In the 20th century, two overriding principles have guided and constrained our educational goals. The most openly and generally accepted principle of schooling is the commitment on the part of both policymakers and the general public to promote democracy through equal educational opportunity for all (Dumke, 1985), although the conception of who "all" includes has had to be broadened several times as the rights of ethnic minorities and women have been recognized. This democratization of education carries the implicit assumption that a citizen must complete a minimum number of school years in order to enjoy her or his civil rights (Illich, 1973). A more restrictive and hidden agenda has kept the ideals of equality and opportunity in education from full fruition. That agenda, the reproduction of the economic relations of the larger society (Bowles & Gintis, 1976), resulted from the demands that a once rapidly industrializing and continuing capitalist society places on our educational system. Our schools have covertly, and often unconsciously, appeared to have been geared toward training the majority of our students to be complacent industrial and service workers while nurturing a privileged minority for potential leadership and leisure.

It is the various segments of society (class, ethnicity, gender, and language)—the social divisions by which people are classified and their status assigned—that provide the most obvious examples of inequality in educational opportunity and achievement. With almost no exceptions, the lower the status of the social division into which one falls, the lower the educational achievement. More than 30 years ago, Coleman and colleagues (1966) challenged the nation to uncouple educational achievement from the social origins of students. Several works document the continuing association between school achievement and class, caste, ethnicity, gender, and proficiency in English. Yet we see little evidence to support the implicit assumption that such differentials consistently favoring high-status populations are a function of immutable characteristics of the low-status populations. Thus, the continuing problem for schooling is that of equalizing educational outcomes for all groups of students served by the schools, independent of the social divisions from which they come. It is entirely possible that the functional characteristics by which individuals may be described do have meaningful relationships to what can be achieved through schooling, and especially to how it can be achieved. However, and most important, in a democracy, the status groups into which persons fall or are assigned should not be determinative of educational opportunity or outcome. This is especially the case in a modern democratic society.

Historically, discussions concerning educational goals and objectives have tended to focus on two major themes: education for the transmission of culture and education for the development of the individual. Currently, those concerns are reflected in two issues around which the goals of education are being debated. The first centers around education as a transmitter of cultural traditions and a related concern with the boundaries of the canon that enshrines those traditions. Unfortunately, the fabric of this controversy is woven with diverse opinions as to which aspects of several cultures are deserving of and essential for such transmission—that is, whose stories and voices are to be heard. The second issue involves differences between those who believe in skill-oriented learning, which focuses on preparation for the eventual demands of the workplace, and those who are oriented toward education as being concerned with the development of the intellect and the individual's capacities for continuing education and adaptation. The debate between those favoring education for the workplace and those in favor of education for broader life processes is by no means new. However, social policy choices have tended to be made in favor of the demands of the workplace for nonaffluent students and in favor of the demands of a general (liberal) education for the more privileged.

Some see the necessity for trade-offs between the culture-transmission and intellect-development functions of education. Changing conceptions of pedagogy and changing demands for competence would seem to indicate otherwise. Findings from modern cognitive science suggest that effective learning and the achievement of understanding result from active engagement with and operation on the relevant knowledge processes and structures in the interest of constructing meanings that make sense to the learner. Such engagement and operations are the vehicles of cognitive development. Because the knowledge processes and structures are derived from the culture, in properly conceived teaching and learning transactions, their transmission is a natural concomitant of intellective development. The problem is that the two are often viewed as separate and competing functions, although they are necessarily complementary.

As we approach the 21st century, our rapidly changing society demands that education fulfill new purposes. The explosion in the amount of knowledge available to individuals and the rapid expansion of advanced technology along with upheavals in political, social, and economic relations throughout the world make it imperative that our schools change, notably in the emphasis on what is learned and possibly on how learning is facilitated. Basic literacy skills are no longer sufficient for meaningful participation in the social order. Multiple literacies—numeric, scientific, economic, cultural, and social, among others, information management, problem solving, and critical interpretation are among the competencies expected of educated persons. Those individuals not attaining a degree of facility in these increasingly essential competencies run the risk of becoming disenfranchised citizens.

The range of traditional and emerging societal demands of education is reflected in a consideration of four broad areas of educational outcomes that we must seek to develop in learners.

1. The first of these outcomes concerns the individual's ability to know, understand, and appreciate oneself, which provides a fundamental reference point from which the individual should be enabled to develop the ability and the disposition to see beauty and find meaning in his or her life and its surroundings. Concurrently and equally a part of this constellation is the generation of a set of values by which one's life choices may be guided. These competencies ultimately enable the individual to apply his or her abilities to the solution of personal and real-world problems, hopefully, with compassion and within the context of considered prosocial values.

2. A fundamental criterion for the educated person is the attainment of critical facility in reading, speaking, and writing. We refer to these as multiple literacies and oralities—that is, the capacity for expression, reception, and critical interpretation of symbolic representations of the world in a variety of experience and knowledge domains. Among the forms of critical literacy and orality considered important are both multicontextual and multilingual communication as part of and contributing to multicultural adaptive competence. The cognitive development of the educated individual must enable the capacity to use abstract symbols to represent other symbols (i.e., tertiary signal system mastery) to the extent that an individual can generate and use alphabetic or numeric formulae to solve problems and generate and use metaphors and other abstract forms to represent relationships as well as real and artificial phenomena.

A second category of literacy basic to participation in our emerging society is quantitative, scientific, and technological literacy. The capacity to understand human relationships and perspectives both interpersonally and in the larger context of the national and international political/economic arena constitutes an important third category. This includes the capacity to understand information concerning the systemic alignments that sustain and reinforce such social divisions as race, class, and gender within the society. The composite mastery of the domains listed above is increasingly referred to as cultural literacy, which, in its widest definition, refers to an individual's command of the information, problem-solving strategies, symbol systems, and currency (instruments of exchange) of the cultures that form the contexts of his or her life. The use of cultural literacy here should not be confused with the more narrow use of the term by Hirsch (1987).

3. It is important that the individual have a body of knowledge with which to work, for critical thinking cannot proceed very far without some specific knowledge structures. It is in the acquisition, accommodation, and storage of chunks of knowledge that new developments and perspectives present new debates. We argue that encyclopedic mastery of knowledge is impossible for most and dysfunctional for all. Instead, what is required is an orientation to major categories of knowledge, access to effective knowledge retrieval systems, and sufficient specific knowledge to enable the framing of appropriate questions and problem-solving strategies. Thus the focus should be on understanding selected basic concepts and the processes by which they function rather than on attempting mastery of the whole of available knowledge. Mastery should be reflected in the depth of understanding of and the capacity to apply basic knowledge concepts from at least one discipline and some concepts from various relevant disciplines.

4. Instrumental to these competencies is the ability and the disposition to access and manage information in its application to problem solving. Ultimately, one must be able to engage specific chunks of knowledge, its multiple representations, and its critical interpretation to make sense of experience and knowledge in the process of applying one's abilities to the solution of real-life problems (Gordon & Nembhard, 1993).

There is little new about such goals of education; rather, basic notions have been cast in modern contexts and language. What is new and challenging in the pursuit of such educational goals is that the expected levels of such achievement be universal and world class; that the systems by which we enable learners to meet these standards of competence be allowed great latitude with respect to how they reach the goals and demonstrate that they have been achieved by all learners; and, most important for this chapter, that the achievement of such educational goals be uncoupled from the social divisions by which we group people and define human status (Gordon & Shipman, 1979). It is to this third concern that the major focus of our attention is directed in this chapter.

EQUITY AND EQUALITY

Traditionally, our society has sought to address the question of equity in education by trying to ensure that all students have equal access to the opportunity for an adequate education. Despite a long history of concern for differences between groups as well as individuals, this conception of equity has rested on the notion of distributive equality: equal access to equal resources. Three pivotal examples are the struggle for school deseg-regation, school finance equity cases, and the *Lau* vs. *Nichols* (1974) decision concerning students with limited proficiency in English. In the first of these, the argument was that forced isolation in school based on race resulted in unequal educational opportunity. In the school finance debate, successful court challenges were initiated by plaintiffs in states including California and New Jersey, arguing the unconstitutionality of inequitable distribution of educational resources resulting from the financing of public schools through property taxes. These cases were argued in the 1970s and early 1980s. (Currently, there is renewed interest in this problem, with new court activity in 25 states challenging inequity in financing from the perspective of the state constitutions.) In the third instance, that of the *Lau* vs. *Nichols* (1974) decision, it was the failure of the school to offer instruction in the language of the student that was considered to result in unequal access to education. In all such instances the concern was with ensuring equal distribution (sameness or comparability) of educational resources.

As noted in the introduction to this volume, the work of Rawls (1971) provides another perspective on the question of equity. Among Rawls's principles of justice are two that are specifically applicable to our discussion of educational equity: the principle of just savings and the principle of unequal distribution in favor of the weakest members of society. The just-savings principle holds that a society is free to limit its distribution of its resources in order to protect some resources for future generations. The principle of unequal distribution is conditioned on its application in the service of the weakest members of society. Thus the accumulation of capital reserves and the building of societal infrastructures, while some members of society suffer, may be justified only in the service of savings for future generations. Under the second principle, since the weakest members of society may require more than others for justice to prevail, resources and services may be distributed unequally to meet their needs.

In a treatise on human diversity, Gordon and Shipman (1979) introduced the concept of distributional appropriateness and sufficiency as essential criteria for equity in human services. Under this notion, educational treatments, like medical treatments, must be appropriate to the condition and characteristics of the person being treated and sufficient to their support and correction. To give all patients sulfa drugs when some need penicillin does not meet the condition of sufficiency. Thus emerges the notion of differential educational treatments in relation to need and circumstance as criteria for educational equity, where justice is defined not so much by treating all in the same way but by the appropriateness and sufficiency of treatment to the functional characteristics and needs of the persons being educated.

CONDITIONS OF EFFECTIVE EDUCATION

What, then, are the components of a program of differential educational treatments related to needs and functional characteristics? Six critical components may be identified:

1. Adequacy of human and material resources
2. Structural organization of schools
3. Quality of teaching and learning
4. Learning behaviors and attitudes of students
5. Support for academic learning: communities and families
6. Affective development

Adequacy of Human and Material Resources

The notion of differential treatment in relation to need implies that educational practices will be adapted to the functional characteristics of the learner. Earlier work on adaptive learning environments (Wang & Walberg, 1985) and individually prescribed instruction (Flanagan, Shanner, Brudner, & Marker, 1975; Glaser, 1977a & b; Klausmeier, 1976) suggests two areas of special need, one having to do with teacher competence and the other with instructional materials. In order that education be truly adaptive, teachers must be able to specify the educational needs of students and the conditions under which they are likely to be met. This means that the teacher functions initially as a diagnostician. He or she must be able to conduct the kind of psychoeducational assessment that specifically informs teaching and learning. This assessment should reveal such features of the learner as areas of prior learning strengths and weaknesses, aspects of temperament, cognitive style and disposition, actual learning behavior, conditions of probable learning task engagement, and sources of motivation and reinforcement. Such teacher assessments take time and talent, requiring that teachers first be taught how to engage in such activity and then freed to do so. The latter may most effectively be achieved under conditions of the personalization of instruction, which enables teacher and learner to relate to each other as persons over some continuing period of time in meaningful teaching and learning interactions. This obviously has implications for the way the schools and classrooms are organized (discussed later), but the most important implications have to do with the competencies of the teacher.

Without detracting from the importance of the human resources that are represented by the professional staff of the school, those resources that are represented by the students themselves must also be addressed. Here two aspects are emphasized: the students' physical and mental health and the quality of the learning behaviors of these students. With respect to nutritional status and physical health, the evidence is persuasive on the relationship between conditions of health and success in school (Birch & Gussow, 1970). Malnourished and sick children are more frequently absent from school and, when there, invest less effort in the work of learning. Similarly, children whose emotional energies are consumed by psychological problems seem to have little intellectual energy to invest in school learning. Even those whose energies are not depleted show levels of distractibility and/or depression that leave little space for academic concerns.

Students share responsibility with teachers for effective teaching and learning transactions. What teachers do is important, but what students do or are enabled to do is crucial. It may well be that the most direct effect of the school experience on students is on their learning behaviors. For effective learning to occur, students must (1) actively engage in the learning experience, (2) spend time on appropriate learning tasks, (3) purposefully deploy their attention and efforts at relevant learning goals, and (4) access and utilize human and material learning resources. These learner behaviors appear to be acquired as a part of the incidental learnings of some students from economically and socially advantaged families. They tend to be notably absent in many children from less privileged backgrounds. In the calculus of resource determination, these health conditions and behaviors of learners must be considered.

This brief overview of human resource needs is intricately interwoven with consideration of material resource needs. Adaptive instruction requires that the range of instructional materials available vary with respect to levels of demand, breadth and depth of content, cultural representativeness of content, learning task specificity of format, flexibility of sequence, user friendliness, and a host of other conditions in response to teacher and learner needs. In the "individually prescribed instruction" model (Glaser, 1977b), a vast library of instructional materials and a special instructional resources manager are required at each site. Under this arrangement, teachers prepare prescriptions for individuals or small groups of students that are filled on a daily or weekly basis by the instructional resources manager. Whether one buys into the management system or not, in this model the available materials begin to approach the magnitude and variety required of a truly adaptive instructional system. Although such a system sounds extravagant, its characteristics are not dissimilar from resources often made available to children of affluent parents to meet special instructional needs. What is different is the aggregate of materials in one place to meet the varied needs of many students. This model respects one of the premises of educational equity: resources that are appropriate and sufficient to meet the educational needs of each learner.

Structural Organization of Schools

A primary concern in the structural organization of schools is the creation of personalized contexts for interaction of all parties involved: student/ teacher, teacher/teacher, student/student, teacher/parent, parent/administrator, and so forth. Among the most important factors that influence opportunities for personal interaction are the ratio of adults to learners, the size of the primary and secondary structural units, and the philosophical purposes served by the overall organization. Student/teacher relations are framed by ratios and continuity, both of which bear on the ultimate investment the teacher is willing to make in his or her students and by the possibility for each student to be known and recognized on a personal basis. A central issue of concern here is the ratio of staff to children in our schools and classrooms. With school populations ranging from hundreds to thousands of students and school staffs reduced by reasons of budget, many students and teachers find the school experience enormously depersonalized. Innovative schools have been addressing this issue by the creation of schools within schools, or family groups that provide opportunities for both greater personalization and a greater degree of relational continuity.

An example of a program that successfully creates a more personal milieu in a large urban school is that of the O'Farrell Community School in San Diego, California. This middle school of 1,320 students is divided into 9 educational family groups, each consisting of 150 students and 6 teachers, that operate with a certain degree of autonomy. The educational family groups span grade levels and traverse the 3 years of schooling together, increasing the opportunity for the development of ties between student and teacher. The curriculum is repeated cyclically over a 3-year period, making multigrade instruction feasible. Importantly, the reorganization and philosophical structure are products of teacher/administrator/parent conceptualization and implementation.

Development of highly capable teachers cannot end with their preservice education. Schools must provide an ongoing and invested development process adapted to the specific needs of teachers in their various contexts. The organizational resources of the traditional school do not prioritize the process of teacher development. Teachers who, often within their first year of teaching, fall below a certain threshold of performance seldom reach a level of success in the classroom that would enable them to learn from interaction with their students. Those who can swim create effective mechanisms that enable them to become better swimmers, but those who cannot swim begin a long process of drowning, putting many children at risk in the process. School structures must have mechanisms to identify and deal with problems, both to improve teacher performance and to defend children from excessive abuse by incompetent teachers. One such mechanism that is being developed comes from teachers themselves, a project of New York State United Teachers. Teachers identified as having difficulty are paired with other teachers, and human and material resources are focused on remediating the teacher's weaknesses. These corrections are much more likely to function in educational units that are small enough to be sensitive to the individuals (students and teachers) who populate them.

Quality of Teaching and Learning Transactions

The resources and structural characteristics of the school do not have purposes and ends that are independent of the quality of the teaching and learning that actually occur in schools. In fact, resources and structures serve to support this teaching and learning. The neglect of attention to these teaching and learning processes is, in our view, a major part of the problem. Even in the presence of reasonably adequate resources and structures, we find limited effectiveness of schooling. As indicated earlier, when Coleman and colleagues (1966) studied the status of educational opportunities for minority and majority populations in the United States, they concluded that these resource and structural factors accounted for little of the variance in school achievement (see page 9). However, additional analyses revealed that while such factors made little difference for the school achievement of students in the aggregate, they significantly influenced the achievement of Black and low-income students (Gordon, 1967). White students' academic achievement seemed to be less affected by the quality of their schools, whereas the academic achievement of minority-group students was found to depend more on the schools they attended. In the South, for example, 40% more of the achievement of Black students was found to be associated with the particular school they attended than was the achievement of White students. There was agreement that these findings indicate that improvements in the quality of schooling (teaching and learning) will make the most difference in academic achievement for the most disadvantaged children.

The initial neglect of attention to the analysis of teaching and learning processes in the Coleman et al. study (1966) led to the misleading conclusion that quality of schools accounted for little of the variance in student achievement and resulted in our giving disproportionate attention to sense of power and to family background as determining factors (Gordon, 1967). It is not that the latter two sources of variance are unimportant. Rather, the point is that the quality of teaching and learning processes also appears to be critically determinant for students from less advantaged circumstances.

The work of Bloom (1968), Edmonds (1979), Lightfoot and Franklin (1989), Sirotnik and Goodlad (1985), Sizer (1984), and others provides convincing evidence of the importance of attention given to the quality of teaching and learning processes. For teachers, these processes include (1) structuring and adapting learning environments, (2) mediating learning experiences, (3) using diagnostic and monitored information to prescribe learning experiences and to inform the improvement of teaching and learning, (4) modeling the behaviors they expect of students, and (5) using processes of assessment and evaluation that are grounded in and facilitative of teaching and learning. For their part, learners need to engage in learning tasks that are appropriate to the mastery of the subject. They must deploy their energies and aptitudes to these learning tasks. They must be enabled to access and utilize human and material learning resources. They must not only engage in but devote sufficient time to appropriate learning experiences. These desired learning behaviors of students are simply extensions of Carroll's (1963) description of aptitude as a function of the time required to learn something (time on task) when the learner is engaged in learning experiences that are appropriate to the demands of that which is to be learned.

The nature of the relationship between teachers and students enables or disables the learning process. Respect, trust, and confidence are vital elements of an enabling relationship, promoting affinity between teacher and student. Those students who stumble on a teacher with whom they develop a close and rewarding relationship, a teacher who can act as a role model and can help them chart a meaningful life course, are lucky, as well as being more likely to set their goals high and to attain them (bearing out many claims that teacher expectation frames the level of student achievement). Where teacher expectation is limited by class, ethnicity, gender, or other biases, equity in student achievement becomes a more complex and difficult problem to surmount.

Students interacting with students need a healthy social climate that reinforces the learning endeavor. The person-to-person learning that goes on between students can be as effective, if not more effective, than teacher/student learning both in and out of the classroom. Positive modeling of learning behaviors between students, emphasized in cooperative learning tasks, is a powerful learning enabler for many students. Negative role modeling and peer pressure, however, can be a factor limiting the achievement of certain groups who see success in the academic arena as a negation of their ethnic and personal identity (Gordon, 1991).

Learning Behaviors and Attitudes of Students

All of the components of effective schooling are not directly referable to schools and the teachers who people them. Because learning is both a process and an outcome that is personal to the learner, the attitudes of learners toward learning and their actual learning behaviors are critical. Attention should be given to the often-neglected variable of "disposition," which refers to the attitudinal and habitual readiness to receive and to respond in specific ways (Gordon & Armour-Thomas, 1991). It is possibly a "habit of mind," to use Gardner's (1993) term. It is clearly a tendency to behave in a certain way and, with some degree of automaticity, to view and engage the environment in certain ways. Some aspects of disposition may be constitutional (see Thomas & Chess, 1977), but most aspects of disposition are, perhaps, best thought of as the products of incidental learning. For example, the disposition to explore, inquire, and examine is thought to be the product of exposure to significant others who model such tendencies, while the tendency toward impulse responsivity (impulsiveness) is thought to be more constitutional in origin. For students whose dispositions do not support serious academic endeavor, we may need to build into the curriculum whatever experiences will be likely to reshape such dispositions.

Four categories of learner characteristics can be identified (Gordon, 1988). Besides the functional and status characteristics with which students begin schooling there are learner behaviors and learning achievements. Disproportionate attention has been given to learning achievements, grades, tests scores, and similar credentials to the neglect of intermediate and enabling learner behaviors—namely, learning task engagement, time on task, energy deployment, resource use, and meta-cognitive and metacomponential strategies. All of these behaviors are learnable, but they are not explicitly taught in school. In some instances, where these behaviors are a part of the naturally acquired repertoire of the student, their relevance to academic pursuits may not be made explicit, resulting in their underuse. In such situations, one of the tasks of instruction is to enable the learner to recognize the existence of these behaviors in his or her own repertoire and to understand their relevance for academic pursuits.

In our own work with inner-city youth, we see "habits of mind" that are highly effective in the achievement of out-of-school ends and that, if so directed, would be equally effective at academic tasks. The challenge is to help these youngsters naturally transfer these behaviors to their in-school pursuits. Where such behaviors are not a part of the learner's repertoire, to be effective, education must ensure that they are learned. However, this may be more difficult than might be assumed. Dispositional behaviors are very likely acquired in highly personalized, effectively important interpersonal teaching and learning transactions. We believe that most such transactions involve informal rather than formal instruction and are experienced as incidentally rather than deliberately directed learning. It is not known whether dispositions can be deliberately taught or whether the conditions necessary for their deliberate instruction can be created in school. Yet if we are correct in the importance that we attach to these dispositional traits, to the extent that they are absent or present and incompatible with academic learning in some of our students, it is in this domain that educators will have to work if equitable educational opportunities and outcomes are to be achieved.

Support for Academic Learning: Communities and Families

More than 20 years ago, Tyler and Wolf (1974) demonstrated that differentials in school achievement between Black and White children as well as between lower- and middle-class children were reduced when they controlled for the extent to which home environments provided adequate support for academic learning. Using a fairly narrow range of independent variables—namely, academic and reading materials in the home, adequate space and time for study, the modeling of reading and other academic behaviors, appropriate school supplies, and the expectation that academic work is taken seriously—they were able to demonstrate comparable academic outcomes across differential status groups that were exposed to equally good schools. Their findings support the notion that an important contribution to the achievement of equality in educational outcomes can be made by factors associated with family and home. But it is not just the economic and educational status of the family that is determinate; this work suggests that it is the family's use of resources and the way that the family functions in support of academic development that is carrying the weight.

Affective Development

The factors involved in the preceding discussion may be represented and integrated in both student and teacher affective outcomes. There is growing recognition that the quality of cognitive development may be limited by the quality of the affective components of behavior; that is, in the absence of a disposition to employ inquiry skills, inquiring behavior in learning may be mechanical in its expression, if present at all. This is the case, in part, because affective development should be thought of as a dialectical force enabling many cognitive functions even as it is influenced by them. Interest, identification, and motivation, as examples, make possible task engagement and problem solving, but the manner in which tasks are engaged and problems are solved influences interest and motivation. Similarly, there are affective functions that it would appear do not become operative in the absence of cognition. For example, some categories of nonhuman animal species show the capacity for affinity for other animals, but we think of humans as being unique in the capacity to feel love. Love as a human affective response may be possible only because of the human cognitive capacity to generate and use symbols to represent feelings for others. It could be that something like love, which we think of as primarily affective in character, is fundamentally cognitive. Or, more correctly, the affective and cognitive components of human behavior, which make possible a construct such as love, are so symbiotic as to make meaningless any efforts at their separation. Thus, this concern with cognitive development must be inseparable from our concern with affective development.

Quite apart from a relationship to cognitive function, attention to the affective components of development in education has a rationale of its own. Human beings are primarily social animals. Although intellectual competence is increasingly required for meaningful social intercourse, without an adequate sense of self and a sense of relatedness to others and without the capacity for empathy and the identification of the values that frame one's life, human life itself would be less meaningful. If these affective components are to receive deliberate and serious attention in schooling, ways must be found to give them more explicit focus and to document their importance in the outcomes of school.

DETERMINING THE ACHIEVEMENT OF EQUITY:
IMPLICATIONS FOR ASSESSMENT, ACCOUNTABILITY,
AND PROFESSIONAL RESPONSIBILITY

In March 1991, the New York State Board of Regents adopted a comprehensive policy statement for improving public elementary, middle, and secondary education. The statement, *A New Compact for Learning* (Gordon, 1991b) is based on the principle that all children can learn and calls for collaboration among parents, educators, state and local governments, colleges, libraries, museums, social service agencies, and community groups in the pursuit of holistic educational reform. The *Compact* lists 10 educational goals encompassing intellectual, emotional, and physical development; societal, environmental, and historical awareness; knowledge development; major domains of learning, skills, knowledge, and values for effective participation in society; and preparation for life in a diverse society in a multicultural world. One of the fundamental principles of the *Compact* states, "Every child in New York State is entitled to the resources necessary to provide the sound, basic education which the state Constitution requires. The requirement is not equality of input, but equity of outcome" (p. 3).

Measures of educational achievement in New York State have long revealed a significant gap in academic achievement between economic haves and have-nots and between members of majority and minority groups. During the 1970s and 1980s, the focus on the achievement of minimum competence in basic skills may have begun to close this gap to some extent. However, as we shift our educational focus from basic skills mastery to the pursuit of excellence (i.e., world-class competence) in all students, we are in danger of widening that gap. This is likely to be the case because less affluent communities and families often lack the resources and sometimes the expertise to invest adequately in education of high quality. For example, the disparity in the investment per pupil afforded by various districts ranges from a low of $3,000 to a high of $18,000, with the most economically privileged pupils being served by those districts with the highest per-pupil investment.

In its concern for the pursuit of excellence and equity in educational achievement, the *Compact* (Gordon, 1991b) asserts that we need not choose between excellence and equity. To that end, three major foci were proposed for the assurance of the attainment of excellence and conditions of equity. These include the provision of resources necessary for all schools to achieve statewide goals and desired learning outcomes and recognizing that children with greater needs require greater resources. Universal statewide standards were proposed along with the strong expectation that all children will meet them. Additionally, the results of assessments of educational achievement were to be analyzed by socioeconomic and racial/ethnic groups to encourage the provision of resources where they are most needed. Although the New York State *New Compact for Learning* is not primarily an equity-oriented document, the implication and expressed concerns of the document challenge the state to define a course of action that will result in the equitable achievement of these goals. Despite vigorous efforts at the implementation of *The New Compact for Learning*, these three conditions were not met and its goals relative to equity were not achieved.

The movement toward universal standards for all students has prompted strong debate among proponents of equity in education. Many of the problems that arise in the attempt to authentically assess the educational outcomes and achievements of populations whose life conditions, experiences, and values differ from those of the hegemonic culture are central issues with which the assessment community is struggling in its quest to forge performance-oriented assessments and standards. Increasingly, it is argued that adequate evaluation of progress toward equity is not possible with the standardized tests and procedures currently in use. Concerned educators are striving to create assessment procedures that allow for diverse ways of preparing, expressing, and demonstrating competency as well as allowing for alternatives and choice in the measurement tasks to be performed and the conditions under which assessment probes are engaged. Assessment that accurately reflects the wide-ranging and diverse achievements of students who differ in many of their characteristics must have the flexibility to take into account diversity between groups as well as diversity within groups.

In any attempt to measure achievement and developed abilities equitably, a primary concern must be the fact that diverse populations have unequal levels of entry into available educational experiences, which themselves are likely to be inequitable. In the past, this has been compensated for by lowering the standards for certain groups, which in effect denies some students the opportunity to even try to achieve equal outcomes. If we set universal standards that are also of high quality in the belief that such standards can be achieved by all students, we must strive to meet the conditions that make that possible. To aid those schools that traditionally demonstrate low levels of student achievement, not only must sufficient resources be made available but assessment processes must be designed that are sensitive indicators of progress in student development as well as accurate measures of actual achievement. It is especially these schools that will require that assessment processes produce more than the traditional indicators of status. What is needed are assessment devices and procedures that capture the processual features of teaching and learning. It is knowledge of the status and especially the functioning of such features that will ultimately inform the improvement of teaching and learning.

A second concern is with the validity and authenticity of assessment measures. The question of validity explores whether a measure really measures what it purports to measure. The question of authenticity asks whether a measure relates in any meaningful way to the reality of the phenomenon in the actual behavior of the respondent. In the days before the field of psychometrics pretty much gave up on demonstrating these constructs, we simply referred to both as "validity." We asked such questions as: Does the test probe measure what it claims to measure? Is the response an authentic and valid expression of the targeted behavior? Solutions to the problem of validity in measurement are generally approached through inference. But the surrogate behavioral expressions from which our inferences concerning ability and achievement are drawn are often such abstract representations that, reported in the aggregate, they do little to inform pedagogical intervention. The emergence of the authentic assessment movement is, in part, a result of widespread awareness of this problem. Despite the enthusiasm generated by this movement, a new and more appropriate system of educational assessment is as yet some years away. Certainly, we cannot afford to put educational reform on hold while we wait for the development of new processes and instruments of authentic and processual assessment. A practical interim solution is to use a thorough *qualitative* analysis of existing standardized tests to identify and uncouple the purposes behind each test item so that this information can be used to better serve the function of informing pedagogical intervention. Unless we thoroughly understand each strand of the bundle, we cannot make the information in the bundle applicable to our pedagogical needs: namely, to describe learner functioning, to diagnose teaching and learning dysfunction, to inform teaching and learning processes, and to promote learner, teacher, and system self-examination as components of an accountability structure that supports professional responsibility in the delivery of high-quality education.

It is, perhaps, this concern with professional responsibility that is the foundation for our pursuit of equity and social justice in education. Recent calls for our schools to become more accountable are understandable in the face of massive school wastage, on the one hand, and the demand that all members of our society become more competitive in global markets, on the other. However, it is unlikely that any externally applied pressure on the schools will lead to the massive increments in educational effectiveness that will be required. To universally deliver the quality of education that is implied in the arguments we have advanced here will require that communities provide more and different resources for education. It will require that students and families behave in ways that are more supportive of academic learning. It will require that our society ensure and make more explicit the universal availability of the rewards of intellectual and social competence. It will require that educators behave differently and work harder. Sirotnik and Goodlad (1985) have suggested that a paradigm shift away from authoritarian conceptions of accountability is necessary if we are to achieve changes of this magnitude. They assert that "the conventional accountability notion suggests authority, manipulation, and control whereas the new accountability responsibility, if you like—suggests leadership, collaboration, enlightenment" (p. 292). If we are to achieve equity and social justice in the pursuit of education of high quality, it will have to be preceded by the assumption of professional responsibility for that achievement on the part of all of us who are involved in the determination of public policy, the financing of our schools, and the processes of teaching and learning.

CHAPTER 6

Characteristics of Learning Persons and the Adaptation of Learning Environments

WITH LIZANNE DESTEFANO AND STEPHANIE SHIPMAN

One of my [Gordon's] most vivid recollections of my childhood is that of my country doctor father standing next to a seriously ill old Black woman lying prostrate on her sickbed with a stream of blood arching from the blood vessel in her left arm that my father had just lanced. The cuff from his sphygmomanometer was still attached to her right arm, and he was watching its gauge as closely as he watched her. After what seemed like an eternity, he stopped the bleeding and placed a cool, wet towel on her head. Her breathing became easier. The mild jerk in her right foot subsided, and she slowly opened her eyes. Later that day, as we drove back home, my father explained that the woman's blood pressure was dangerously high, and that he had to let some of the blood out to relieve the pressure. "If we could have gotten her to a hospital, we might have tried something else, but out here we have to be adaptive," he explained.

I often think of my father as he went through the countryside, adapting what he knew about the healing art to the needs and conditions he encountered in his patients. I think about the other country doctors of that period and before, letting blood to get rid of impurities in the system and performing other procedures we now know to be useless if not dangerous. And I think about us, their counterparts in education, as we seek to practice the art of teaching, adapting what we know—often under less than optimal conditions—to the needs of our pupils. I dream about the day when we shall know more about teaching and learning and about the needs and conditions of learners, and be able to look back with amazement that we were able to do as much good and as little harm as we did in a profession that has yet to establish its bases firmly in the sciences of behavior and pedagogy.

INDIVIDUALIZED INSTRUCTION: PRACTICE AND RESEARCH

We observe that good teachers often adapt and individualize instruction in order to address the great diversity in the student population and in learner-relevant and nonrelevant traits. Many researchers are concerned with the potential of individualized instruction and attribute-treatment interactions (ATIs). Yet the diversity of learners outweighs the diversity in curriculum design and instructional practice, and only modest complementarities exist between our emerging knowledge of functional and status characteristics of learners and our knowledge of curriculum development and pedagogy. Our best-developed adaptations to individual differences are concerned with learning rate, interests, or combinations of developed abilities, achievement, and background experiences (Gordon, 1979).

In the United States, the oldest and most common approach to dealing with individual differences is homogeneous grouping by age, sex, race, and general ability in school, grade, classroom, and activity units. Although grouping by age remains the norm, grouping by sex, race, and general ability has become less common at the school, grade, and classroom levels. This is partly due to democratic concerns regarding the unequal allocation of resources and academic stimulation among such groupings. It is recognized that grouping by these latter categories into classroom units does not result in homogeneous groups; it simply reduces variation in a classroom on one dimension. Lately, grouping by ability into autonomous classes has come under attack because most of the research on grouping practices has shown no universal academic benefits to low-, medium-, or high-ability groups over what they would have achieved in similar but mixed-ability classrooms. In addition, some of the affective outcomes from such groupings have been rather insidious, stemming from the social-class character of the resulting structure, especially when confounded with race and sex segregation (Esposito, 1971). Thus, education programming has turned to individualized learning systems that serve children of a wide variety of ability groupings in the same classroom.

Gagné's (1974) system of identifying the hierarchical cognitive requirements of an educational task has had a tremendous impact on the best of these individualized learning systems. In stressing the importance of a careful analysis of the steps in learning, he laid the groundwork for teaching a child any concept or skill whose prerequisites can be carefully identified. In learning hierarchically arranged information and skills, it is presumed that the individual characteristics of importance are the rate and quality of the achievement of the prerequisite skills and information.

Gagné recognized different kinds of learning (signal, stimulus-response, chaining, verbal association, discrimination, concept and role learning, and problem solving), each requiring different modes of presentation and teacher prompts and/or direction to be most effective.

This process, then, is an example of transforming the task to meet the demands of both the kind of learning involved and the student characteristics considered most relevant to the task at hand, regardless of the child's performance on some measure of intelligence or a more global type of achievement measure. The assumption is that children fail at an educational task only because it is inappropriately presented or it is mistakenly assumed that the children have the identifiable prerequisites. Therefore, children take a pretest on the material to be mastered and, according to the information received regarding their acquisition of the prerequisites, they follow the universal sequence of steps for that material, although they may start at earlier or later steps than their peers. Gagné (1974) has formed highly precise but generalizable rules for teaching particular "bits" of learning within any hierarchically structured topic relative to the particular bits of learning the child has already acquired, thus creating a system for individualizing education on the basis of prior achievement.

A few centers have used this concept of individualizing education according to prior achievement as the basis for large-scale federally supported individualization programs that are implemented in school systems across the nation. Although the emphases of these programs differ with regard to the different ages of the target group, all lean heavily on the goal of individual mastery of behaviorally prescribed objectives; the choice of alternative presentations of instructional material; frequent pre- and post-testing with regard to achievement level; the special training of teachers, administrators, and support personnel for data management and for counseling and diagnostic services; and integrated teamwork in administrative and management procedures. The intent of each program is to improve student achievement outcomes and interest in schooling. After the 2 or more years required to complete implementation and adjustment, all programs appear to do very well, especially with regard to the achievement of their low- and middle-ability groups. Cost varies, since many of the testing and data-processing functions require the use of computer terminals for the efficient use of personnel time (Talmage, 1975). However, despite the relative success of many of these programs that plan learning experiences based on prior achievement, findings from a 3-year study conducted by Nojan and her associates suggest that further delineation of student learning characteristics is a critical need in individualizing instruction and adapting learning environments (Nojan, Strom, & Wang, 1982). Ideally, in addition to prior achievement, learning environments that are truly adaptive should be systematically sensitive to a variety of learning behaviors associated with individual pupil characteristics such as affective response tendencies, cognitive style, motivation, and identity.

Periodically, articles by teachers appear in applied educational journals describing how they have met the call for individualization within their classrooms. A hodgepodge of methods and theories of diversity has emerged out of the pragmatic quest to deal adequately with the obvious range of individual pupil characteristics with which teachers are confronted. Presumably, these are highly sensitive and conscientious teachers who, whether they do or do not read the educational psychology journals, are making systematic observations and judgments concerning their pupils that are congruent with the findings of educational research. Hunt (1975) is convinced that good teachers have an intuitive sense for the differential characteristics of their pupils and adapt their teaching behavior to their perceptions of those characteristics. Unfortunately, we must conclude that these teachers depict rather uncommon classroom procedures, and that most public education in this country is individualized only to the extent of providing readers with texts on a few different reading levels, combined with some separate instruction for small reading groups within a classroom unit.

That the ATI paradigm is not more present in curriculum development is not surprising since the knowledge regarding learner characteristics is complex and contradictory, and furthermore, there is little evidence of its validity and no guidelines for its application. Despite its tenuous nature, the paradigm continues to demonstrate a persuasive logical relationship between learner characteristics (attributes), learning experiences (treatments), and learning outcomes (interaction results).

ATI research has been overwhelmingly the expression of concern regarding the importance of individual differences for learning and teaching (Cronbach & Snow, 1977; Endler & Magnusson, 1976; Glaser, 1977a). It is best characterized statistically as the comparison of the regression slopes of a variable from individual behavior onto an educational outcome variable under two or more contrasting educational treatments. Two kinds of interaction are defined by plotting the calculated slopes, for the range of the ability measured, on the same graph. In the ordinal interactions, one treatment is associated with significantly higher criterion scores than the other treatment for a section of the aptitude range, with an insignificant difference between the two treatments at another part of the range. In the disordinal interactions, the slopes actually cross so that at one section of the aptitude range, one treatment produces significantly higher results, whereas the other treatment produces better results at a different part of the aptitude range.

The ATI knowledge base is so confused because certain factors make difficult our understanding of individual and group differences and ultimately our appreciation of the value to pedagogy of the ATI paradigm. These same factors help explain why there appears to be little empirical support for the very logical and commonsense notion that differences in human characteristics should be associated with differences in the effectiveness of various educational treatments. In addition to these methodological, operational, and technical reasons for the lack of clarity in this area, one of the reasons why the empirical evidence in support of this notion is so limited may be that the conceptual work in support of the logic of the relationship has not yet been done. As Rothkopf (1978) has observed:

> It would be a mistake to expect too much from methodological reform alone. Both hands, the statistical and the conceptual, are needed to plow the field of aptitude x treatment interactions in teaching. The reasons for weak studies and incoherent results derive chiefly from our inadequate conception of the learning person. We need more psychological insights to provide us with working hypotheses about significant aspects of teaching and how they interact with personal abilities. (p. 708)

Glaser (1977b) in some ways anticipated the Rothkopf (1978) criticism in a little book that is pregnant with pedagogical ideas. In his *Adaptive Education,* Glaser recognizes that the combination of available alternatives provided in systems of schooling and the decision-making procedures used to place individuals in these alternatives are the fundamental characteristics by which educational enterprise can be described and analyzed. He then uses these characteristics to describe the ways in which aspects of teaching can be adapted to individual diversity.

Glaser (1977b) outlines five models of educational enterprise that are not mutually exclusive and, hence, are combined in a variety of ways at different levels of education:

Model One: Selective with Limited Alternatives. Individuals come to an educational setting with an initial state of competence. Through informal and formal means, this state is assessed, and on the basis of that assessment, a decision is made to place the student in the standard educational environment or to designate the student as a poor learner for whom some special treatment is required. The activities carried out in the standard learning environment are generally limited in the alternative modes of learning provided and emphasize the particular abilities addressed in the initial assessment, to the exclusion of other abilities. Because the selection process is geared to include those students with a relatively high performance in the abilities required to succeed in the given educational environment, the environment can remain fairly rigid.

Model Two: Development of Initial Competence. The second model has the same characteristics as Model One: selection procedures and a learning environment. In Model Two, however, not only are individuals assessed with respect to presence or absence of abilities that allow participation in the program, but some diagnostic decision is made about the nature of those abilities. For individuals whose initial state of competence is not sufficient for selection, an educational environment is provided to develop their competence to a point where participation in the program is maximized. In this way, through some combination of prior and continued monitoring and instruction, entry abilities are modified so that the number of individuals who succeed is maximized. A student is forced to adjust to the standard program with the help of supplemental instruction, implying that the deficit lies in the learner rather than in the learning environment.

Model Three: Accommodation to Different Styles of Learning. Model Three attempts to respond to the limitations of Model Two by providing alternative flexible educational environments and instructional methods that accommodate to different learners' abilities at entry into the program and throughout the course of learning. As information is obtained about the learner, decisions are made to enhance probabilities of success in alternative instructional environments with various learning opportunities. The procedures by which instructional methods are altered for different students is based largely on teachers' intuition and expertise. This process can be improved by increasing the range of diagnostic, instructional, and organizational resources available to teachers.

Model Four: Development of Initial Competence and Accommodation to Different Styles of Learning. The fourth model considers the combination of the second and third models. In this case, achievement is maximized both by improving the initial state of competence and by providing multiple environments so that abilities and instructional environments can be matched and so that there can be movement across the alternate environments as the individual develops the skills useful to learn in each context.

Model Five: Alternate Attainment Possibilities. In the previous four models, the educational goal reflected the emphases of the elementary school, that is, to teach basic literacy to all students. Model Five contains a variety of educational outcomes usually associated with higher education. Multiple goals encourage the development of different constellations of human abilities and reward many different ways of succeeding.

It is not unreasonable to identify the selective, limited alternative Model One with past and prevailing educational practice. Currently, intelligence and aptitude have emerged as the significant entering abilities that are assessed to the exclusion of most other individual characteristics. The assessment instruments used are not designed to determine different ways in which students learn best or to identify basic competencies necessary to learn various kinds of tasks in various environments. Model Two attempts to introduce flexibility and seeks success for a greater number of students by developing initial competence.

It is not until Model Three, however, that the concern for the interaction between instruction and individuals, which is the crux of the Rothkopf (1978) criticism, becomes apparent. Glaser (1977b) indicates that Model Four—providing the development of initial competence and accommodation to different ways of learning—offers maximum adaptability of aspects of teaching to individual diversity in the elementary years. Model Five—offering multiple educational outcomes—maximizes success in the upper grades. A cognitive psychologist who is uniquely sensitive to many of the practical concerns of classroom teachers, Glaser goes on to describe and give specifications for the design, delivery, and management of teaching and learning transactions consistent with these models. However, even Glaser's very advanced concepts fail to provide adequate conceptions of the learning person.

DIMENSIONS OF HUMAN DIVERSITY

Human learners are more than cognitive beings. Human behavior is also influenced by affect, by motivation, by identity, by environmental press, and indeed by various manifestations of status, for example, sex and gender, social and economic status, ethnicity and race, and language and culture. An adequate conception of the learning person requires that we understand each learner from each of these dimensions of human diversity as well as from the collectivity of these dimensions as they are orchestrated in the lives and behaviors of learners. Our efforts at isolating significant treatment effects in relation to differential aptitudes or attributes, as well as the limited effectiveness of adaptive and individualized education, may simply reflect our continuing insensitivity to such single and collective dimensions of the person whose learning we seek to affect. What do we know about these dimensions of human diversity in learners and what relevance do they have for the design and management of teaching and learning transactions?

Socioeconomic Status. Socioeconomic status accounts for that component of subjective recognition of shared similarities that is related to income, style of life, education, occupation, and the acquisition of corresponding modes of life, or prestige of birth, for an aggregate of individuals. The realization that socioeconomic status dictates class in a hierarchical society is an essential component of human history. For Marx, much of human history is rooted in the class struggle. It is this struggle that gives rise to class consciousness. This concept allows for changes in the individual, since the subjective component of consciousness of socioeconomic status makes class an active, emergent force in history. Empirical sociologists concerned with the relationship between class and educational achievement do not give emphasis to this notion of class. Rather, they use class to designate a relatively fixed set of assumed characteristics and social hierarchical positions. This latter use of the term has made for rather dubious causal assumptions since class as an indicator of social hierarchical position indicates how one is likely to be perceived and treated but provides little information about the functional dimensions of one's experience and behavior. The work of Mercer (1973) and Wolf (1966) suggests that it is the functional dimensions that make differences in educational achievement, and socioeconomic status is not a reliable indicator of these dimensions.

Sex and Gender. Sex and gender are often colloquially used interchangeably but are used here to refer to the biological (sex) and social-role (gender) characteristics by which distinctions are made in the identification and socialization of females and males. In discussing sex differences, we refer only to those characteristics that can be directly linked to the biological structures and functions of one of the two sexes, whereas gender is used in the discussion of socially assigned or adopted role functions. There appear to be few if any educationally relevant behaviors that can be traced to the biological aspects of sex. However, several of the behavioral differences observable in the learning behavior of boys and girls can readily be attributed to differences in gender. In addition, these differences in sex-related, socially assigned, or adopted role functions also serve to influence the ways in which boys and girls are treated, what is expected of them, and what is allowed. Thus the educationally relevant characteristic is gender rather than sex.

Ethnicity. Ethnicity is used to refer to one's belonging to and identification with a group that is characterized by such attributes in common as physical characteristics, genetic and cultural history, belief systems, and sometimes language. Although often used synonymously with race, ethnicity does not specify biological race (Caucasian, Mongolian, or Negroid) but may be used to refer to a group that shares, among other things, a common gene pool. Ethnicity may be assumed, inherited, or assigned. As used in this chapter, ethnicity includes the growing concern with the self-interest of a group as a manifestation of ethnicity. As Ogbu (1978) has indicated, ethnicity often functions like caste, in that it determines a position in the social order from which its members cannot escape. Since ethnicity is so often associated with status, it is the status phenomenon that has the greatest implications for education. In the United States, ethnic status determines in large measure the nature of one's access to educational opportunities. Because of stereotypic thinking, it influences what is expected of the ethnic group member; and, because of biases born of the castelike nature of ethnicity, how one is treated in educational settings is significantly influenced by one's ethnicity. Thus, although ethnicity provides us with few leads for pedagogical intervention, it does strongly suggest the nature of some aspects of educational conditions and circumstances.

Culture. Culture is that complex experiential whole that includes knowledge, belief, art, morals, law, custom, and any other capabilities and habits acquired by humans as members of society. The total pattern of human behavior and its products embodied in thought, speech, action, and artifacts is dependent on the human capacity for learning and transmitting knowledge to succeeding generations through the use of tools, language, and systems of abstract thought. As a descriptive concept, culture is a product of human action; as an explanatory concept, it is seen as a dialectical cause of human action. In a more colloquial sense, culture is the mores and way of life of a people. Cultures differ. Some are more influenced by technological developments than others, and some are more complex; but no group of people is without its culture. Cultural "deprivation" is a misnomer. With respect to education, the culture of the school may complement or be alien to that of some of its students. Bridging and second-culture learning present the largest challenge for education; failure to achieve an effective level of complementarity is the greatest threat (see Chapter 3).

Motivation. Motivation has been traditionally defined as a personalistic variable reflecting the ability of a person to sustain effort in the absence of extrinsic rewards, or as a prompting force or an incitement working on a person to influence volition and action. It is the second definition, which gives emphasis to forces acting on a person, that better reflects the definitional emphasis utilized here. We see the prompting force as residing within persons and within stimuli. The process is reinterpreted to refer to the acquired ability of stimuli contained within situations to sustain the performance capability of certain individuals. It is in the nature of human organisms to act and react. The ability of stimuli to arouse and sustain human action is the motivating force. In the context of this definition, in education it is the responsibility of the learning experience to be motivating and not of the learner to be motivated. Obviously the conditions and sources of motivation differ for different learners.

Language. Language, conceptually defined, is a systematic means of communicating ideas or feelings by the use of conventionalized signals, sounds, gestures, or marks having understood meanings. In a deeper sense, however, languages are collections of symbolic representational repertoires and their appropriate milieu (setting, topic, social status of participants) for realization in speech or other communication modes. The language system(s) used is thus the vehicle for expressive and receptive communication. In addition, the language system provides the schemata around which mental functions gain meaning. Language competence, then, is a necessary condition for effective education. Educational experiences are more effective when there is congruence between the language of the school and that of the learner. However, learning is not rendered impossible simply because there is a lack of congruence.

Identity. Identity, in common parlance, refers to what stands out about a person and how the person defines himself or herself. It has been defined as the unity and persistence of personality reflecting the individual comprehensiveness of a life or character. Here a distinction is drawn between basic and qualitative identity. Basic identity is the nonreflective state in which existence is taken for granted, or in which the sense of existence leads to feelings that all is well. Qualitative identity refers to the sense of completeness, synthesis, and continuity by which persons perceive in themselves a character of a particular kind. Of the characteristics that learners bring to learning situations, it is, perhaps, identity by which most of the components of individuality are integrated. To the extent that one's characteristics are consciously orchestrated in the interest of learning, it is probably around identity that such patterning occurs.

Operating at the core of sense of self, identity is the wellspring for sense of efficacy and ultimately for effort applied to learning.

Cognitive Response Tendency. Cognitive response tendency, usually called cognitive style, is used to refer to relatively consistent patterns characteristic of an individual in the manner and form rather than the level of perceiving, remembering, and thinking. The most commonly utilized categories are abstract and concrete functioning and field-independent and field-dependent styles. Since style connotes a higher degree of stability than is supported by the evidence, the term tendency is frequently used in preference to the term style.

Affective Response Tendency. Affective response tendency, identified generally as temperament, is used to refer to relatively consistent patterns, characteristic of an individual, of emotional responses to a specific stimulus situation. Aspects of temperament such as characteristic tempo, rhythmicity, adaptability, energy expenditure, mood, and focus of attention are most often referred to in the literature, and are given emphasis in most discussions. However, affective responses also include stylistic variation in processes such as attribution, personalization, projection, and cathexis. Cognitive response tendency and temperament speak to the *how* of behavior, defining for the most part the manner in which behavior is deployed in response to stimulus situations. It is the relative consistency in these response tendencies that leads us to type individuals and to anticipate reactions. In learning and other developmental situations, it is thought that the complement between response tendency and situational demands facilitates development, while conflict and contradiction tend to challenge and may distort the course of development. With respect to education, Shipman and Shipman (1988) argue that one of the purposes of education is to extend the repertoire of response tendencies available to the learning person.

Health and Nutrition. Health and nutrition refer to the status of the biophysiological equilibrium of the organism in its environment. Often underestimated as variables of importance to education, health and nutrition influence attentional behavior, available energy, and stability of response potential, as well as such ordinary factors as school attendance and availability for instruction.

Environmental Press. Environmental press refers to the influence of living and nonliving phenomena that surround the individual. Specifically, press is what these phenomena can do to the subject or for the subject—the power they have to affect the well-being of the subject in one way or another. There is a distinction between the press that exists objectively for a subject (alpha press) and the press that a subject perceives (beta press). The environment may be thought of as objective or subjective. The objective environment can be defined to include, but not necessarily be exhausted by, the alpha press. However, it may be the attributed character (beta press) that is projected onto the environment by the perceiver that gives environmental press its special role as a determinant of the individual's engagement in and response to educational intervention. Thus the ecology of learning situations is being increasingly viewed as important. However, it is the social and personal meanings of these situations that may be of greatest importance to the learning person.

ORCHESTRATION OF ATTRIBUTES

The knowledge base relevant to understanding these dimensions of diversity has been explored and the possible implications for education have been explicated (Gordon, 1988). In the course of the completion of this work, it became clear that, as important as each of these learner characteristics may be, it is not in their unilateral but in their multilateral impact that their importance for teaching and learning resides. Learners do not bring their unique characteristics singly to bear on teaching and learning transactions. Rather, they bring these characteristics to bear on learning behavior in dynamically orchestrated patterns or clusters. It appears that it is these orchestrations, and not the individual attributes, that influence the learner's approaches to learning problems, the strategies and skills that are developed in response to learning task demands, the directional deployment of effort, and, ultimately, the nature and quality of task engagement, time on task, goal-directed deployment of energy, resource utilization, and efficacious behavior. Thus, it may be important that the teacher know the dominant features of each pupil's cognitive style, temperament, sources of motivation, identity, and so forth, but even more important that the teacher be sensitive to the stimulus conditions and situational constraints under which aspects of each of these domains change.

One could say that we are dealing with learner attributes at three levels: traits (cognitive style or temperament), instrumental behaviors (strategies, directed effort, skills), and intermediate outcome behaviors (time on task, resource utilization), the product of all of which is achievement. Instead of focusing on a specific manifestation of cognitive style, for example, it may be necessary to study several components of cognitive stylistic preference as they are orchestrated in learning strategies and to focus the manipulation of educational treatment on these strategies rather than on style. We have earlier suggested (Gordon, Wang, & DeStefano, 1982) that it should be noted that even single-domain clustering or patterning may reflect too limited a conceptualization. Messick (1982) suggests that human traits in learning behavior may be best understood as encompassing cross-style and cross-domain (for example, affective or cognitive) patternings that are not necessarily constant across situations. What is being suggested here is the real possibility that preoccupation with the learner's tendency to utilize a specific manifestation of a single domain or even the learner's utilization of multiple expressions from a single domain is counterproductive. Rather, a better conceptualization of the principle of behavioral individuality must include dynamic and dialectical relationships, within and between domains, selectively integrated into response tendencies.

It is entirely possible that multiple manifestations of styles or response capabilities may be present simultaneously, with some expressions more readily available, some more actively incorporated into habit patterns, or some attached by prior experience to specific stimuli or situations. Specific instances of learner behavior may then be the product of deliberate or fortuitous selection from the repertoires of possible responses. Leona Tyler (1978) has written:

> The core idea is that each individual represents a different sequence of selective acts by means of which only some of the developmental possibilities are chosen and organized. . . . As Whitehead pointed out, the fundamental realities are actual occasions in which indeterminate possibilities are transformed into determinate actualities. (p. 233)

Our learner behaviors are examples of Tyler's "determinate actualities." They are the results of selective acts through which multiple manifestations of diversity (Tyler would say individuality) are orchestrated. To seize on unitary components of those orchestrations may be an error. But the adaptation of instruction to those orchestrations may pose a greater challenge than the pedagogical sciences foundational to education currently enable us to meet.

ISSUES SURROUNDING ADAPTIVE EDUCATION

In what directions, then, do our current knowledge and experience enable us to move? In answering this question, let us examine three issues: (1) What needs are served by existing models? (2) To what is it that education should be adaptive? and (3) What are the demands placed on teachers of an appropriately adaptive education?

1. *What needs are served by extant models of adaptive education?* The spirit of adaptive education seems to provide greater support for humanistic approaches to instruction. Its focus on individuals rather than on groups seems to ensure that individual pupils are less likely to be ignored, whether their individual learning needs are addressed or not. The customization that we have achieved does seem to serve the needs of some pupils, since individualization tends to broaden the achievement spectrum.

Yet, extant models are still too narrowly prescriptive in that they are sensitive singly to pupil characteristics. In many cases, diagnostic information on pupil characteristics reflects a concern for curriculum rather than for the functional nature of the learning person. We have not fully exploited the area of cognitive psychology that addresses the affective and cognitive processes by which pupils mediate their own learning or by which learning can be mediated. This knowledge base may offer us a greater understanding of the learning person and, through that understanding, the development of an appropriately adaptive education.

2. *From the perspective of learners, to what should education be adapted and for what purpose?* Clearly, these questions cannot be answered independently. That to which education should be adaptive depends on the purposes to be served and the characteristics of the learner.

One can use current theory and common sense to hypothesize about the relative importance of different learner characteristics as the purpose of educational tasks changes. For example, when the primary purpose is to enable mastery of content and skills, adaptation to developed abilities and prior achievement may be most important. Interest, motivation, and affective response tendency may not be as salient, but probably should not be ignored. Adaptation to sex, ethnicity, and social class may be marginally helpful but probably would not be crucial. On the other hand, when the purpose is to learn how to learn and to systematize mentation in problem solving, adaptation to affective response tendencies and cognitive style may be highly important while prior achievement, developed abilities, and status characteristics may be less important. When the purpose is to develop appreciation and a sense of efficacy, it may be that interests, motivation, and identity are the salient learner characteristics to which adaptation must be responsive and that, in some cases—such as when the purpose is to develop understanding of process, relationships, and meanings—blending of all learner characteristics may be required.

Unfortunately, it is unlikely that the matching process is that simple.

What is to be adapted to and the purposes for which education should be adaptive are not static phenomena. They can change over time and across learning situations, making it essential that adaptive education be recognized as dynamic, dialectical, and transactional in response to Tyler's (1978) "determinate actualities."

3. *What are the demands on teachers of an appropriately adaptive education?* If adaptive education is to serve learners rather than teachers and if, to do so, it must be dynamic, dialectical, and transactional, to deliver adaptive education may place responsibilities on teachers that are far greater than they are currently prepared to assume. It becomes necessary to speculate about the qualities such teachers should possess and what regimen of training might facilitate these qualities.

Let us return to the example of the "country doctor," the best of whom were prepared in the tradition of the Viennese physician—broadly educated, richly cultured, with a good knowledge of human anatomy, some appreciation of physiology and biochemistry, and a keenly attuned medical intuition. Using limited diagnostic technology, they had to depend on judgment and wisdom informed by considerable experience. It may be that the teachers we need for adaptive education must be broadly educated, sensitized to diverse cultures, with a good knowledge of human behavior and its development, some appreciation of the science of pedagogy, and a keenly attuned pedagogical intuition. Using limited diagnostic technology, they may have to depend on their judgment and wisdom informed by experience.

But given the requirements of a truly adaptive education, these professional practitioners of the art of teaching may not be good enough. They may now stand where the country doctor stood, soon to be replaced by scientifically educated pedagogues. For while teaching may forever be in part an art, its foundations can and should rest on the sciences of human behavior. Pedagogical practice and adaptive education in particular must be informed by those foundational sciences. The orchestrations that we have suggested as being at the core of adaptive education cannot otherwise be systematically arranged.

CHAPTER 7

Perspectives on Counseling and Other Approaches to Guided Behavior Change

I consider myself something of a radical in the field of counseling. Although I identify with the profession and have chaired a university training program in the field, I maintain that our profession ought to be done away with or at least radically changed.

For a great number of years people who have been motivated to help other people with their problems have gone into the ministry, social work, guidance, counseling psychology or psychotherapy, influenced by such assumptions as these:

- Educational, personal-social, and psychological problems tend to be reflections of aberrant conditions or patterns of function peculiar to or within the individuals or groups in whom the problems are manifested.
- Personal-social, particularly verbal, interactions or relationships are the essential vehicles by which insight, changed attitudes, and changed behavior are achieved.
- Abrasive, difficult, or deprived atypical complex conditions of life are destructive to wholesome development and people should be protected from them.
- Understanding or rather the acceptance of an explanation of one's problems in the context of one's reconstructed history or some psychodynamic assumption leads to resolution or reduction of the problem and changed behavior.

I call these assumptions because the evidence to support them is sparse if not nonexistent. They are not postulates developed as the result of tested hypotheses. They seem logical and reasonable enough, yet I have serious questions about each of them.

Adapted from the Invited Address, Division of Counseling Psychology, American Psychological Association Convention, Miami, FL, September 1970.

INTERACTIONS BETWEEN HUMANS
AND THEIR ENVIRONMENT

I am increasingly convinced that most human problems are reflections of disturbed interactions between individuals or groups and the environmental field in which they exist. Under changed environmental conditions, the particular problem may not be manifested. There are some conditions or disorders in human subjects that will result in aberrant behavior no matter what the environmental conditions, but for most of the garden-variety maladjustments, problems, and unhappiness, it is my view that they reflect or signal environmental conditions that are incongruent with the desired human condition.

I seriously doubt that artificial or clinical social interactions are the sources of changed attitudes and changed behavior, except in those interactions where new conditions are created that require changed behavior and result in changed attitudes and feelings.

I am fully persuaded that one's consciousness, one's attitudes, and one's feelings are products of environmental encounters. Here, environment is defined to include the physical environment (objects, things, people), the perceptual or affective environment (those aspects of the environment to which one responds, including objects as well as conditions such as poverty), and the conceptual environment (including ideas such as mystic forces, love, friendship, obligation).

Without these encounters, these human organismic-environmental interactions, human consciousness, and possibly even human life would not exist. Our tendency to focus exclusively on the interpersonal interactions of the counseling contact, and to treat them primarily as history, assigns greater power to individuals than I can accept, even if these individuals are counselors or therapists.

The difficult and complex conditions of life that we blame for maladjustment and from which we would protect our clients may not be the culpable agents. In recent years I have been considering the possibility that the destructive element is the sense of powerlessness that so often accompanies these conditions. I am less convinced than I used to be that poverty is demeaning; it is the sense of powerlessness that is so often forced on the poor in an effort to keep them poor that is demoralizing and destructive. It is not so much the fact of being Black, or the segregated experience that has been our lot, that is handicapping to Black people. It is the sense of powerlessness that this society has systematically imposed on Black people in order to exploit them.

We have some tangential evidence to support this hunch. The Black Panthers were only a minor source of irritation to the nation as long as their bag was Blackness and Black pride. White America was even willing to tolerate some "hate White sentiment." But when the Panthers started talking about and working for political power and economic change and moved toward collaboration with non-Black, politically radical groups, they became the nation's number-one enemy and the object of political genocide and police murder.

I really don't need to discuss my reservations concerning the extent to which explanation or "understanding" contributes to problem resolution or changed behavior. Our casebooks are full of examples of clients who can hold forth with explanations of their conditions. Some of them are better at psychodynamic formulations than many of us. These efforts at fiction or reconstruction of history do make some of them and many of us feel better, but I don't see a lot of evidence that they are making our clients live better. I do see people living better as they become involved in the assertion of power, as they participate in changing the environmental interactions that dominate their lives.

Humankind has existed on earth for millions of years. Until recently, most of us have assumed that humankind will somehow continue to exist. However, our attention is increasingly called to the possibility that what the destructive forces of the natural environment have been unable to do in the contest between humans and nature, our changes in the physical environment may quickly do. We now come face to face with the possibility that without radical shifts in our relation to our physical environment, humankind may be destroyed by the pollutant-induced changes in that environment. What may not be as clearly recognized in this increased environmental awareness is the equally urgent need to correct and prevent further pollution of the social or spiritual environment.

The advanced technology of modern communication has created a condition in which the contradictions of complex social orders; the atrocities of interpersonal, intertribal, and international conflicts; the inequities inherent in practically all of our social systems; and the richness of our cultural and technical accomplishments constantly bombard the human spirit with relentless assault and stimulation. Human beings, accustomed to far simpler social environments, have reacted to these inputs with habituation or adaptation. As these inputs increase in complexity and intensity, the process of habituation is likely to accelerate and the processes of adaptation become more complex. Some observers see these processes reflected today in the growing insensitivity to social and moral indignation or shock; increasing insulation and isolation in personal-social interchange; alienation from the concepts, institutions, and affiliations that heretofore have provided stabilizing points of reference; and disaffection, or less of a sense of faith in nature, society, authority figures, or in oneself as continuing influential forces.

These adaptations are probably enabling us to exist in a progressively threatening environment. They may also be the mechanisms of our extinction, since adaptive behavior at one stage of development may be counteradaptive at another. Reptiles once started on a course of evolutionary adaptation. They gained in number and complexity of protective structures until, as dinosaurs, they dominated the earth and the sea. But the adaptive armor developed in order to survive the rigors of that premammalian period became too heavy a superstructure to be supported by the accessible environmental resources. Or to put it differently, the dinosaur may have become extinct because its adaptation to one aspect of the environment precluded its effective utilization of another aspect that was an essential source of sustenance. Similarly, the protective adaptation of the human personality to the rigors of the increasingly polluted social environment may result in our isolation from essential sources of support for our personal and spiritual survival.

What seems, then, essential to the continued development and survival of humankind is a concern with reciprocal adaptation. Our survival will increasingly depend on our capacity to adapt to our changing environment as well as on our ability to adapt the environment to our special needs, without accelerating the production of pollutants. It is the latter half of this proposition that in part distinguishes humans from such animals as dinosaurs. Humans are capable of conceptualizing their environmental requirements and planning the modification of their environment to meet those requirements. Humans are the only living creatures who combine the capacity to perceive reality, to change reality, to anticipate the outcome of their perceptions as well as their efforts at change, and, thus, to design and to some extent to control their interactions with the objective and subjective realities of their life. It is in the quality of these interactions that human destiny, individually and collectively, is determined.

However, humans may be unnecessarily limited in their pursuit of this process by their self-doubt, alienation, or disaffection, or by mistaken concepts of environmental and developmental plasticity born of chauvinistic pollutants in the social environment. For example, the work of Jensen (1967) and Herrnstein and Murray (1994) promotes a predeterminist and recalcitrant view of behavioral development in the human being (see Chapter 2). In spite a proliferation of refutations and rebuttals stemming from a humanistic rejection of the racist implications of these assertions as well as from a scientific concern with the inadequacies of the research

and methodology, the nature–nurture or heredity–environment controversy is far from dead. There are at least three reasons why the issue keeps
cropping up. First, we are simply not able to provide a definitive answer
to the question. Second, while this work is open to methodological criticism, the explanations advanced by environmentalists have generally
been equally sloppy. Third, it is clear to most of us who are involved in
this area of study that a dichotomous approach to this problem is fallacious. Even the view that gives a certain percentage of influence to one
or the other is misrepresentative of the dialectical interaction between
genetic and environmental forces in behavioral development.

What concerns us here, however, are the practical implications of the
two positions. The dominance of the conception of behavior as genetically
determined has led us to place a tremendous emphasis on intrinsic factors
in predicting performance. The behavioral sciences in the Western world
have been dominated by preformationist or projectionist views of the
genesis of behavior, in which potential has been estimated on the basis of
ethnic characteristics and static measures of function. The implicit assumption is that the observed level of performance is an accurate projection of some intrinsic pattern rather than a reflection of the interaction
between these patterns and external forces. It has become too easy to say
that a student is not performing adequately because of a lack of intelligence, or, equally disastrous, a lack of motivation. Our estimations of capacity have grown out of our knowledge of how people with similar characteristics have performed in the past. But this is an obvious tautology,
since, at least as concerning behavior, we can judge capacity only through
performance. Thus, we are in effect saying that because this individual
and other individuals "like him or her" have performed in a certain way
in the past, they are "determined" to do so in the future. Such estimates
say nothing about future performance under changed environmental conditions.

It is my opinion, and I am glad to say that of a number of others, that
greater attention must be given to extrinsic factors in development and
learning. Most obviously, since at present we are only able to manipulate
the environment and can do nothing to change genetic structure, it
would be well to concentrate where we do have the power to affect
change. Viewed from this standpoint, the task of the counselor or behavior modifier is to set the goal of performance at the level of necessary
competence, to analyze behaviors and behavioral environments to determine the conditions necessary for the achievement of competence, and
then to manipulate environmental interactions so that performance can
more likely reach that level. This requires that we recognize that there is
a reciprocal interpenetration between whatever is given in the organism

and whatever is given in the environment, that the environment is increasingly subject to change by the organism (human), and that the organism is continually subject to change by the environment. The interaction of the two produces or fails to produce involvement, which in turn influences performance. When environmental encounters are structured to complement the needs of the organism, the environment is considered supportive and optimal development is more likely to be achieved.

We have noted that human beings, more than any other creature, have the power to change the environment to suit needs, and therefore are not limited, like lower animals, to changing only themselves to ensure survival. Keeping in mind this need for reciprocal modification, what, then, are the dimensions of the relationship between the individual and his or her environment that are essential for continued adaptation and development? What is required is a complex balance, which must be maintained in three essential areas. The first dimension involves the balance between congruence and incongruence, which must be maintained in such a manner that the organism and environment are "at home" with each other, yet still in a state of sufficient tension that the relationship and its components do not become static. Thus, it is necessary to maintain enough incongruence between the human and his or her environment to ensure this minimum tension, but always at the risk of an incongruence so great as to be confusing, frustrating, disruptive, and potentially destructive.

In what might be called the constancy-change dimension, the nature of one's interaction or experience with his or her environment must be sufficiently stable or consistent to allow for orientation of self with objects and phenomena. At the same time, a certain level and capacity for change must be maintained so as to keep the system dynamic, and to support a perception and acceptance of change as an essential existential process. This state, which I choose to call dynamic-constancy, thus provides for change while at the same time providing logic and stability on which the organism can depend. A central task of human intelligence in dealing with change is to recognize its many features. There exists at all times a minimum requirement of regular but modest amounts of change, which may occur without dissonance and may allow for easy adaptation. However, there are certain times when radical change may be required as necessary for the development of some phenomena. This degree of change may be necessary to dislodge a recalcitrant force or to reenergize a moribund system. The problem, of course, is to recognize the circumstances that call for which kind or what degree of change.

A third dimension involves the collective/idiosyncratic-needs balance, which we seek when we deal with the problems of recognizing, allowing for, and respecting individuality within the context of the essential requirements of group survival. Obviously, it is not beneficial to either the individual or the society if one is developed in such a way that individual needs are no longer compatible with the survival of the group. On the other hand, group life is threatened and certainly will not be enriched if no provisions are made for the idiosyncratic needs and interests of the individuals comprising it.

The need for the establishment and maintenance of these three areas of ecological balance or personal-politico-social homeostasis has implications for what we do in the process of helping people with their problems. An approach that combines ecological and psychological concerns is indicated. The field of counseling has been greatly influenced by the traditional concern in psychology with the characteristics and behavior of individuals and groups. Psychology has tended to neglect the study of the characteristics and behavior of environments in which people develop and learn. Our strategy has been to work on the individual directly to make a change within the individual and seldom to modify the environment or to involve the individual in the deliberate modification of the environment to more appropriately complement personal unique developmental needs.

THE DEVELOPING PROFESSIONAL FOCUS ON ENVIRONMENT

Our profession in many ways parallels that of the physician and as such may be moving in a direction similar to the development of that profession. One of the earliest conceived goals of medicine was the control and elimination of evil spirits, with the witch doctor standing as the symbol or practitioner of the "science." In a sense, guidance in its early days was also concerned with evil spirits as causative agents, with moralistic exhortation serving a function parallel to the witch doctor's incantations. It was not by accident that the religious leader was the first chief dispenser of guidance and continues to function actively in this field.

A somewhat higher level of scientific procedure was reached in medicine with the introduction of herb therapy, which involved the identification and administering of substances in nature that seemed to be associated with recovery in the infirmed; in the guidance field, information came to serve a similar purpose, with the emphasis on supplying the specific information thought necessary to adjustment and decision-making. In guidance, the parallel to medicine's treatment with herbs was our treatment with information.

As scientific knowledge increased, surgery became the primary technique in medicine, its purpose being to correct disordered physical conditions causing illness or interfering with normal functions. Surgery so dominated the profession that its importance came to be reflected in the title "physician and surgeon." Similarly, counseling came to be the technique of central importance in guidance, the procedure being directed at emotional disorders causing maladjustment or interfering with functioning. Counseling so dominated this profession that "counseling and guidance" came to be the common title by which the profession is known.

With the development of the germ theory of illness, germ control became a central concern of medicine, and growing success in the control and treatment of germs accounted for major strides in the profession. Similarly, anxiety control became a concern in the field of guidance when anxiety came to be considered a central feature in maladjustment, emotional disturbance, and mental illness. The treatment and control of anxiety greatly influenced the practice of guidance despite many admonitions that this technique constituted psychotherapy and was beyond the scope of guidance. Nonetheless, there hardly exists a counselor who does not directly or indirectly turn his attention to the control, treatment, or utilization of anxiety in his work as a guidance specialist.

The next development in medicine, supportive therapy, was made possible as a result of germ theory. By enriched nutrition, by control of environmental conditions so as to reduce the competing demands on the system, or by the introduction of drugs that directly attacked germs or provided support for the system, supportive therapy was aimed at strengthening the organism as it naturally combatted germs. The field of guidance was influenced by similar methods, also known as supportive therapy and also utilizing drugs for treatment of certain conditions. Just as germ theory influenced the course of medicine, so anxiety theory led practitioners in the guidance field to develop supportive procedures designed to provide psychological support as the individual struggles with anxieties, or to structure the environment so as to reduce the competing demands on the individual, or even, as in chemotherapy, by the introduction of sedative drugs, to attempt to insulate the individual from the disruptive effects of anxiety. We have not yet discovered, in this area of chemicals, treatment for anxiety itself.

Germ theory was also responsible for a further development in the field of medicine, public health. When correction of diseases through the application of germ theory proved to be inadequate, it became clear that preventive measures were needed. Medical specialists began to turn their attention to the treatment of conditions that produce disease; when malaria became a hindrance to the exploitation of underdeveloped peoples by the so-called civilized countries, attention was turned to the control of the mosquito and the swamps in which it breeds. When the source of tuberculosis was understood, steps could be taken to correct the conditions out of which it developed. The effort to change was influenced by a similar concern for mental hygiene and community mental health. As the causes of emotional disturbance and mental illness were increasingly recognized to derive from the life experiences of the victims, the mental hygiene movement became prominent in the schools. Increasingly, mental hygiene specialists and the communities they served turned their attention to eliminating conditions that might create problems or interfere with wholesome development. Racial and economic discrimination became a matter of public concern; the concept of the democratic, as opposed to the authoritarian, classroom was given some attention. The theories of Dewey gained prominence, and educators came to recognize the importance of the students' learning to appreciate themselves or their relationships with other people. The conditions under which people lived began to draw almost as much concern as mental illness itself, and all aspects of school service were seen as part of these conditions, influencing the children equally with their classroom experiences. It should be emphasized, however, that at this stage the ideas and theories were considerably more honored than their practice.

This concern for the prevention of disease and disorder through control of physical and social health conditions came to be reflected in an equal concern for developmental processes. In medicine, for example, pediatric specialists are trying to change their image as a group of doctors concerned only with diseases of children to that of a medical specialty concerned with the child's total course of development and the contribution this makes to health or illness. Pediatricians on the cutting edge of the field are increasingly viewing themselves as specialists in environmental and developmental medicine. As such, they are concerned with the monitoring and management of developmental processes and related environmental conditions to the end that optimal health conditions prevail, and with the manipulation of these processes and conditions to the end that disease and malfunction are corrected. We see a similar trend in guidance, where the natural and directed development of young people is progressively seen as the field's principal concern and where the study and manipulation of environments are increasingly viewed as crucial vehicles for the achievement of guidance objectives. Concern with theories of career development and those theories underlying social development reflect the growing emphasis in the field on understanding the developmental process as a first step toward the goal of directing that process. In my own work, drawing on philosophical-materialist concepts, I have argued for years for greater attention to the influence of environmental-organismic interactions on development and the need for guidance specialists to concern themselves with the analysis, design, and control of environmental encounters. When this concern is combined with an understanding of the developmental process and the two are used to complement each other rather than being left to chance, we will find that we have provided the basis for more successful guidance work. That means the opportunity for making real differences in the lives of young people.

This concern with environmental encounters in both medicine and guidance, and a reconsideration of the nature-nurture controversy, should lead to greater attention to the interaction between intrinsic and extrinsic factors involved in the development of human behavior. This concern with the interactive nature of these many factors is likely to lead to a confluence of interests and division of labor between medicine and guidance—both being concerned with human developmental ecology, with medicine focusing on physical and biophysiological functions and guidance focusing on psychological and sociopolitical functions. The quality of function is then seen as largely determined by the nature of individuals and their reciprocal relationships with the vectors operative in their existential field (their perception of the people, objects, conditions, structures of their environment).

For both of these professions, the history of knowledge and of human development makes it clear that the dynamics of the ecosystem (the living community and its nonliving surroundings, both in their objective reality and as their subjective perception) should be the ultimate joint concern. In my more radical moods, I would recommend that counseling be abolished as a professional area and incorporated as a special skill and function in a new profession. I would call it "human developmental ecology," or perhaps advocate its union with the new field calling itself "environmental psychology" or "ecological psychology." I consider the group of functions that are critical to the achievement of the goals of our profession as being more appropriately encompassed by human developmental ecology.

ECOLOGICAL MODEL:
UNDERSTANDINGS AND IMPLICATIONS

In order to understand the relevance of the ecological model, it is helpful to review the role that the system plays in providing the physical, psychosocial, and sociocultural phenomena necessary for one's successful adjustment to one's environment. Within any system, both supportive and restrictive forces are present, facilitating or interfering with reception of the basic life supplies and thereby placing the population at varying degrees of risk. It would appear then that the central functions of physical, mental, or social health workers are to assess these forces and examine their interactions to the end of intervening with preventive measures to restore the homeostatic balance between individuals and their environment. This is not an easy task. In its essence, it is similar to the task of applied biology that ecologists have been attempting since the days of Haeckel (1866, 1892).

Basically, the ecological model provides a synthesizing function when superimposed on a social system. By providing a conceptual frame encompassing the human and nonhuman environment, the model offers a framework for gathering data of a multidisciplinary nature without disturbing the natural interplay of environmental forces. Rather than the operant approach of behavioral psychology, which attempts to control certain forces and concentrates on events and processes in reference to contrived data, ecology employs a transducer data system in which conditions "in situ" are assessed. This kind of dynamic analysis is needed by the behavioral specialist who is trying to examine many of the environmental forces impinging on the individual's behavior and also the status of his or her adaptation to the environments in question—school, home, community, and so forth. While the individual is being understood, the model simultaneously permits the worker to examine the environment, looking for ideas for changing the total structure, redefining the goals and exploring the ability of the system to survive in its present state, and assessing the ability of the student to survive in that state, as well as the potential of both for changed existence in improved states.

In addition to integrating the physical, psychosocial, and sociocultural milieus, the ecological model is based on evolutionary principles stressing the process of development. By allowing the analysis of both structure and function, the model is congruent with the developmental nature of the learner. An essential weakness in our work has been our focus on the assessment of the individual in terms of achievement level, personality type, and measured intelligence, procedures that arbitrarily freeze and extract isolated evidences of development or "learning," negating the dynamic character of the teaching-learning and developmental processes. The result is that we view the data as they are received—in static categories—while what is more helpful to the improvement of the developmental process is the way in which the person is functioning in the maintenance of progressive equilibrium.

Guidance, in accordance with other professions concerned with the actualization of human potential, is moving to an even greater emphasis on primary prevention while continuing to support both secondary and tertiary methods of interaction. Primary prevention seeks not simply to lessen the impact of harmful forces or even to immunize the population to their effects, as do tertiary and secondary methods, but also to eliminate them from the environment.

At first, the focus of the ecological model on the individual primarily as a member of a community or other organizational system may seem incongruent with our professed concern with the development of the individual. But such concern does not limit the worker to interacting with individuals only as members of groups. The ecological model permits us to be truly respectful of the individual by giving greater attention to the multiple forces impinging on him or her and to help the individual grow through the adequate definition and control of the effective environments that are unique to him or her. Evidence mounts to suggest that a substantial impact in reducing risk can be made on individual development by altering deleterious aspects of the system in which the individual functions. The developmental-ecological model makes understanding the system and its multiple interactions as important as understanding the individual, and makes control and modification of the system crucial to the development of the individual and uniquely appropriate as a model for the reconceptualization of approaches to guided behavior change.

What are the professional tasks of guided behavior change? They should be:

1. To make available to human subjects expanded alternatives for choice referable to their development
2. To optimize decision behavior in these expanded situations of choice
3. To facilitate development and movement toward the objectives specified by these choices

Each of these has a dual focus, one on the individual, the other on the field in which the individual exists. Having been greatly influenced by the early medical model, counseling has focused almost exclusively on the individual—what does he or she bring to the situation? What predictions can be made relative to the individual's function? What can we do to change the individual? The early individual psychological model is now being challenged by the developmental-ecological model as a more appropriate frame for the conceptualization and implementation of guided behavior change. Put simply, the choices an individual makes and the quality with which these choices are implemented are largely dependent on the nature of the interaction between whatever is given or possible in the individual and that which is given or possible in the system in which the individual functions.

Within this framework, it is possible to examine some of the implications for counseling and guidance, right now and in the future:

1. The logical first step is a shift from appraisal of individuals to appraisal of environments or individuals in environments, with attention to such questions as the nature of the conditions of learning and development and the reciprocal relationship between this individual and his or her developmental-learning environment. The new focus calls for a shift from the study of pupils or clients to the study of systems—the family as a social system, the school as a social system, the factory or office as a social system, and education and development as social processes.

2. Also required is a shift from the assessment of behavioral product to the assessment of behavioral process. With less emphasis on quantitative summary and classification, the guidance specialist will examine the nature of intellectual and social functioning for the individual and describe those functions qualitatively.

3. This shift in focus of appraisal will result in a movement away from prediction to prescription; the more sophisticated and sensitive appraisal process will provide information for prescription or design of learning experiences and learning environments. This should be followed by a shift from identification and placement in available opportunities to the creation of and placement in appropriate opportunity situations.

4. The guidance function should be vastly broadened from our traditional concern for the discovery of the talented few to the development of talent in all. This entails a fundamental commitment to those policies and practices that ensure universal optimal development.

5. We will also need a shift in method from didactic exhortation to discovery and modeling as vehicles for learning, with more attention given to use of naturally occurring or contrived environments to provide interactions supportive of learning and development in specified directions.

6. The ecological model implies a shift from interpretation to environmental orientation as the principal focus in counseling and other forms of directed learning. The skills the behavior-change specialist helps to develop in young people should come to include the use of environmental cues and relationships to analyze and interpret behavior and experiences, to manage information, and to bring order to confusion and chaos as an essential step in problem solving.

7. Emphasis on consultation should be greater than emphasis on counseling, and the focus in consultation should include active efforts to

influence persons and groups who have the power to make necessary and relevant changes in the conditions that determine the course of the student's life.

8. In addition to these changes in focus and method, a significant consideration is style: What is needed is a shift from diplomacy to advocacy. Our clients don't need to be apologized for and have their troubles explained away; they need to be more actively involved in the decision-making processes that control their lives. Their rights should be more appropriately defended and opportunities for meaningful involvement should be more vigorously advanced. Equally important, the role of the guidance specialist should not be that of ambassador for the establishment—conning students into cooperation with the system—but that of ombudsman for students, thereby protecting the individual and collective students from accidental, incidental, or intentional abuse by the establishment or its representatives.

9. Finally, we will need to bring about a shift from a primary concern with socialization to a major concern with politicization. Probably one of the most important contributions we can make to the optimal development of young people is to help them to learn not only what is expected of them by the social order—the traditional concern of socialization—but how they can effectively use themselves in relation to other people to cope with the systems that in large measure control their lives.

CONCLUSION

Increasingly, I see social-coping and systems-management or systems-maneuvering skills as the skills essential not only to the development of an adequate concept of self but also to future survival. This means that participation with students by the behavior specialist in the politicization process is raised to the level of urgency.

In the present climate, we, as institutional representatives and professionals, appear to be contributing more to the separation of the politicization process from the main line of education and development. Our young people are moving vigorously on this front without us. And too many of us have lined up behind the protectors of the status quo. While conservation is an essential process and can be a respectable stance, in the present period too many of our young people see this concern with maintaining what is as a camouflage for advancing executive, judicial, and police repression. Under these conditions, when they proceed without more mature guidance, their need for politicization sometimes leads them to express their protest in irrational and explosive ways. But as a professional behavior specialist concerned with their development and equally concerned with change, I cannot turn my back on their endeavors or join the opposition. I must join with them and hope to influence them and that they will influence me. With them I raise the clenched fist— symbol of protest, symbol of determination, symbol of hope that power and compassion will embolden the hearts and minds of the people.

CHAPTER 8

Toward an Equitable System of Educational Assessment

The most fundamental issues concerning human diversity, equity, and educational assessment have to do with the effectiveness and sufficiency of teaching and learning. When teaching and learning are sufficient and truly effective, most of the problems posed for equitable assessment as a function of diverse human characteristics become manageable. It is when teaching and learning are insufficiently effective with the universe of students served that problems arise in the pursuit of equity in the assessment of diverse human populations. Thus, it can be argued that the problems of equity in educational assessment are largely secondary to the failure to achieve equity through educational treatments. However, the fact that these problems of equitable educational assessment are only secondarily problems for assessment does not mean that they should not be engaged by the assessment community, even if they cannot be solved through assessment alone.

It is not by accident that existing approaches to the standardized assessment of educational achievement are insufficiently sensitive to the diversity of the student populations served and to the pluralism of society. The prevailing standards by which academic competence is judged are calibrated in large measure against either (1) what most persons at a specific level of development can do or (2) what society agrees is necessary for students to meet the demands of increasingly challenging levels of work. That some persons have greater difficulty than others or seem unable to achieve these standards is generally thought to be a problem of individual and group differences in abilities or productivity, not a problem of the appropriateness of the assessment instruments or practices used. Despite educators' efforts to be responsive to diverse learner characteristics and pluralistic social standards, the prevailing wisdom suggests that there may be limits to what can be done to make the design and develop-

Adapted with the permission of Howard University Press. Copyright © 1996 by Howard University Press. *Journal of Negro Education, 64,* 3, 1–13.

ment of assessment technology and procedures more inclusive. The assessment process may be made more instructive and supportive of diverse learning experiences, the varied contexts in and vehicles through which students can demonstrate their competencies may be determined, test items may be made more process-sensitive, and less emphasis may be given on tests to narrowly defined products. Yet, in the final analysis, the assessment procedure is ultimately most likely to reveal the effectiveness of the teaching and learning to which students have been exposed. Thus, diversity and pluralism may have more serious implications for teaching and learning than for equitable assessment technology and practice.

Increasingly, we live in a world that places multiple and concurrent demands on our competencies. More and more, all of us are called on to function in multiple contexts, cultures, and languages. The most effective among us are multilingual and multicultural. Thus, pedagogical intervention in this day and age must be responsive to this diversity and pluralism in order to meet the criteria for educational sufficiency and effectiveness. Equitable assessment must be influenced by these developments, even if it must be less responsive to both than it is to educational intervention. However, this differential in potential effectiveness, which favors teaching and learning, does not eliminate the assessment community's responsibility to be responsive to the complex realities, problems, and challenges of population diversity and contextual, cultural, and linguistic pluralism.

One source of this complexity is the ubiquitous distortions that flow from classism, nationalism, racism, sexism, and other forms of chauvinism in our society. Traditionally, these distortions have been seen as unrelated to the processes of education and educational assessment in the United States. The tendency on the part of most Americans has been to focus on the impact of racism or sexism on persons who are the targeted victims of such communicentric biases (see Chapter 11), rather than to focus on the social processes and institutions that reflect those biases. However, Americans in all segments of society are victims or possible victims of these "isms." The distortions and otherwise negative fallouts affect practically every aspect of our lives. Nowhere is this more obvious than in our efforts to educate diverse populations effectively and to assess the educational needs and outcomes of Americans whose life conditions, experiences, and values differ from those who have achieved hegemony in this society.

To the credit of many of the recent efforts at reform in education and the education measurement communities, several educational researchers have agreed to try to engage seriously the possible implications of human diversity in order to develop more adequate and perhaps more equitable systems of education and assessment. Implicitly, these researchers have agreed to try to make teaching, learning, and assessment procedures more authentic with respect to what is known about learning and human competence, as well as to the educationally relevant characteristics of the various populations whose members must be educated and assessed. This concern with pedagogy has concentrated on the establishment of higher standards for all students and the diversification of approaches to the achievement of these standards.

The concern with authentic measures has focused on the development of assessment probes that require performance—that is, respondents must demonstrate competence and understanding in solving problems or explaining relationships. However, this shift toward higher achievement standards, away from more static measures of ability and toward performance measures of developed competence, may not be sufficiently responsive to the student diversity at hand. Concern for authentic and effective assessment reform may also require recognition that the members of various populations live their lives in multiple contexts. Further, it demands awareness that authenticity may vary not only with population characteristics but also with these varied contexts. Thus, competence must be achieved and measured by multiple criteria met by persons functioning in multiple contexts. This is readily seen with regard to languages, as those who are monolingual are increasingly disadvantaged in a multilingual world; or with regard to cultures, as those who see and react to the world through monofocal lenses are threatened with marginalization.

Although diversity and pluralism have not been reflected in our society's concern for universal standards of achievement, the language of authenticity has crept into some of the planning for reform in assessment. In an earlier period, concern for authentic assessment would probably have referred to a concern for validity, reliability, and attention to ensuring that standardized procedures were adhered to. Today, however, educators are likely to be concerned with more complex psychometric problems long known to confound assessment processes, such as the problems of test bias, which, though they have been addressed to the satisfaction of many psychometricians, continue to frustrate some educators and advocates for civil rights. Others presently debate questions about whether to use standardized tests at all. The argument they advance is that more traditional standardized test items tend to misrepresent the changing nature of knowledge and the processes by which knowledge is acquired and utilized. Some of the most negative critics of such tests argue that traditional procedures and tests penalize not only our weakest students but many of our society's most creatively intelligent members as well.

Still other educators are ready to concede the importance of having some measures of what persons know and know how to do, yet they continue to insist that it is possible to develop assessment procedures that provide a more appropriate reflection of the ways in which people think, learn, and work, and that are less dependent on recall and regurgitation. Another school of thought includes those who are sympathetic to standards and assessment but insist that it is immoral to begin by measuring outcomes before we have seriously engaged the equitable and sufficient distribution of inputs (i.e., opportunities and resources essential to the development of intellect and competence).

Contemporary educators confront the questions of reform in teaching, learning, and assessment in the face of complex psychometric, pedagogical, political, economic, psychological, cultural, and philosophical problems. However, there appear to be few who are prepared to engage such complex problems from such a broad range of perspectives. Most tend to approach these issues from an isolated disciplines-to-be-mastered perspective and from the point of view of personal biases and the hegemonic identity of the dominant group. Generally, reference to hegemonic identity relates to the ubiquitously distorting effect of a dominating communicentric bias—the tendency to see the world from the perspective of one's narrow group membership and interests and to generalize from that truncated perspective to other communities and their people. This communicentric bias is reflected in approaches to class, culture, ethnicity, gender, and language—to name but a few examples of the most blatant areas.

In recent decades, spokespersons for the interests of several nondominant groups have begun to remind the educational community that sources of identity and socialization have important influences on the development of the character of human adaptive functions and learning. They argue that such variables influence what is learned, opportunities to learn, the ways learned information is stored and retrieved, motivation to produce and utilize mental products, and more. If these advocates are correct (and I think they are), these variables must influence educators' and our society's conceptions of competence with respect to knowledge, intellect, and technique.

VALIDITY AND DIVERSITY

Many years ago, when the late Bob Thorndike and the marvelous Anne Anastasi were trying to teach me psychometric theory, they insisted that I and their other students take questions of validity seriously. In one of the last talks I heard Anne give, she was complaining that psychometric theorists and technologists seem to have given up on the validity question. Indeed, current practice seems to treat validity through assumptions, or rather, through assumptive bias. Commonality and homogeneity or difference and heterogeneity are simply assumed these days. However, the question remains: How are these assumptions influenced by racism, sexism, classism, or, in the case of language, nationalism?

In our efforts to better understand the influence of these assumptions and communicentric biases on human development, my colleagues and I have recently begun an examination of issues related to human diversity and pluralism in society, focusing especially on their implications for the achievement of a higher degree of equity and social justice in U.S. education and on the assessment of educational achievement generally. Because these issues are far more complicated than is often reflected in public debates, it may be useful here to clarify what I mean by such constructs as diversity, pluralism, and equity, and to identify some of the possible ways in which I believe a concern for population diversity and pluralistic outcomes can influence teaching, learning, and assessment.

The Meaning of Diversity

Diversity in human characteristics refers to differences in status and function. Status defines one's position in the social hierarchy and often determines one's access to sociopolitical power and material resources. Status also influences the amount of access one has to societal opportunities and rewards. It influences how individuals are treated, what society expects of individuals, and, too often, what individuals expect of themselves. Traditionally, differential status has been assigned based on social class, caste, ethnicity, race, gender, sexual orientation, language, national origin, and a host of other less prominent social dividers.

Diversity in functional characteristics—which include such traits as culture, cognitive style, temperament, interest, identity, and motivation—refers to the "how" of behavior, the manner in which behavior is manifested, and the way people act. These characteristics may be colloquially associated with certain status groups, but one's manner of behavior is not invariably associated with status.

The Meaning of Pluralism

Pluralism refers to the social demand for the demonstration of multiple, concurrent competencies in situationally relevant contexts. As such, it implies the recognition of diverse routes to the mastery of both universal and population-specific standards. Pluralistic demands are most readily

recognized with respect to cultures and languages. In our rapidly shrinking world, those who are bilingually and multilingually competent have
clear advantages over those who are monolingual. Though some people
fight chauvinistically against such global trends, thoughtful persons cannot fail to recognize the importance and advantage of multicultural competence and multiperspectivist thought.

The Meaning of Equity

Care must be taken to make clear the difference between equity and
equality. Equity speaks to and references fairness and social justice; it requires that the distribution of social resources be sufficient to the condition that is being treated. Equality, on the other hand, connotes sameness
and the absence of discrimination. Rawls (1971) eloquently reminds us
that one of the fundamental tenets of social justice provides for an unequal distribution of social resources that favors the weaker members of
the society. In societies that include unequal members, equal distribution
may not be equitable. For example, if one person needs penicillin and the
other needs tetracycline, and the hospital gives both penicillin, the two
people have been treated equally, but it certainly cannot be claimed that
they have been treated equitably. Or, if one person needs three doses and
the other needs one dose of the same medicine, and both are given one
dose, then they have been treated equally, but one has been deprived of
what is sufficient to his or her needs, and thus has been treated inequi-
tably.

Implications for Pedagogy

When applying the constructs of diversity, pluralism, and equity to education, the implications are much clearer for pedagogical intervention than
for assessment. We educators are just beginning to become sensitive to
the possibility that educational productivity can be improved by diversify-
ing students' opportunities to learn by providing more time on task, more
cooperative and individualized learning, more diversity in material and
modalities, more culturally relevant learning demands and situations,
and so forth. Though we recognize the limitations of differential attribute
treatment interaction (see Chapter 6), we continue to search for the
power of teaching and learning experiences. However, with respect to
assessment, we have only recently begun broader exploration of alternatives to standardized tests and their traditional use.

    For some time now, I have argued that standardized tests serve rather
limited purposes (Gordon, 1977). Yet I have also maintained that when

the criteria of eligibility are narrowly drawn, standardized tests are highly effective in the selection of persons who meet certain criteria under certain specified conditions. So long as test items mirror those competencies that are privileged in test takers' learning situations as well as those in their work or subsequent learning situations, standardized tests are excellent instruments for predicting future functioning. It is when the criteria become more diffuse and the indicators of competence become more diverse, when the frames of reference for the persons being tested diverge, that standardized tests become problematic, their validity in selection weakened, and the reliability of their predictions lessened.

From evidence of behavioral differences that are thought to be associated with differences in cultures (Hale-Benson, 1986; Harrington, 1988), one can conclude that children who come from different cultural groups and whose socialization experiences differ from those of the dominant group are likely to experience school differently. It is sometimes implied that these differences are related to nondominant-group students' differential functioning in school. Thus, persons concerned with assessment are presently exploring the possibility that such differences influence these students' engagement and performance on tests of educational achievement (Gordon & Armour-Thomas, 1991). However, caution has often been expressed concerning the tendency to overgeneralize and stereotype nondominant groups with respect to these alleged differences (Gordon & DeStefano, 1984). Within all of these populations can be found wide variations with respect to behaviors. Even when it seems to make sense to expect to see a high frequency of certain behaviors in a particular group, one would be wise to recognize the equally high possibility that individuals in any group may vary from the patterns attributed to the group. However, this interplay between group and individual differences and the high potential for overgeneralization about them should not distract from meaningful consideration of group and individual differences in learning and other behaviors to which teaching, learning, and assessment should be responsive.

DIFFERENTIAL IMPLICATIONS OF DIVERSE CHARACTERISTICS

Earlier in this chapter I noted that the human characteristics associated with the social divisions and cultural identities by which students are often grouped may be usefully divided into two categories, status and function. It seems reasonable to assume that these different categories of characteristics may have quite different implications for educational intervention as well as for assessment. With respect to intervention, one's status might suggest that attention be directed toward administrative issues such as access, expectation, opportunity, resource distribution, and reward. On the other hand, aspects of the functional characteristics might suggest that teaching and learning transactions should be customized to reflect such issues as cultural identity, cognitive style, interest, prior knowledge, and language form as well as usage. However, we probably should not expect to affect educational achievement directly through interventions in teaching and learning that reflect diverse groups of learners' functional characteristics. Rather, we may immediately influence the quality of such learner behaviors as time on task, energy deployment, task engagement, and resource utilization through our adaptations to the functional characteristics of various learners. It is these learner behaviors that may be more directly related to educational achievement. Our prospects may be much more limited in the area of educational assessment because, after all, it is to the achievement of the common as well as the idiosyncratic standards that the educational enterprise is directed.

Despite criticisms of and lingering problems with the extant standardized tests, they need not be totally discarded. They have some utility and can be made even more useful. Given the low current estimates of the utility of normative and standardized approaches to achievement testing and the equally low likelihood that we will soon be rid of standardized tests, what can be done to improve on the current state of the assessment arts?

In recent decades, a great deal of work has gone into the development of test-item pools that tap a variety of intellective functions. Unfortunately, these items have been grouped, presented, scored, and analyzed with a view toward gross classifications of success or failure, distribution of the examinee population over the statistical bell-shaped curve, and communicentric predictions of who will or will not succeed. Notwithstanding, these instruments and procedures can be made to serve other purposes. The data from these same instruments can be analyzed to accomplish the following:

1. To identify, through logical analysis, the dimensional or categorical functional demands of selected standardized tests
2. To determine the rationale utilized in the development of each of several tests to identify the conceptual categories for which items were written and in which item response consistencies might cluster empirically
3. To determine the learning task demands represented by the items of selected tests and classify those demands into functional categories

4. To appraise the extent to which selected tests provide adequate coverage of the typical learning task demands found in educational settings
5. To utilize the categories produced by any or all of the above strategies in the metric and nonmetric factorial analyses of test data to uncover empirical dimensions of test responses

The dimensions referred to in the last point could be interpreted in the context of item clusters derived from the conceptual and task-analytic strategies described above to ascertain the extent to which they provide an empirical foundation for those clusters or require a reconceptualization of response processes. The empirical dimensions could then be used to produce individual and group profiles reflecting across the several categories or factors. The first four tasks are intended to unbundle existing standardized tests and to reveal their factorial demand structure. Each of these steps contributes to the last task, which involves the analysis of performance data to reveal diagnostic patterns that become the basis for the profiles used to inform instruction.

With these same instruments, we could also explore possibilities for adding to quantitative reports on the performance of students reports that are more descriptive of the patterns of achievement and function derived from the qualitative analysis of existing tests. Existing instruments could be examined with a view toward categorization, factorial analysis, and interpretation to determine whether the data from standardized instruments could be reported in descriptive and qualitative ways. For example, response patterns might be prepared differentially for (1) information recall (to reflect rote, associative, and derivative forms) and (2) vocabulary (to reflect absolute and contextual forms).

Going beyond the mining of data from extant tests, we might explore the development of new tests, test items, and procedures that lend themselves to descriptive and qualitative analyses of cognitive and affective adaptive functions in addition to wider specific achievements. In the development of such new tests, attention could be given to the appraisal of

1. Adaptation to new learning situations
2. Problem solving in situations that require varied cognitive skills and styles
3. Analysis, search, and synthesis behaviors
4. Information management, processing, and utilization skills
5. Nonstandard information pools

In the development of new testing procedures, attention could be given to the appraisal of

1. Comprehension through experiences, listening, and looking as well as reading
2. Expression through artistic, oral, nonverbal, and graphic as well as written symbolization
3. Characteristics of temperament
4. Sources and status of motivation
5. Habits of work and task involvement under varying conditions of demand

In the development of tests and procedures designed to get at specific achievements, attention could be given to

1. Broadening the varieties of subject matter, competencies, and skills assessed
2. Examining these achievements in a variety of contexts
3. Making open-ended and unstructured probes of achievement to allow for the assessment of atypical patterns and varieties of achievement
4. Assessing nonacademic achievements such as social competence as well as coping, vocational, artistic, athletic, political, and mechanical skills

The implementation of this modest proposal would contribute to making our tests more useful and their use more equitable. The information that such analyzed data would make available could inform interventions directed at greater educational effectiveness and sufficiency. But we can do more.

Because the issues surrounding diversity and pluralism are far more complicated than is often reflected in the public debates, it may be useful to identify some of the possible ways that a concern for population diversity and pluralistic outcomes affects teaching, learning, and assessment. It is becoming more and more obvious that these sources of variance influence students' motivation to engage academic learning and to master its content. They also influence students' opportunities to learn and to be reinforced by academic competence and literacy as well as affect the conditions in and under which students acquire knowledge and develop attitudes toward various disciplines. Further, they impact on the nature of the processes by which academic attitudes, knowledges, competencies, and skills are assessed. These and other adaptive behaviors are certainly influenced by such social divisions as race and gender, yet an exclusive focus on racism or sexism may be less useful for our purposes. Instead, a focus on the implications of diversity and pluralism might better enable us to address the relevant concerns.

Class, cultural, racial, ethnic, gender, and language diversity are all possible influences on the manner in which knowledge is acquired and the manner in which academic attitudes and knowledge are elicited by assessment demands. It is not clear how much attention we should give to other aspects of diversity such as cognitive style, motivation, and temperament. What is clear, however, is that if achievement is ever to be adequately assessed and assessment information ever to be used to improve education, effective ways must be found to accommodate relevant sources of diversity in the revised assessment probes. A related issue concerns the question of pluralism, particularly regarding the requirement that students meet different standards in the multiple contexts in which they live their lives.

Obviously, purposes, perspectives, and goals influence what is learned as well as what students are willing to produce. Thus, the assessment problems surrounding this aspect relate to the appropriateness of examination probes to the purposes, goals, and standards of the students being examined. Concern must also be raised about the appropriateness of a standardized examination to a context that is pluralistic, as well as the extent to which the standardized context can be made to accommodate pluralistic ends without distorting the purposes to be served by the examination. Ideally, students should be able to function in multiple contexts and meet multiple standards—the fact of pluralism in our society makes that necessary; however, current approaches to assessment do not address this problem explicitly.

The efforts aimed at the reform of curriculum and instruction have made little progress in substantively attacking the problem of equitable opportunities and outcomes. There are several reasons for this, some of which go beyond the processes of education and measurement. Family support for learning and the state of the nation's economy are examples. It may well be that the accepted approaches to teaching, learning, and assessment are insufficiently reflective of or responsive to the wide diversity in the characteristics of today's learners and the pluralism of the cultures from which they come. Thus, in the continuing development of systems of curriculum and assessment, the challenge posed by a serious concern for equity is the development of systems of teaching, learning, and assessment that bridge (1) the diverse characteristics of learners, (2) the pluralistic demands for social competence, and (3) the universal standards for human competence—all of which are increasingly characteristic of democratic, postmodern, technologically advanced societies. Though many seek to do this bridging effectively in the interests of all students, the very least for which students should settle is the uncoupling of the achievement and demonstration of educational adequacy and excellence from the different social divisions and cultural identities with which they are associated.

The intersections between teaching, learning, and assessment processes present an interesting paradox. We in the education and educational measurement communities are just beginning to recognize well-established principles and practices in both instruction and educational measurement as being dysfunctional to what is currently viewed as effective teaching, learning, and intellectual productivity. As a result, we are faced with a situation in which our professional practices and the assessment of these practices may get in the way of the ends that are the purpose for their existence.

In teaching, too many of us continue to be caught up in the didactic paradigm, in which demonstration and transfer of knowledge and skill are the dominant modalities. We do so even though modern cognitive science represents learning as a process by which learners selectively experience elements of their own worlds, conceptualize and assimilate symbols and relationships, and ultimately construct their own knowledge and its meanings. The end toward which such cognitive development should be directed is the honing of the ability to interpret critically, understand from more than a single perspective, and apply one's intellect to the solution of novel as well as practical life problems.

In assessment, the assumption has been that because teaching and learning are concerned with the transfer and assimilation of knowledge and skill, the assessment process should sample the pool of acquired knowledge and skill. This logic seems to be based on the related assumption that if one can produce on-demand evidence of having mastered the assimilated knowledge and skill, one not only knows but can use the knowledge and skill whenever required. This basic conceptual model for assessment seems to ignore findings showing that the traditional assessment process is also heavily dependent on the ability of the persons being tested to recall and symbolically represent knowledge and to select iconic representations of skills. Resnick (1987) and others who have compared students' intellective work in and outside of school have concluded that although the traditional assumptions may be correct and may operate adequately for some learners, vast differences exist between the ways in which mental exertion is experienced in school and in real-life settings. In real life, learners actually perform rather than producing samples of their repertoire of developed abilities. Moreover, they generally work with others to solve problems and often complement their own knowledge and skill with that of others. Even more likely in the real world is the collective production of new knowledge and technique in response to experience with real problems that have special meaning to those encountering them.

When we put these differences together with the relatively low correlations between test scores and real-life performance, we must consider that there is some dissonance between educational assessment and the processes of optimal intellective functioning. Thus, much of what we educators have done traditionally in instruction and assessment is increasingly viewed as being nonsynchronous with optimal conditions for learning and sustained mental productivity.

It is perhaps the changing nature of the populations served by mass education in the United States and the changing criteria for what it means to be an educated person that have forced greater attention to this paradox. When the population was more homogeneous and U.S. society could absorb its school failures in a nonconceptually demanding workforce, the reality that schooling did not work for some of our members seemed less important. As the proportion of persons for whom school did not work increased, and as we became aware that even those learners for whom schools once were adequate presently are not being enabled to function at the intellective levels appropriate to changing societal demands, the potential crisis became more obvious. Teachers and schools became the targets of closer scrutiny. Concern for how both teachers and schools could be held more accountable began to gain the focus of public attention. Because what teachers and schools produce is believed to be reflected by the achievements of their students, and because it is these achievements that were increasingly viewed as inadequate, attention also came to be focused on educational testing and other processes by which judgments about the outcomes of schooling are made. This closer scrutiny seems to have revealed to serious observers the contradiction between what is happening in teaching and assessment, on the one hand, and what should be happening optimally in learning, on the other.

It is the increased awareness of this implicit paradox that appears to have made long-recognized weaknesses in the technologies of educational measurement almost as prominent on the nation's educational agenda as concern for the quality of educational achievement itself. Federal and state departments of education, education professionals, psychometricians, and the public at large are in considerable ferment concerning the need for reforms in education, increased accountability regarding the quality of education, and more effective ways to measure educational outcomes. Out of this professional and political context have emerged calls for a strategy involving curriculum-embedded assessment (CEA), with educational portfolios as its most prominent and widely practiced model.

CURRICULUM-EMBEDDED ASSESSMENT AND STUDENT PORTFOLIOS: PROMISES AND POTENTIALS

Curriculum-embedded assessment is responsive to the paradoxes identified in this chapter in several ways:

1. It assumes little or no separation between teaching, learning, and assessment, and treats them as continuously interacting components.
2. It assumes a system in which teaching, assessing, record keeping, criticizing, evaluating, exhibiting, and reflecting all serve to enable and enhance learning.
3. It eliminates the competition for time between the demands of the instructional process and the assessment process.
4. It utilizes instructional materials/practices for assessment and assessment instruments/procedures for instruction.
5. It is heavily dependent on students' engagement in and performance of real tasks and projects as opposed to their engagement in symbolically and iconically representative behaviors or memory exercises.

In a system of teaching, learning, and assessment so configured, the documentation of, reflection on, and accessibility to the records of these educational experiences and students' performances are crucial. The student portfolio serves these functions; however, discussions concerning portfolios suffer from the many different and confusing conceptions concerning what they are and how they should be used. For educators, the term *portfolio* has come to be used to refer to a system for the collection of information concerning (1) the teaching, learning, and assessment experiences of students; (2) selected products of these experiences; (3) samples of on-demand and sustained measures of performances; and (4) students' and others' reflections on their experiences, performances, and products. The portfolio is both a system for keeping records and an instrument of instruction and evaluation. Because it can be the stimulant for and vehicle of student and teacher reflection, it is also a teaching device. The value of the portfolio as a means by which teaching, learning, and assessment can be viewed and operationalized as integrated processes is paramount.

Despite the critical nature of these several functions, important tensions have surfaced in the development and use of portfolio assessment systems. Whereas one type of portfolio and the materials it holds may adequately serve one function, they may not serve another function well at all. Fortunately, much of the current work on portfolio-system development is directed at models that serve several functions concurrently. Additionally, many portfolio systems have been developed for the purpose of monitoring educational achievement outcomes, and educators are apparently torn between the use of those that focus on the measurement of growth and those focusing on the comparison of students' achieved status on a given dimension with an external standard or with a multiple-student standardized norm. This latter conflict detracts from recognition of portfolio systems' potential to reflect the diversity of students' experiences and products. It also makes the use of portfolio-type data in comparative evaluation more difficult with regard to the creation of uniformly calibrated standards when student contexts, experiences, and the content of performances differ.

CONCLUSION

Diversity, equity, and pluralism may have greater implications for pedagogical intervention than for educational assessment. However, this does not mean that we educators have no responsibility for trying to make educational assessment more appropriate to the characteristics of the persons being assessed. The challenge to educational assessment is the development of measurement devices and procedures that are capable of the following:

1. Engaging students from diverse backgrounds and experiences in assessment situations that are capable of eliciting performances and products appropriate to standards that are both universal and pluralistic
2. Providing assessment opportunities that are embedded in and complementary to teaching and learning experiences
3. Supporting the diverse learning and performance contexts necessary to the optimal expression of variously developed and expressed abilities
4. Managing and presenting information in ways that are meaning-

ful and useful to a variety of audiences, but especially to teachers
and students, in the improvement of teaching and learning
5. Enabling reliable and valid judgments concerning the quality and
adequacy of students' diverse developed abilities, documented performances, and collected products

Here again it is useful to distinguish between status and functional
characteristics. There is little in the differential statuses of learners that
should require changes in the design and management of educational
assessments, but there may be several ways in which teaching, learning,
and assessment can be made more appropriate to the functional characteristics of students. It is essential that we understand and agree that concern for diversity, pluralism, and equity rests on a commitment to universal standards of competence. The same standards should be applied to all
populations, even though we may not be able to agree on differential indicators of change or on what constitutes a satisfactory rate of progress
toward those standards for a given population. Standards or criteria for
competence or mastery cannot be based on learners' different entry or
exit characteristics. Population-specific norms may be useful in planning
pedagogical intervention, but they are irrelevant to the certification of
educational achievement. If we are to measure progress, our instruments
must be sensitive to changes within specific populations but referable to
the universal standard.

The task then is to find assessment probes (test items) that measure
the same criterion from contexts and perspectives that reflect the life
space and values of the learners being tested. Our indicators must be valid
with respect to the criteria used. They must also be capable of eliciting
culturally indigenous behaviors that reflect appropriate and incremental
movement toward the chosen criteria. Doing this will require that educators find ways to provide students with learning and testing opportunities
that are appropriate to the standards, equivalent to the standards, and
adequate to evoke relevant and sufficient responses. These goals may be
achieved by (1) paying attention to the engagement potential and interest
power of our probes; (2) ensuring the relevance of diverse reference
points; and (3) identifying the capacity of items and tasks to be mapped
onto the diverse groups of learners' existing schemata, styles, and response repertoires.

This kind of item fluidity or flexibility demands that some agreement
be reached concerning the core knowledges, competencies, and understandings that are fundamental to developing intellect and preparing our
students for responsible citizenship. Further, it compels our society to permit learners some choice with respect to how and in which knowledge,

competence, and understanding subdomains they will learn or demonstrate their competence. Thus, options and choices become a critical feature in any teaching, learning, and assessment systems created to be responsive to equity, just as processual description, diagnosis, and learner enablement must become central purposes behind these systems.

Woven throughout the range of concerns raised in this chapter is an overarching concern with teaching and learning as constructivist, interactive, reflexive processes, especially as they are applied to the successful education of diverse populations. It is precisely this concern that has prompted attention to the challenges posed for traditional instruction and assessment in their use with diverse learners who are increasingly called on to meet demands for plural competencies. Several states have begun the specification of standards for the common elements of the school curriculum, yet considerably less attention has been directed at the establishment of standards for the delivery of educational experiences. Not much progress has been made on the development of standards for the more pluralistic components of the learning experience beyond modest progress in bilingual and multicultural education. The greatest deficiencies remain in efforts to specify what is required to help teachers and schools provide the teaching, learning, and assessment experiences that will enable all and diverse students to meet universal as well as pluralistic standards of educational achievement. Such efforts must necessarily incorporate consideration of the following:

1. Diversity in teaching, learning, and assessment experiences, tasks, contents, contexts, demands, and referents
2. Flexibility in the timing of teaching, learning, and assessment entry points (e.g., the time spans allowed for learning and performance)
3. Multiplicity in the perspectives to which students are exposed as well as in the perspectives students are encouraged to express, and which are accepted, with the requirement that they engage in comparison and justification
4. Critical sampling from canonical and noncanonical views, knowledges, and techniques
5. The use of hypertext (i.e., embedded substantive and/or procedural knowledge) with the requirement that the absent element be provided
6. Choice, involving self-selected and teacher- or examiner-selected options for the demonstration of what is known
7. Opportunity to identify with the indigenous experience examples

of canonical knowledge and technique, and with the canonical examples of the indigenous

8. Individual and cooperative learning and performance opportunities

9. Self-designated tasks from learner- or examinee-generated inventories of knowledge, skill, and understanding

Obviously, meaningful ideas are only just beginning to be generated about the ways in which teaching, learning, and assessment and their technologies must change if they are to become more equitable. However, the emergence of educational strategies such as curriculum-embedded assessment and the use of portfolio systems provide a culture and technology in which teaching, learning, and assessment can be adapted to the diverse characteristics of and plural demands on students. The mechanical adoption of these strategies as fads will do little to achieve that end. The challenges to and tasks of instituting equitable systems of educational assessment will require the persistent dedication and vigilance of all of us who are involved in the education of our young.

PART III

Cultural Diversity and Education

Culture, as I discussed earlier, refers to the medium in which an organism develops, and it is also the medium that humans create for their own development. Culture is thus socially constructed at the same time that it is constructive of human behavior and consciousness. Culture describes and prescribes the thought and behavior of a group of people. It defines what one does and how one does it. It also provides the schemata that frame and enable the feelings and thoughts about what one does. Cognition is dependent on culture because it is one's culture that provides the content and the context for thought, even though the cognitive processes may be enabled by biologically determined capacity and physiologically mediated functions.

Culture has emerged as a central focus in my intellectual work, and this interest is represented by the three chapters in Part III of this book: Chapter 9 discussing the impact of culture on the sciences of pedagogy, Chapter 10 analyzing the raging controversy around representation of diverse cultures in the curriculum, and Chapter 11 examining the relationship of cultural and other forms of bias on the production of knowledge. It is the representation of diverse cultures in the curriculum that has received the greatest amount of public attention. But the publicly debated issues are the wrong ones. The real issues for education in the relationship between cultures and the curriculum have more to do with how we use the study of accumulated knowledge and technique to develop intelligence in humans than with whose history shall be taught or in what form. Four of these issues recurrently are addressed in this book.

The first of these issues concerns the responsibility of pedagogy for the development of intellect. Unlike earlier conceptions of education, which stressed the responsibility of teachers for the transfer of knowledge, techniques, and skills to students, I have embraced the conception of education as being concerned with the development of intellect—the expansion of the student's ability to think. There are two fundamental problems when one is concerned with the development of intellect. One has to do with the learner's capacity to deal with perspectives, and the other has to do with the student's capacity for critical interpretation. Piaget (1973) argues that one of the highest levels of cognitive function involves the capacity to see the world through the eyes of other people—the capacity to develop perspectives with respect to the things that I view. The enablement of critical interpretation builds on this capacity for handling multiple perspectives, including the weighing of differential knowledge interests to arrive at understanding.

A second issue concerns the importance of going beyond knowing to understanding. This position privileges the view that simply acquiring information and even mastering it is not the essential function or purpose of education. To arrive at understanding is the pedagogical task in the service of intellective competence—hence the struggle with the tensions between breadth of curriculum content coverage and depth of understanding of the basic concepts in each and across knowledge domains. The concern here is that if through multicultural education, through the study of science, or through any curriculum domain, one is concerned with the development of intellect with an emphasis on the capacity to develop perspectives and understanding, one can no longer focus on comprehensive mastery of all the knowledge available on any subject. Rather, we need to move more and more toward broad orientations to knowledge and in-depth understanding of basic concepts. Thus, one of the major recommendations from many curriculum reformists is that we begin to focus on some central concepts that should be treated in specific content areas from a variety of perspectives, using a variety of examples—not primarily to ensure the representation of all perspectives, but to ensure that students have an appreciation for the fact that concepts can take different forms or can be manifested in different ways and in some instances may even be fundamentally different as one moves from people to people, from situation to situation, from context to context. It is my view that the basic concepts should be dealt with from varied perspectives, and that students be encouraged to use this richer information in their assumption of responsibility for arriving at critical judgments.

A third issue with which we must deal is the issue that I call personalization. Here, two subconcepts are involved. One is relevance and the second is sense-making. The notion here is that learning is likely to proceed more efficiently for learners if it is personalized. We are distinguishing between individualization and personalization. Personalizing the learning experience means it is made a part of me, is made relevant to who I am; it becomes a part of my effort to try and make sense out of things. So whether we are studying the social sciences or literature or biology or chemistry, I am likely to learn it much more effectively and much more efficiently if I can find some relevance in that material for who I am, or for where I am coming from, and if it contributes to my effort at making sense out of my experience.

The fourth issue involves a concern for diversity and humanity—diversity because humans are so diverse, but humanity because we are all so much alike. Here, the focus is on people and the understanding of people, and a focus on culture and the understanding of cultures—our two principle vehicles for doing this. Understanding that there is a multitude of ways in which people differ, while studying people for people's likeness to me and the unlikeness to me, is one of the best ways of appreciating that diversity. Trying to understand what people are about, what they are trying to do, and the variety of ways in which they have gone about trying to make sense out of their worlds—trying to make adaptations to the world—would be a principal vehicle for getting at the kind of education that increasingly will be required for survival in the era of increased globalization of cultures and economies. So I argue that human beings are not only different, they are also quite interdependent; they are enormously varied, but share a great deal in common. The function of education is to help these human beings to better develop their intellects, and in the process of doing so we turn to the pluralistic demands on people as well as to their many variations. I use the construct *pluralism* to refer to the fact that each of us has to function in a variety of contexts. Increasingly, we have had to learn to speak the languages of other folk and we have tried to understand the differences that, say, women bring to a situation as opposed to what men bring to a situation. The ways in which my having been born and reared in North Carolina may have shaped who I am may differ considerably from the ways in which a youngster who is born and grows up in Watsonville, California, functions in the world and constructs his or her identity. It follows, then, that intelligence, depth and breadth, personalization, humanity, and diversity are the principle issues that have driven my particular approach to the treatment of multiple cultures in education.

CHAPTER 9

Culture and the Sciences of Pedagogy

The knowledge on which educational practice is based is about where the field of medicine was at the turn of the 20th century. The end of the 19th century and the beginning of the 20th was a period marked by an explosion in the growth of the knowledge of anatomy, biology, biochemistry, physiology, and other sciences foundational to medicine. The report of Abraham Flexner to the Carnegie Foundation for the Advancement of Teaching in 1910 is generally credited with being the catalyst for radical changes in the nature of medical education. That report focused attention on many inadequacies in the preparation for professional practice of medicine in that period. However, there was a growing awareness that the training schools for the preparation of physicians were out of touch with the changing base of knowledge necessary for medical education and the practice of medicine.

Scholars of the sciences foundational to medicine were not to be found in these medical training centers. In these schools, laboratories for the study of the relevant sciences were reported by Flexner (1910) to be primitive and underequipped. The conceptual and exponential bridges between theoretical knowledge and clinical practice were not a part of the curricula of these medical training centers. By 1925, most of the 155 training schools had been closed or brought into university settings where scholars of the emerging knowledge base were present. What resulted was the elevation of the medical sciences and medical education in the United States to world-class status.

Today, at the end of the 20th century, we see a similar explosion of knowledge concerning the pedagogical sciences. We have seen radical changes in the behavioral sciences, the cognitive sciences, the computer sciences, the social sciences, and even in the way some of us think about the humanities. We are beginning to recognize how much these sources of knowledge are shaped by context and perspective, on the one hand, and how deeply they are embedded in particularistic cultures on the

Adapted from a paper presented at a meeting of the American Educational Research Association, New Orleans, April 1994.

other. The tradition of respect for the authority of knowledge in these disciplines stands side-by-side with skepticism concerning its completeness as well as the extent of its applicability. Some of our schools of education have scholars who are masters of these changing disciplines, or at least familiar with some of the implications of such changing knowledge and technology for the practice of teaching and learning. However, my own sense of the conditions, resources, and practices of schools of education in this country leads me to conclude that the preparation for the professional practice of pedagogy is about where the preparation for the professional practice of medicine was 100 years ago: out of touch with the knowledge base essential to it.

Pre-20th century medical education had been deeply rooted in the preparation for the practice of medicine as an art. The prevailing model was the old Viennese physician, wise and artfully skillful. My father was one of those physicians. With his sensitive hands, ears, and eyes, and the gifted intuition born of years of practice as a country doctor, he gained a reputation in rural, segregated southern North Carolina for being "Black as hell but a damn good doctor." That was an expression we heard from a couple of White men one night as they talked about him. He did almost no laboratory work; he could not read X-rays. He carried most of the portable medical equipment he owned in a small black bag. He read one medical journal and four or five ragged medical books. Were he alive today, he would be lost in the modern medical setting. Yet he helped a lot of people and he was considered "a damn good doctor." Medical education had to be revolutionized in order to break out of the model of which my dad was an exemplar. It also had to be revolutionized to accommodate a changing knowledge base. Education or pedagogy may find itself today in the same position.

THE PEDAGOGICAL SCIENCES

Now what is this relevant knowledge base of which I speak? What is this body of knowledge we assume that teachers have or must have? Pedagogy has to do with the design and management of the teaching and learning transactions involving subject matter (i.e., content knowledge) and academic appreciation, skills, and understanding. I will have little to say about content knowledge, not because it is unimportant but because my concern is with the identification of that procedural knowledge essential to the design and management of teaching and learning transactions. I think it is what Lee Schulman (1987) calls "pedagogical knowledge." I refer to its core as the pedagogical sciences. It encompasses both the behavioral and the social sciences, as amplified by the arts and humanities. Those behavioral sciences are anthropology, biology, and psychology. I consider the social sciences to be economics, history, political science, and sociology. But this classification is almost arbitrary in that many of these disciplines overlap and some could be called behavioral or social or both. (Sociology, for example, is more correctly both a behavioral and a social science.) What is important is that in their totality they represent the knowledge, methodologies, and perspectives essential to pedagogical understanding and practice.

Yet, when one examines the literature of these disciplines, the seminal work is rarely conducted by educational research scientists, and the cutting edges of knowledge production and application are underrepresented in the curricula of our schools of education. To make matters worse, postmodern thought and the politics of changing demography have resulted in changed perspectives on the knowledge represented in these disciplines. Concepts once thought to be invariant and universal are now much more susceptible to contextual and situational phenomena. Realities once taken for granted are increasingly recognized to be mediated by particularistic attributions, by existential states, by perspectives born of differential experiences. Cultural diversity once entertained for its exotic appeal is beginning to be recognized as essential to the integrity of most epistemological endeavors. Thus the knowledge referenced by these disciplines is in a state of flux.

CULTURE AND THE BEHAVIORAL AND SOCIAL SCIENCES

Let us examine the intercept between culture, on the one hand, and the behavioral and social sciences, on the other. In doing so I turn first to two of our most seminal pedagogical scientists, Piaget and Vygotsky—radically different in their perspectives, almost contradictory, but complementary in the processual implications of their thinking. Piaget (1973) posits the genesis of cognitive function as occurring largely within the developing person. Proponents of the heritability of intellect can cite his formulations to support the idea that cognitive capacities are more or less preprogrammed in the individual's genetic material.

Operating from a cognitive-structural perspective on intellectual development, Piagetians emphasize the structural nature of human cognition: sophisticated logical mental structures genetically programmed to unfold in response to experience. Piaget (1973) maintained that there are four major stages of cognitive development, each characterized by unique structural features enabling qualitatively different modes of cognitive function. He posited four constructs as the mechanisms through which cognitive development proceeds: assimilation, accommodation, equilibration, and schema. Assimilation, accommodation, and the movement from concrete to formal operations are represented as the unfolding of natural processes in consequence of maturation.

Vygotsky (1978), by contrast, asserts that cognitive abilities emerge, develop, and are displayed within a sociocultural milieu. Similarly, Geertz (1973) assumes an interdependence of contexts and cognition when he argues that the human brain is thoroughly dependent on cultural resources for its very operation. Those resources are, consequently, not adjuncts to but constituents of mental activity. Followers of Vygotsky posit the genesis of intellectual function outside the developing person in the interactions between the person and the social environments to which he or she is exposed. It is through these interactions that knowledge and cognitive skills are transmitted, nascent cognitive abilities are cultivated, and cognitive behavior is modeled, encouraged, and rewarded.

But when we ignore their positions on the genesis of cognitive abilities, and focus on the processual features of intellect implied by these theories, the two pedagogical scientists appear to be elaborating different features of the same process. Assimilation and accommodation are what the developing person does with the content and meanings of environmental encounters. These encounters are the vehicles by which knowledge and skills are transmitted. It is through these encounters that cognitive behavior is encouraged, is cultivated, and is rewarded. Embedded in these encounters is Vygotsky's (1978) social scaffolding, which enables movement from concrete to formal or abstract operations. The mental processes facilitating this cognitive growth have been called generalized event representations or scripts used in social interaction, which are similar to the Piagetian notion of schemata.

It is to Vygotsky (1978) that we generally turn for the functional bridge between culture and pedagogy. But the processual conceptions of both theories highlight the critical role of culture in our understanding of what it is to know and to understand, as well as to enable knowing and understanding in others. Thus, teaching and learning are explained partially by the cultural mediation of the opportunities for both.

My central message has to do with the interpenetration of two areas of study, that is, the intersection of culture and the sciences of pedagogy. There are many seeds from which this interpenetration notion grows. The pedagogical sciences can be conceptualized along a continuum from experimental, through correlational, to interpretational science. Those in psychological circles remember that in 1957, the Cronbach presidential address to the American Psychological Association spoke of the two disciplines of psychology, the experimental and the correlational. If Cronbach were writing that paper today, I think he would also talk about interpretational science. I think he would argue that we have three divisions of, or approaches to, psychology. One is based on experimental work. One is based on the analysis of correlations between natural or contrived phenomena. And, borrowing from the critical theorists, critical psychologists, and cultural psychologists, I think we would have to recognize that knowing and understanding require some of us to worry about the interpretational analysis of phenomena.

Interpretational analysis really goes back to the work of Kurt Lewin (1935) in the 1930s and 1940s. He held that behavior can best be understood as a function of dynamic interaction between individual and environment. His colleague Murray (1938) amplified the idea, specifying alpha and beta presses of environment. The alpha presses come largely from the physical environment. The beta presses emanate internally, from what their external phenomena and events mean to us individually. Both, Murray insisted, are important to understanding human events.

Dollard (1935) contributed to interpretational analysis by insisting that phenomena can be understood only in context. In so doing, he laid the groundwork for using the case study as a method for investigating social as well as individual clinical phenomena. Some years later, Tom Pettigrew (1968) helped by making an eloquent case for the importance of supplementing quantitative work with qualitative, and vice versa. The power of social predictions is greatly increased, he showed, when the quantitative data undergirding them are amplified with qualitative data.

Others, too, have done interpretational analysis in the Lewinian tradition. Barker (1968) and Barker and Wright (1949) and the ecological psychologists have insisted that behavior can be understood only in terms of the context in which it takes place. All of this work has led me to an affinity with contextualism and perspectivism.

CONTEXTUALISM'S THEMES

Four basic themes are involved in contextualism: the emergent and processual features of social reality and social action; the central relevance of intentionality and sociocultural referents to communicative practices; the various contextual contingencies and boundaries (e.g., historical, sociocultural, idiopathic) of knowledge production and dissemination; and the culturally embedded qualities of scientific labor itself. Let us examine these themes.

Nature of Human Activity

The first concerns the nature of human activity itself. Contextualists assume that human acts are dynamic, transactive, and dialectical. Reality is not assumed to be stable or necessarily ordered. Contextualists argue that humans impose order on the world's phenomena, and that those phenomena are not necessarily intrinsically ordered. They are constantly changing—that is, the imposed order is continuously changing as it is constructed and reconstructed by those of us who experience it, each of us influenced by the context in which phenomena are encountered.

All of these claims are intended to argue the importance of the cultural contexts in which people live. It is our cultural experiences that shape our intentions, and that mold the ways in which we shape our environments. Such a view rejects the idea of individuals as simply passive or reactive. Rather, humans are seen as self-conscious, reflective, and transformative, as well as reactive, beings. We are not only reacting to environments, but we are also intentionally creating those environments. We know that one of the characteristics of culture is its capacity to shape behavior. Yet another of its characteristics is its capacity to be shaped and created by human behavior. Cultures have this double-edged, bifocal characteristic. We are born into cultures and they shape us, but we as human beings create cultures. Cultures are constantly in the process of being changed. So context is by no means a fixed or stable phenomenon. Examining human behavior from photographs—from still pictures captured at one point in time—without sensitivity to the fact that a photograph pictures an isolated incident that may have changed since we snapped it is a mistake.

Human activity interacts with changing sociocultural contexts that can either facilitate and allow, or constrain and frustrate, behavior and development. This is terribly important. We must remember that there are social structures out there that facilitate development for some people. There are also social structures—sometimes the very same structures—that facilitate development for some people but inhibit it for other people. Any careful analysis of behavior must look at those reciprocal, dialectical, sometimes contradictory relationships that link context and developing behaviors.

To further complicate the situation, those structures that facilitate or frustrate have to be understood from the perspective in which they are seen by various people. When I seek to reward a youngster, if my reward—my reinforcer—is not perceived by that youngster as a reinforcer, then it may be a frustration and an interference rather than a facilitator of the desired behavior. Yet in so much of our work, using relatively narrow lenses we reward rather mechanically, and remain insensitive to the fact that for different people, coming out of different backgrounds and cultures, things we think of as rewards may actually be interferences/penalties.

Banks, with his colleagues (Banks, McQuarter & Hubbard, 1979), has done some very interesting related work. He worried about the phenomenon of delayed gratification and the way in which it is treated in the literature. It is traditionally thought that low-status people—Black people, for example—are less able to delay gratification than are White people. Banks was troubled by this notion and began to research it. He finally concluded from experiments he conducted that when the *interest power* of the reward is held constant, the differential in delay of gratification in the diverse status groups disappeared. What traditional approaches had done in running experiments on the question was to hold the reward constant. But it is the interest power of the reward that is the trigger, not the reward itself.

Nature of Communication

A second assumption underlying contextualism pertains to the nature of communicative acts. Since human communication occurs within and relates to its surroundings, context must be examined in order to understand communication. We recognize that intentions underlie most communicative acts. We also understand that intentionality is often influenced by context, by the situation in which it occurs. Thus, even interactions that have the same reference points may rise from the different situations of participants. The judicial sciences are far ahead of the social sciences in recognizing this. We penalize people differently if they harm someone by accident rather than by intention. We are beginning to recognize that in the analysis and understanding of behavior, and the understanding of communications as behavioral acts, the intention behind the communication certainly has to be taken into consideration if the message is to be understood. Furthermore, human acts involve relational processes where the act incorporates—that is, reflects and affects—the sociocultural context.

Let me elaborate. To understand the act, you have to understand its sociocultural elements. Each act reflects such elements as well as impacts on them. Things never remain constant; they are constantly changing. Human actions are dynamically and dialectically related to their context. One act influences subsequent acts. So goes the process, much in the same way as proprioceptive processes in which a response in one part of the organism stimulates a different response in another part of the organism, and produces feedback to change the original response.

One of my former students, Dominque Esposito (1971), used to refer to these "dynamic and interacting" processes as dynamic blending. In his elaboration of the notion, he argued that one of the reasons we do so little research in this tradition is that we simply do not know how to deal with that ever-changing dynamic situation where the dependent variable at one moment is independent and at another moment is dependent. However, if we are to understand the dynamics of human behavior, somehow we have to come to grips with that fact of dialectical interaction and find ways to deal with it.

Nature, Origin, and Boundaries of Knowledge

The third basic theme of contextualism involves epistemological questions having to do with the nature, origin, and boundaries of our knowledge. The contextualist position holds that more than one explanation can be applied to the same behavior because of differences in context, circumstances, and temporal factors. If we follow Keil (1990), different explanatory positions can also flow from differences in existing constraints. Keil is a cognitive psychologist who examines how prior knowledge constrains the development of subsequent thought—how the constraining circumstances surrounding the behavior shape the behavior itself. He is arguing that the constraints have to be understood to allow us to understand the behavior.

Such a concern with context suggests that indifference to prior history, indifference to the current situation, or ignorance of attitude and perceptions leaves us with incomplete pictures. Recall my earlier reference to the importance of attributional phenomena, such that insufficient attention to the idiosyncratic meanings of an experience can result in misunderstanding the behavior. No matter how accurately I describe the situation that I am observing, unless I understand it in the same way as do those who are involved in it, I am likely to misunderstand their response.

I was first alerted to this concern by Don Medley of the University of Virginia. In my Head Start research days, we were trying to understand what goes on in Head Start classrooms. We developed rather sophisticated devices for observing and documenting teacher and student behaviors and environments. Don looked at our instruments and was troubled. He argued that if you really want to know what is happening with these students, you need to know what *they* think is happening. While professional conceptions of what is going on may be important, what students are responding to is what *they* perceive as going on—and what the investigator needs to know is what those perceptions are.

Principles and theories cannot be universally valid, then, because the contexts to which they refer are constantly changing, and they involve vastly different historical and sociocultural meanings across persons and situations. There are always cognitive limitations, because any representation of reality will always be biased by historical dynamics, and in relating to some aspects of "reality," other aspects are necessarily omitted. It is terribly important to remember that when I fix my vision and turn my lenses to reveal one aspect of a thing, there are just loads of other things that I do not and cannot see.

Cognitive developmentalist Elsa Haussermann (1957) acknowledged this in her psychological assessments of work with youngsters who had suffered neurological impairment. She asserted that the task of the psychological examination was to determine under what conditions a youngster can accomplish particular tasks, and under what conditions is it difficult or impossible for him or her to do the tasks, rather than to simply determine whether he or she can accomplish tasks in the standard condition. She is suggesting that maybe we have to worry about the validity of our hypotheses under a variety of conditions, in a variety of contexts, and from different perspectives.

Cultural Embeddedness of Science

The fourth basic theme central to contextualism is a belief in cultural embeddedness of the scientific enterprise itself. Scientists play an active and dialectical role in the process of knowledge production, not an objective, passive, or removed one. Since the world consists of highly complex interactions of multiple and dynamic factors, there can be no single complete representation of reality or of specific human behaviors. What the scientist does is (1) try to deconstruct specific phenomena within particular sociohistorical contexts and (2) play an active role in the process of conceptual reconstruction to generate social science knowledge. In a sense this is an extractive process in which the scientist extracts meaning about complex phenomena from neat little experiments. What this process provides is a single view of the world. This view in a different context, or these events as seen from a different perspective, may give us very different results.

I am reminded of a talk that Donald Hebb (1975) gave to the American Psychological Association. He was talking about the elegance of some of our research strategies, and the brilliance of some of the designs and analyses we bring to bear in our work. He suggested that there is a problem in bringing such elegance to bear on questions that should not have been asked in the first place. He was complaining about the absence of good theory in a lot of our research, and about our tendency to substitute very elegant designs and analyses for this lack of good conceptual work. There is a real potential for loss as we so reify the phenomena we are studying that we in effect destroy their meaning.

CRITICAL PSYCHOLOGY

I turn now to some of the work of critical psychology and critical interpretation. An early entry was Edmund Sullivan's brilliant little book *A Critical Psychology* (1984), in which he attempts to apply critical theory to psychology. From this perspective, critical interpretation is a central purpose of psychology as a discipline. Sullivan offers critical interpretation not so much as a substitute for empirical work, but as an essential addition to more traditional approaches to knowledge production. Critical interpretation is analytic in that it deconstructs not only the problem, method, and findings of inquiry, but also the purpose, the intent, the underlying values, and the knowledge interests served by the object of investigation. What critical theorists are suggesting is that on reading or designing a piece of research, it may not be enough to look at the relationship between problem, method, and findings. The intentions and the knowledge interests of those who do the work are also important.

I like to remind people who cannot recognize it that I am an African-American male, born in the United States in the 20th century, and that these things influence me and what I do. They influence the way I think about things. When I identify a problem to investigate, I bring my African-American, 20th-century, male person to bear on it. That person is likely to be somewhat different from some of my colleagues who do not share my particular background and identity. Looking at the work of others and at my work, the critical theorists would argue that it is important that you know that this work is done by Ed Gordon and that other work is done by, say, Mary Anne Raywid, and that the perspectives that each of us bring to our work may be different. Most important is that those perspectives may influence our respective findings as well as our interpretations—even though we may like to think of findings as being objective.

The perspective an investigator brings to his or her work can influence how the question is posed and how the investigation is designed (see Chapter 11). These factors can also influence findings, rendering them less objective than we are inclined to think. So as a responsible scientist, I owe it to you to remind you—and maybe even more important, I need to remind myself—that the conclusions I come to are the products of a specific perspective I have brought to the problem. Thus, the problem, the method, the findings, can never be separated from context. The three are synthetic or constructed. Consequently, special attention must be given to the intentions that drive the behaviors of those who study as well as those who are being studied. Since intent must always be inferred, and we do not yet have good ways of measuring it, concern with intent involves interpretation. We argue for critical interpretation.

In looking for intent, the critical interpretationists are critical of the mechanical and biological metaphors they find have guided most behavioral science theory. They are arguing that we may have looked too narrowly for our explanations for behavior. We may have used the mechanical metaphor excessively in looking for one thing causing the other, or the biological metaphor with its implied unidirectional linear relationships. Both are primarily concerned with explaining how things work. Instead, the critical interpretationists propose that we also have to be concerned about the *why* questions, about why things work. Here we have to focus on meanings. I often cite the difference between efforts at identifying the mechanisms by which aging can be explained and a search for understanding of the meanings of growing old. When the question is "What are the factors associated with growing old?" social scientists can identify these. But if you want to know the meanings of growing old, I would go to a good novel, a piece of poetry; or I would talk to a person of my age. The meanings of growing old are quite different from the *mechanisms*, even though both are important to understanding aging or critically interpreting the behavior of aging persons.

Critical interpretationists turn often to the personal metaphor. They ask, "Who and what is this person?"—a question that they claim requires the "I–Thou" dyad. They argue that too much of our work has focused on the hypothetical and counterfactual autonomous person. When we stop to think about it, none of us can exist as individuals outside of relationships to other people. Human beings are essentially social beings. We derive our existence and are able to maintain it—we achieve our survival—out of our interactions with other people. It is I–Thou rather than just "me" or "I" or "you." It is the social force that drives the interactions within and between these dyads that ought to be the subject of our investigations.

CULTURAL PSYCHOLOGY

It is from such ideas as contextualism and interpretivism that a new subspecialty in the sciences of behavior is emerging. Some refer to this work as cultural psychology. Stigler, Shweder, and Herdt (1990), in their anthology entitled *Cultural Psychology,* present a collection of essays by 14 different writers. This is a school of thought that is being born rather than one that already exists. It asserts that cultural psychology is the psychology of intentional worlds—the intentional worlds of the I–Thou dyads that drive behavior. A cultural psychology aims to develop the principle of intentionality

> by which culturally constituted realities (intentional worlds) and reality-constituting psyches (intentional persons) continually and continuously make each other up, perturbing and disturbing each other, interpenetrating each other's identity, reciprocally conditioning each other's existence. (Shweder, 1990, p. 3)

Therefore, I am constantly in the process of creating you as I try to understand you, because what I have to do in order to understand you is to create an image of you, a vision or image of you in my mind. You may share my image or parts of it or you may deny it, but my mental images contribute to my identification of you and vice versa. In addition, we may be reciprocally conditioning each other's existence as well as each other's images. Now these are very mushy realities with which to deal. It is easy to understand why the related conception of knowledge is disconcerting and why educators have not rushed to embrace it.

Cultural psychology suggests that the narrowness with which the social sciences have approached human behavior is dysfunctional. That is not to say there are no common or universal characteristics of human beings that such paradigms might help us to understand. But the richness of the diversity may escape us because of the narrowness with which we study human beings.

Mental representation and intention are crucial to a psychology of culture or the interpenetration of culture and the sciences of behavior. A prominent characteristic of the human mind is its capacity to create its own realities. We do not know if other forms of animal life are capable of it, but certainly one of the many features of human beings is this capacity to transform things conceptually. If B. F. Skinner (1954) had been able to incorporate this notion into his conception of behavior, he would clearly have earned the title of our greatest psychologist. It is his blindness on this point that limits my own regard for his position.

Human behavior is not simply a function of that which is observed and reinforced. Rather, behavior is a function of what the mind does with stimulation and what the stimulus does to the mind. Even the nature of the reinforcement can be transformed by this human mind, so that what

I offer as a punishment can be transformed into a reward or a neutral contingency. In one context, a condition may be perceived as positive, in another it may be negative. What one group of people perceive as an opportunity, some others perceive as a challenge or an obstacle. Thus this concern with intention and mental representation is a crucial one. Minds that create realities function in intentional persons. Organized human behavior is explicitly or at least implicitly purposeful; actions are intended to achieve certain ends.

What we produce, and how, and often why we produce it, as well as the meanings we collectively assign to it—all of these are culturally constituted realities reflecting intentional worlds. The question is just how these intentional worlds, and the individual human intentions that appear so important, relate to socialization contexts such as ethnic, gender, language, and class groupings. Human survival and human behavioral development involve intentional acts, which are facilitated or frustrated by context. Context includes social structures. Social structures affect things like opportunity, resources, discrimination, rewards, arbitrary constraints, political power, health care, education. To understand behavior one has to understand it in relation to those social structures that are part of the context in which behavior develops and exists, especially as that behavior is influenced and represented by identification with one of these ethnic, gender, language, or class divisions.

Consequently, it is necessary to study human intention and human agency—that is, the actions of humans—as they are mediated by these social structures. To do this requires that we heed context, perspective, and the dialectical interactions specific to the behaviors under study. The intersection between culture and the sciences of behavior requires that we conduct these kinds of investigations.

THE IMPLICATIONS OF A CULTURAL PSYCHOLOGY

Let us turn to a few practical suggestions or examples of how such a focus might be played out. I would argue that the very first thing we have to do is to find ways to incorporate the serious study of the pedagogical sciences described here into the preparation of professional educators. I am not advocating that we necessarily have our students study more anthropology or psychology or economics. Rather, what I am arguing is that we must find ways to approach their knowledge in transdisciplinary fashion. By transdisciplinary I mean the sort of merger accomplished in political economy where what one deals with is the interaction between political and economic forces in accounting for events. The economic analysis and the political analysis combined will not suffice, but with the interpenetration of these ways of knowing, the explanatory power of the two disciplines becomes greater than the additive power of the two. The emerging field of cultural psychology does the same with anthropology and psychology.

We have to find ways to bring the several disciplines of pedagogy together in more creative ways than simply the additive examination of each. The phenomena of the world do not separate themselves out for psychologists, anthropologists, and sociologists. These disciplines are just lenses through which phenomena can be viewed. What we need to find now is ways to put those lenses one on top of the other to better understand the phenomena we would know.

A second task is the incorporation of the sciences of pedagogy into the preparation of education professionals as culturally relevant and situated knowledge rather than as decontextualized disciplines separated from the cultures in which they are embedded. I do not want to suggest that psychology or sociology or anthropology for Black folks is different from the psychology or sociology of, for example, folks of Asian, European, or Latin descent. But somehow the study of these disciplines must be approached with sensitivity to diverse cultural contexts.

A third concern is to lure into the education professions people who can learn, manage, and live with dynamic, contextual, and, yes, even relative knowledge. Some need knowledge that is much more fixed or absolute. They have little tolerance for ambiguity. But the real world is not so absolute. Rather than black and white, what I see are many shades of gray. The older I get the more ambiguous I think things are. It becomes clearer to me that unless I can deal with ambiguity, I cannot deal with the realities of the world. I hope we can help the people that we bring into this profession to learn these things, to manage them, and to mediate such learning in others. This may mean that the quality of minds that we invite into pedagogy will have to be elevated, which in turn introduces a lot of political and economic implications. To draw more able minds to the practice of pedagogy, we may have to radically change the rewards.

A fourth implication of cultural psychology is enabling educationists to recognize and treat knowledge and technique from multiple perspectives and in diverse contexts. We can no longer look at a piece of knowledge or a particular technique (way of doing things) and assume that it is universally applicable. Nor can we assume the objectivity of either the producer or the situation out of which it was produced. When I formulate a problem, or a practice and application, what I do in the process is to bring all the stuff that is Ed Gordon to it, and Ed Gordon has some biases. He sees things in particular ways. Others may see them quite differently.

Their use of the same material, the same technique, the same idea, may be different from mine, and what is important is that the professional educator will have to recognize and live with that fact. Edmund Gordon's competence then may have to be judged by his capacity to transcend the context and perspective that are his own. He must be able to put himself in the places where others are sitting, as he tries to understand phenomena—and most particularly in the places where the people he teaches are sitting.

A fifth concern is to develop and nurture wise professionals who are scholars of the sciences of pedagogy that inform pedagogical practice, as well as scholars of pedagogical praxis that should inform the continuing production of knowledge. When I first joined the faculty at Teachers College some years ago, Robert Shaefer was dean. Shaefer used to talk about education as inquiry and about the developing scholars of the practice of education. He was one of the people who rejected the separation of basic from applied research. He thought they should be equally privileged and of equally good quality. He urged those of us who worry about practice to be scholars of practice. I would hope we can produce educators who are scholars of the sciences and practice of pedagogy. But teaching and learning are very personal and relational enterprises. As such the profession requires a command of knowledge and technique that enables both personalization and relational adjudication (Gergen, 1990). Pedagogical science and praxis, mediated by cultural perspectives, can move our profession in that direction, enabling understanding of the interpenetration of culture and the sciences of pedagogy.

CHAPTER 10

Human Diversity, Cultural Hegemony, and the Integrity of the Academic Canons

WITH MAITRAYEE BHATTACHARYYA

Questions concerning the appropriate treatment of diverse human experiences, identities, and perspectives in the curricula of our schools have achieved prominence in the debates over curriculum development in recent years. As manifestations of diversity in human characteristics have become more obvious and are experienced as being ubiquitous in the lives of all members of the society, the facts of human diversity and cultural pluralism have become a significant source of social concern. As the special interests of diverse subgroups have been increasingly expressed in the political arena, the problems for education have been exacerbated and the debate has been accelerated. It is in this context that concern for Afrocentric and multicultural education has become the focus of so much attention and often uninformed debate.

Afrocentric education can be thought of as a response to or corrective for what has been perceived by some as Eurocentric education, with the latter's history of having preempted the academic canon by imposing standards for knowledge content and validity that are associated with the cultures of Northern Europe. Proponents of Afrocentric education insist that the long and rich history of the peoples of Africa and their cultures are legitimate foci for academic study, and that all students, especially students of African descent, should have the opportunity to be exposed to such studies. Additionally, the critics of an exclusive or excessive focus on Western civilization (Eurocentric knowledge) argue that such a truncated approach to knowledge is a distortion of reality and must be corrected. In both approaches, the tendency exists for a single perspective and knowledge community to be the focus for curriculum organization. Thus, it is the contending validities and priority claims of each that are often debated.

Adapted with permission of Howard University Press. Copyright © 1992 by Howard University Press. *Journal of Negro Education, 61*(3), 405–418.

A report to the New York State Board of Regents (Gordon & Roberts, 1991) argued that such a juxtaposition of claims misrepresents the problems. In this report, the problems are defined as having to do with (1) the juxtaposition of concern for human diversity, cultural hegemony, and the integrity of the canon and (2) the pedagogical question of how knowledge and human experience are organized and used through education to enhance the development of intelligence in human beings. In other words, how do we protect and enhance the integrity of the academic canon under circumstances of diverse human and cultural characteristics, on the one hand, and a hegemonic culture, on the other? If education is concerned with the development of intelligence in learners, rather than the simple transfer of knowledge and skills, how can its social studies curriculum be organized and directed at such cognitive enhancement? Conceptualized in this way, concern with Afrocentric, Eurocentric, and multicultural education is more appropriately seen as raising problems in epistemology and curriculum development than as debating questions of what is politically correct, whose canon is it, or which voices should be heard.

Several questions follow from such a reconceptualization of the problems. They include:

- What is the nature of the diversity, and its pedagogically relevant dimensions, to which schooling and the curriculum must be responsive?
- What are the nature and relationships of cultural hegemony, cultural diversity, and cultural pluralism in the United States? What are the relationships between diversity, pluralism, hegemony, and the integrity of the canon?
- How have our conceptions of intelligence, knowledge, and education changed?
- What are the relationships and influences of these changed conceptions to the nature of the canon, to curriculum, and to teaching?
- What implications do these conclusions have for the treatment of cultural and ethnic identities, and for the development of cultural and historical materials in the service of education?

THE NATURE OF DIVERSITY

Diversity in the origins and other characteristics of its people has been and continues to be a fact in the United States. We are obviously a nation of many peoples. Additionally, we are perhaps unique as a democratic nation that has marched, from its beginnings, under the banner of "E Pluribus Unum" ("one from many"). The United States was created with democratic principles as fundamental and on the basis of respecting group differences. As such, while other nations have sought to create one from many by force, the United States sought to do so by common will, at least with regard to the groups of original European colonizers. The peoples of northern Europe, who originally settled in what is now the northeastern part of the United States, exemplified the ideals of tolerance and commonality—although in that earlier period their diversity was more obvious than it is perceived to be now.

While these diverse European groups have grown less culturally diverse and more homogeneous, the diversity of the U.S. population and the differences between groups in this land have continued and increased as other peoples, from perhaps every major geographic region in the world, joined the nation. The population presently includes diverse peoples who are not nearly as unidirectional in migration to the United States as were the earlier European settlers. Both the attitudes and the movements of these diverse peoples have become more bidirectional. That is, many travel back and forth between the United States and their countries of origin and also maintain strong ties with their original lands, their cultural roots, and indigenous traditions. There is also greater movement toward attitudinal bidirectionalism in diverse groups who are seeking to preserve, to revive, and to reconstruct their cultural origins. Moreover, our recognition of human diversity today is not limited to variations in national origin, religion, race, and ethnicity; it also includes the diversity of gender, sexual orientation, caste, class, and language. Cultural diversity in a sense refers to all of these social divisions. Each of these means by which persons identify themselves (or are identified) comes to be associated with specific belief systems, behavioral styles, mores, and/or ingroup characteristics that are the partial basis for identification. It is to these indicators of cultural group identity that schooling is called to be responsive.

CULTURAL HEGEMONY, CULTURAL DIVERSITY, AND CULTURAL PLURALISM IN THE UNITED STATES

As the variations among the U.S. citizenry have multiplied and as the meaning and the nature of diversity have evolved, support for homogeneity, or assimilated oneness, has decreased. On the other hand, pride in and celebration of uniqueness or human diversity have increased. Stated differently, while there has emerged a hegemonic culture in the United States—as manifested in the dominance of "cultural elements, values, and worldviews that tend to be associated with our European ancestry alone" (Gordon & Roberts, 1991, p. 30)—there has been some decrease in the disposition toward this homogeneity. Concurrently, there has been an increase in the pride group members hold in their own origins and their need to celebrate these origins.

The need to celebrate uniqueness in our society, interestingly enough, is at issue not because it is necessarily a new phenomenon, but in part because of the progress the society has made toward democratization. Many groups lived in such isolation until the 20th century that opportunities to celebrate various groups' uniquenesses were plentiful. I [Gordon] recall that, as a young African-American lad growing up in a semi-rural Black ghetto in North Carolina, it did not matter much what was going on in the White communities because I had little contact with them or access to them. In such protected isolation, Black people celebrated their Blackness and its cultural elements. However, by the middle of this century, with the dismantling of legalized exclusion and forced separatism, more direct contact was occurring between ethnically diverse groups in public places; and by the 1960s and 1970s, there was significant commingling.

While this democratization of the social order resulted in increased contact between groups and reduced ethnic isolation, it also resulted in reduced opportunity for the celebration of cultural diversity and of uniqueness. This occurred because the social order was conceived under the European-assimilationist standard rather than with the idea of embracing and maintaining cultural diversity. Thus, in mainstream (less officially segregated) America, there were reduced opportunities for diverse cultural expression and celebration in protected enclaves. This development forced the demand for such celebration in public (desegregated) institutions.

A second consequence of this development was that, initially, social distinctions and, later, education were racialized. Groups were largely conceived of and categorized by gross and generic social divisions such as Black/African American, White/European American, Red/Native American, Yellow/Brown/Asian American, and so forth, whereby the cultural diversity within these peoples was geographically regionalized and subsumed by mistaken conceptions of race. The recognition of culture and cultural diversity was increasingly bypassed by the insistence on creating and using the word *race* specifically to categorize and hierarchize peoples—to the point today that how residents of the United States perceive their ethnic identity contributes to their cultural identity. The construct of race, though only several hundred years old and still as ill-conceived as it ever was, is now primary in the minds of the world's peoples. As a result of this racialization, attempts to democratize the educational system in the United States have revolved around either allowing or continuing to disallow Blacks the equal opportunity to assimilate, rather than around allowing or continuing to disallow them the equal opportunity to learn. This has resulted not in increased opportunities for Blacks to integrate and learn as equals as much as in opportunities for them to assimilate, play "catch-up," or resegregate in opposition to the White establishment's "standards."

Nevertheless, group awareness of other groups grew with the measures toward democratization, as the peoples of the United States began to hear each other's desires for the opportunity for public expression, representation, and celebration. Most of us have acknowledged the humanity of people without property, of people of African descent, and of women. If we think of voter participation in governance as a part of being a full citizen, then, to our nation's credit, the reflection of our respect for all people's humanity, at least with respect to suffrage, is evidenced in our history of broadening the number and category of persons to whom citizenship has been extended. Religious diversity has also become a fact of life in the New World; we no longer physically go to battle in religious wars. Today, we not only have greater diversity; we have greater acceptance of diversity as a fact. Unfortunately, we also have greater potential for conflict. The U.S. society has been rapidly overcome by a modernity (i.e., efficiency of communication, transportation, commerce, and technology) that has served to destroy the cultural enclaves in which ethnic identities were formerly celebrated and maintained. This destruction has forced interaction and assimilation. Although this modernity heightened economic competition, it did not eliminate the influence of tribal loyalties in favored economic, political, and social advancement. The English language and the associated culture of northern Europeans have achieved hegemony. Thus in the modern nation-state, the public assertion and protection of cultural/ethnic identity appears to be perceived as essential to cultural survival. As most structures of the society have become hostile to subcultural retentions, most members of society feel the need, as a means of survival, to assert the values of their own cultural identity. These several factors have occurred together and have changed the context for the nation with respect to its population diversity.

DIVERSITY, PLURALISM, AND HEGEMONY, AND THE INTEGRITY OF THE ACADEMIC CANON

As a consequence of these factors, we see on the education agenda the emergence of debate concerning the appropriateness of a canon that primarily reflects the hegemonic culture and that argues the uniquely superior character of Western civilization and its consequent centrality in any curriculum (Kagan, 1990). Some of the main questions in this debate over the facts of cultural hegemony, cultural diversity, and cultural pluralism concern the adequacy of the existing academic canon; the permeability of its boundaries; and whether or not, to what extent, or how satisfactorily it credits and includes diverse knowledges. The debate involves questions of inclusiveness, representation, and social justice, as well as those of pluralism and sound pedagogical practice. Together, such questions result in challenges regarding equal access to and participatory inclusion in quality educational opportunity.

At the same time, in contrast to such questioning, there are strident voices expressing resistance to change. For example, Schlesinger (1991) argues that what has made this country great is the coming together of people under a single banner. He fears the assertion of diverse identities will disunite America, and calls attention to the potential for divisiveness that is grounded in any attempt to deemphasize the hegemonic glue that has held the nation together. From Schlesinger's perspective, what people may have given up (or have been forced to give up) to fly that single banner is beside the point. However, this aspect is not at all trivial or inconsequential. The stripping of one's identity is demeaning, even genocidal, especially when one's caste status makes it impossible for one to accept the hegemonic identity. The reason the United States's "unitedness" is today so precarious may be that it does not rest on a solid foundation of respect for personal identities or cultural pluralism.

Some have recently called our attention to the current disunity in eastern Europe, as if it were the result of the honoring of diversity in those countries. To the contrary, those conflicts are partly a reflection of earlier efforts to impose homogeneity on the people of eastern Europe through the assertion of military and political power rather than the prior honoring of diversity through education and the practice of inclusionary and participatory democracy. It is then not so much the dismantling of the *unum* that causes strife, but the neglect of the *pluribus* and the absence of social justice. (Moreover, it is a mistake to think *unum* exists where it is imposed, for the imposition itself indicates the existence of *pluribus*.) In this connection, it is the United States's failure to respect the diversity of its peoples that may lead to its disuniting, not the enlightened study of the sources of identity in its many peoples. The United States as a nation of many peoples must function to honor diversity, not suppress or hide it. Though having undergone democratization, this nation has yet to truly recognize and honor, through participatory inclusion, the diversity and interdependence of its many groups.

Over the years, this neglect has erupted in political insurrection and, in all likelihood, such unrest will continue as long as diversity is neglected.

CHANGING CONCEPTIONS OF INTELLIGENCE, KNOWLEDGE, AND EDUCATION

The problems of importance here are not simply issues related to demographic changes, associated political pressures, and concern for the unity of the nation. The facts of cultural diversity and contending claims for the validity of knowledge present us with critical pedagogical questions. To understand these pedagogical issues, it is necessary to examine changing conceptions of knowledge as well as changing conceptions of pedagogy. Both are in part epistemological issues involving such concepts as the nature of understanding, consensus and existential realities, and contextualist and perspectivist thought.

As mentioned earlier, Wallace (1961) has proposed three purposes of education—for moral development, for the development of skills and techniques, and for the development of intellect. When one considers these fundamental purposes of education, one is forced to give primary attention to the development of intellect, which involves more than the transfer of knowledge and skills. Although Wallace ranks these purposes differentially in relation to the stages of societal development, intellect—as the parent of all else that is uniquely human—is the quintessential human characteristic. Education directed at the development of intellect requires that one cultivate the capacities for perspective taking and the achievement of understanding. In Piaget's (1973) stage theory of cognitive development, the abilities to view phenomena from the perspectives of others and to manage more than a single perspective are placed quite high in the developmental hierarchy. The achievement of understanding is so important because understanding is an essential manifestation of intellectual competence. It also influences human behavior. Indeed, understanding could be viewed as the ultimate reality because to understand any phenomenon is, with respect to it, to know and appreciate it: What is it? From whence does it come? Why so? What more? How to? Why not? And what if?

After reading a beautiful book entitled *Paths Toward a Clearing* (Jackson, 1989), I [Gordon] wrote the following note to myself:

> "The correct view" will always be a futile exploration, because the truly noble
>   inquiry may be a pursuit of a clearer and sometimes different perspective,

from which—in the company of other perspectives—we may begin to approach explanation and understanding.

Jackson, an anthropologist, borrows the "paths toward a clearing" metaphor from Heidegger to refer to the problem of humanity's search for truth. Because truth is relative (i.e., dependent on the context in which it is developed or experienced), investigators in anthropology and in the study of cultures must recognize many truths in the search for meaning, which is often grounded in the behaviors and experiences of those being studied. Jackson questions whether meanings can be understood in the absence of an investigator's having lived the experience of the person(s) whose behavior he or she is trying to understand. It is clear, however, that to view another's observed experiences through too narrow a lens is to fail to see much of that which is available and essential to understanding.

One way of seeing is also a way of not seeing. What the understanding observer seeks are clearer and different perspectives, different ways of seeing. Let us take as an illustration the differences between an explorer and a hunter in a forest. The hunter enters the forest in search of something very specific, usually an animal. Consequently he or she is likely to look for and see animal tracks. Hunters are likely to look in those places animals are prone to inhabit. The explorer enters the forest in search of a better understanding of the forest. As such he or she is more interested in seeing the whole of the forest and in exploring its subtleties. The explorer is interested in finding paths that lead toward clearings because it is from the clearings that one gets broader and different perspectives than from down in the bush. Metaphorically, there are certainly many "paths" to the "clearing" of understanding. As such, when one clearing is found and appreciated, explorers seek still another and another until they have an understanding of the entire forest.

Existential realities and lenses honed by attribution shape and influence the way any phenomenon is viewed and make for differences in the ways phenomena are perceived. Thus, one must not forget that knowledge is both informed and formed by existential and attributional realities as well as by the consensus reality (that which all can agree on). That is, what one person may attribute to a phenomenon may be quite different from that which his or her colleague may attribute to the same phenomenon. For example, according to our work on the "defiers of negative prediction" (Gordon & Song, 1992), more than half the respondents indicated that they never thought of themselves as poor although they came from poverty-stricken families. How these respondents perceived their reality depended on how they experienced that reality and the attributions they assigned to it. The objective condition was poverty, yet the existential condition was something else. The special meaning of the condition to those who experienced it seems to have influenced their behavior and development. Thus, one must seriously consider the possibility that the specific information or knowledge one has derives its importance from one's own understanding of it. What individuals do with their knowledge is based on what they understand it to mean. Problems arise, however, when one person's existential meanings contradict those of the consensus; yet, as far as teaching and learning are concerned, whether one's special meanings are right or wrong, they must be addressed if learning is to be effective and meaningful.

The implication for teaching, then, is that the work of teaching centers around learning to understand, on the part of both the student and the teacher. In the parlance of modern pedagogy, teaching and learning thus become the exercise of the collaborative construction of meanings and their critical interpretation. In the pursuit of sense-making then, it is fallacious to try to find "the one" truth. Examining this point further, one observes that usually when one arrives at truth, it is generally seen to be that which most people agree on. However, on closer scrutiny, one begins to see that many truths are true only because they represent the reality around which people can gain consensus at the moment. The conception of truth, then, is not so absolute as it is contextual, temporal, and relative.

This tension between existential and consensus reality mediates our conceptions of both truth and understanding, which in turn influence the changing nature of conceptions of knowledge. Increasingly, knowledge is seen as fluid, dynamic, dialectical, evolving, and temporal. Any serious epistemological analysis requires that one take into account contextualism, existentialist meanings, perspectivism, and relativism in examining the genesis and interpretation of knowledge. These changing conceptions of the nature of knowledge are influencing the ways in which pedagogy is conceived and practiced. In education, teaching and learning are rapidly moving away from instruction by didactic methods of knowledge and skill transfer to the more maieutic methods of guided and mediated construction of meaning and the exploration and interpretation of knowledge and techniques. Increasingly advocated is a shift from breadth and comprehensiveness of factual coverage and content mastery to the pursuit of in-depth understanding of core concepts in which "less is more," from group instruction to cooperative learning, from the individualization of instruction to its personalization (i.e., grounding the learning in the lived experience and values of the learning person).

Such conceptions as these may appear to be floating anchors, lacking in stability, divorced from the realities of schooling, and difficult to deal with. In the traditions of the scientific method and some of the most honored values of established scholarship, they simply are not practical or feasible. For example, to "do" science one must hold variables fixed from one experiment to the next in order to see relationships. To reason logically, one must first agree on and hold constant the constraints within which an argument is to be pursued. When objects are in constant motion or subject to infinite variation, analysis becomes difficult if not impossible. However, valid knowledge and meaningful understanding may require no less than that we work with such dynamic and dialectical phenomena. Instead of relying on established ideology and dogma (either one's own or that of others), one must develop or adapt theories and postulates that are grounded in both the consensus and the existential realities that frame the experiences of diverse peoples. Through such work societies may come to see that despite the great diversity, the fundamental facts of human existence may be generic in their meaning while yet different in the situational manifestations toward which chauvinistic attention too often has been directed.

CHANGED CONCEPTIONS OF THE CANON, CURRICULUM, AND TEACHING: RELATIONSHIPS AND INFLUENCES

In applying these ideas to the canon and curriculum development, we advocate the elevation of the questions in Afrocentric, Eurocentric, and multicultural education from "whose canon?" "whose history?" and "whose voice?" to "how do we better enable learning and the development of intellect in our students?" Multiculturalism and multiperspectivism are thus seen as vehicles for enhancing intellectual competence in all of our students. Despite the political nature of the educational debate involving social and economic equality, equal opportunity, the centricity of Western civilization, and the inclusion of diverse histories and voices, our argument for multiculturalism does not focus on these issues alone. Rather, multiculturalism is seen as extremely important for its contributions to the enablement of effective pedagogy and to the ultimate achievement of the primary purpose of education—that is, to nurture the development of intelligence.

Knowledge, science, and education may not have to be revolutionized before society can become more sensitive to diverse human characteristics, contexts, and perspectives, or before education can be improved. Revolutions are difficult to come by and usually are unselectively destructive. Within the current debate concerning the nature of the canon and the curricula through which it is taught, there is room for a great deal of expansion, change, and reform. But in what ways? How will society know in which directions to proceed? What is society to use as signposts?

If the integrity of the canon is understood and agreed on as one point of reference that should remain as an anchor, a new a set of criteria is needed to guide these changes. In this context integrity is taken to mean wholeness, soundness, completeness, and the lack of deception. Therefore, the following are proffered as criteria by which the integrity of the canon is to be judged:

1. The canon should reflect the comprehensiveness of knowledge. Knowledge should not be context-bound; rather it should be both universal in its applications and capable of being assigned general applications. This is one of the elusive goals of scientific methodology. Presently, however, understanding and application are usually situationally bound. They require sensitivity to contextual phenomena and are often related to the perspective provided by the position from which a phenomenon is investigated. Demands for relativistic knowledge thus seem to conflict with our desires for absolute knowledge; similarly, efforts to know and understand seem to require both inclusive and exclusive categories. The result is the emergence of paradoxes that appear both unresolvable and essential to the comprehensiveness of knowledge. Yet, while the criterion of comprehensiveness creates a tension between the absolute and the relative, this tension need not immobilize human thought. It can be the driving energy behind knowledge production and critical interpretation.

2. The canon should contribute to the conservation and stability of knowledge, techniques, and knowledge products. Verbal and written symbol systems and other cultural products are the foundations for the continued development of human societies, and human beings cannot afford to lose access to them. All such systems and products deserve to be considered for membership in the human archives, but because such inclusiveness is nearly impossible, some system of selection is justified. However, to avoid arbitrary or chauvinistic exclusion, our criteria of measurement and the rules for determining validity and acceptability for inclusion must remain flexible and dynamic. At the same time, the core of the canon should remain relatively stable over time to enable replication, reflection, critical analysis, and critical interpretation between multiple investigators and situations.

3. Notwithstanding, the canon must be characterized by the capacity to accommodate change. Its boundaries must be sufficiently permeable to permit expansion and constriction in response to the new or different information, perspectives, or technologies. As Kuhn (1970) asserts, paradigms change as a result of changing experiences and different views of

phenomena. Similarly, the canon must respect and accommodate contextualist, existentialist, universalist, and relativist conditions of validity as they may be differentially applicable depending on the nature of the knowledge and the purpose for which that knowledge is to be used. However, this accommodative capacity of the canon must not be an excuse for the rejection of falsification; a part of the canon must always be the evidence that a particular assumption, finding, or theory has as yet failed to be confirmed.

4. The contents of the canon must be accessible to a broad range of audiences. No matter how brilliant the findings and statements of scholars, if the means by which those findings are represented to others serves only to keep other scholars (and those outside the academy) from understanding, then the findings do not meet a crucial criterion of the canon. The canon should be interpretable by persons who are interested and willing to prepare to use it.

5. The canon must reflect a functional and meaningful relationship between prior knowledge and the requirements of new knowledge. This is recognized as a condition of effective learning. A requirement for inclusion in the canon must be based on the functional characteristics of the content rather than its ritual characteristics. Thus, the dogmatic nature of new content is insufficient rationale for its inclusion; however, a specific bit of dogma may be justifiably included because of its historical significance.

6. The canon must reflect the aesthetic and nutritive value of knowledge, respecting intellectual behavior as an art form and intellectual stimulation as the nutrient of mentation.

A canon so conceived would be a living document, more protean than concrete, designed not so much to protect and conserve knowledge and technique as to enable learning and the development of intellect.

CULTURAL AND ETHNIC IDENTITIES AND MATERIALS IN THE SERVICE OF EDUCATION

Efforts directed at developing and utilizing such a canon will be neither simple nor easy. The issues that will arise as a result of these efforts will be complicated partly because they are simultaneously epistemological, political, and practical. They are epistemological in the sense that they challenge traditional notions of the very nature of knowledge or at least the categories of knowledge that may be included in the canon. Conceptions of the nature of knowledge are indeed changing, with more voices contributing to the canon and being recognized as such. However, for many the introduction of new conceptions of the nature of knowledge is threatening because it challenges knowledge systems with which we have become familiar. It forces new ways of thinking about the world and ourselves. It requires that educators teach across disciplines, across cultures, and with heightened sensitivity to context.

The issues are political in the sense that knowledge is power. Struggles to expand, change, and control knowledge—and access to it—are struggles to change the control and distribution of power and ultimately the distribution of resources. There is a long history of conflict over the control of what is to be included in the canon and reflected in the curriculum (Cremin, 1989). Repeatedly in the history of the nation, questions have been debated concerning the purposes of education and the content with which educators are to pursue their goals. As different segments of the U.S. population have gained voice, the values honored by the society have changed, as have the goals of education and the ways in which schools function. The current debate over Afrocentric, Eurocentric, and multicultural education and about what is to be included in the canon is a continuation of this political struggle concerning who will control knowledge, what students are expected and allowed to know, the ways in which students are enabled to think, and with what resources they will be enabled to participate in society. The manner in which these questions are answered will not only influence what schools do; it will also determine the nature and extent of the power and resources that will be under the control of students when they become adults.

The political issues are further complicated by the changing demographics of our nation. It may well be that the projected shift from a nation in which persons of European ancestry constitute the majority to a multicultural nation where such persons are a numeric minority is such a psychological threat to the present majority group as to make their rational accommodation to it a political impossibility. Accommodating such change is already viewed by some to mean the disruption of the social order and the disuniting of the nation (Schlesinger, 1991).

The issues are practical in the sense that the implicit changes will require the development of new instructional materials, the reeducation of a huge teaching staff, and the redesign of much of our existing curricula. These changes in curricula will involve not only their content but also their functions and the nature of the assessment of curriculum outcomes. Such practical changes will not be well served by a political decision to substitute one dogma (Afrocentric knowledge) for another dogma (Eurocentric knowledge).

What is required is professional and scholarly effort directed at better understanding human cultures, the knowledge and techniques by which they are represented, and their utilization in the processes of education, which is, again, the development of human intelligence and not simply the transfer of information and skill. In the report to the New York State Board of Regents (Gordon and Roberts, 1991), some of this work was begun. In addressing needed changes in the New York State social studies curriculum, they concluded that a few fundamental concepts should provide the focal points for the curriculum; and that applications, context, and examples should be drawn from multiple cultural sources, different perspectives, and diverse identity groups. Such experiences through the curriculum enable students to examine quite varied kinds of evidence in pursuit of different ways of understanding. Students learn to draw from several alternatives and perspectives on their way to arriving at wise judgments and the reconciliation of differences.

In this context, the goal of multicultural education is to enable students to develop their intelligence and to function as human and humane persons (Gordon and Roberts, 1991). In pursuit of this goal, seven fundamental concepts are identified as focal points for a social studies curriculum that is responsive to the concerns of multiculturalism:

1. Democracy: [Viewing] democratic ideals as the foundation of American society.
2. Diversity: Understanding and respecting others and oneself.
3. Economic and Social Justice: Understanding personal and social responsibility for economic and social systems and for [their] effects.
4. Globalism: Recognizing interdependence and world citizenship.
5. Ecological Balance: Recognizing responsibility for the global neighborhood.
6. Ethics and Values: The pursuit of fairness and the search for responsibility.
7. The Individual and Society [Participation]: Seeing oneself as a participant in society. (p. viii)

The members of the Gordon and Roberts (1991) committee were especially cognizant of the widely held concern that efforts aimed at giving greater attention to multicultural issues will interfere with or preclude educators' attention to the nation-building functions of education. Committee debates raised the point that several years ago social studies courses were called "citizenship" classes, and that these classes covered how the U.S. government works, the responsibilities of citizens, and so forth. Such a curricular focus is no less important today, but what is the true nature of citizenship? One of the prime tenets of democracy is the principle of government with the consent of the governed. However consent cannot be considered to be real consent unless it is informed consent, which

> requires understanding born of critical analysis and synthesis and critical interpretation . . . [which] do not arise from training in established traditions . . . [but from] exposure to diverse opinions, multiple perspectives, and situated histories . . . [involving] comparative analysis, contextual validation, heuristic exploration, and judicious reflection. (p. 30)

For some, this concern for common elements in the interest of *unum* means neglecting the diversity that is so much a part of the nation's peoples. Despite what many see as the primary need for nation building, there is no necessary conflict in serving both *pluribus* and *unum*. However, what historically have been offered as the "common elements" of our nation's heritage are in reality hegemonic cultural traditions drawn from a truncated conception of knowledge as a product of our European ancestry alone. To better serve both *pluribus* and *unum*, the nation should consider "the flowering of human civilization" not as the singular achievement of peoples of European descent, but as

> the culmination of cultural and technological developments from virtually every part of the world . . . as we uncouple specific human achievements at one point in history from the immediate and sometimes fortuitous context in which they have been presumptively "first" observed. (Gordon and Roberts, 1991, p.30)

A multicultural education directed at the development of intellect in learners and the support of nation building should thus be directed at (1) the inclusion of diverse cultural elements and the assimilation of common values; (2) the accommodation of different perspectives and the correction of erroneous information; (3) the appreciation and celebration of those things that make us distinct as well as those that make us one; (4) the achievement of comprehension and understanding of the meanings of experiences and the lives of self and others; and (5) all of these in concert in the interest of developing the capacity for critical interpretation and informed consent. To quote Gordon and Roberts (1991):

> We want our students to become thinking participants in, rather than trained validators of, decisions concerning the affairs of the nation. Such richly intelligent beings are very likely to recognize and respect the important things that we share in common as well as the unique things that make us different. (pp. 30–31)

CONCLUSION

High on the list of goals for education in a democratic society is the enablement of intellective development and, ultimately, understanding of the diverse peoples of the nation. The United States is diverse with respect to its population characteristics and pluralistic with respect to its standards; therefore, such intelligence and understanding must be functional in more than a single context. Increasingly, we in the United States are required to function in more than a single language, adapt to the demands of more than a single culture, meet the behavioral demands of more than a single situation, and understand the symbols and rituals of people other than those with whom most of us have been socialized. It is from multidisciplinary, multiculturalist, and multiperspectivist learning experiences that competencies of this order are developed. Diverse approaches to knowledge are necessary to help students in the United States gain the ability to see issues from a variety of perspectives. It is from this broader view that they will be enabled to discharge responsibility for their future judgments and decisions. From this point of view, rather than intellectual effort directed at the discovery of singular truth, their efforts can be directed at the discovery of truths as these components of knowledge may be shaped by the contexts in which, and the perspectives of the persons by which, they have been developed.

Educational goals of this order are not likely to be well served by an exclusive emphasis on Afrocentric or Eurocentric education, although either could provide the core around which a truly multicultural education can be developed. No matter what core knowledge is chosen as the vehicle, however, educators are beginning to realize that the teaching of dogma (either hegemonic or resistant) is no longer appropriate for the optimal development of learners. It is to teaching for the development of competence in critical analysis, critical interpretation, and critical understanding that modern pedagogy has turned. In the final analysis, the integrity of the academic canon may have to be judged by the extent it enables such teaching and learning.

CHAPTER 11

Coping with Communicentric Bias in Knowledge Production in the Social Sciences

WITH FAYNEESE MILLER AND DAVID ROLLOCK

Over the past two decades, we have experienced heightened concern about the underrepresentation among the contributors to knowledge production. Within the American Educational Research Association (AERA), the concern has focused on the paucity of minority participation in social science and educational research. Minority-group members share this concern but are even more concerned with the impact of this underrepresentation on the character and nature of the knowledge that is produced:

1. Much of the social science knowledge referable to Blacks, Latinos, and Native Americans ignores or demeans their characteristics.
2. This knowledge often presents distorted interpretations of minority conditions and potentials.
3. The resulting knowledge base appears to be unnecessarily limited in its capacity to appropriately inform efforts to understand and improve the life chances of such people.
4. The knowledge base itself may be distorted and truncated as a result of these missing perspectives.

In response to these and other concerns, the AERA has created the Committee on the Role and Status of Minorities in Educational Research and Development. In addition, the association's special-interest groups focus attention on aspects of these concerns. In most of the social science disciplines, ethnic caucuses have been organized within the respective associations to address special minority interests. In psychology, a separate organization has been created that is devoted to the special interests of

Adapted with permission of The American Educational Research Association. Copyright © 1990 by The American Educational Research Association. *Educational Researcher, 19*(3), 14–19.

Black psychologists. Frequently, more attention is given to the representational and political aspects of minority status within the disciplines than to the conceptual and methodological implications of oppressed minority-group status for research in these disciplines. As the Taskforce on the Relevance of the Social Sciences for the Afro-American Experience, a small group of our colleagues periodically met over a period of 3 years to address some of these issues. We produced two published papers that began to discuss conceptual and methodological issues (Gordon, 1985; Stanfield, 1985). Much of the thinking reflected in this chapter is based on our experience with that task force.

We will identify five issues that make solutions to the problem of minority-group underrepresentation and its impact on knowledge production in education and social sciences difficult to achieve. After brief comments on each issue, we have a few proposals that might ultimately reduce the problem. Because so much of the problem is deeply rooted in the racist, political, and economic structure of the larger society, we doubt that the problem can be eliminated. The five issues are as follows:

1. Knowledge, technology, and the production of knowledge are cultural products and are not culture-free.
2. Knowledge production operates within communicentric bias frames of reference, which dominate and enable it.
3. Communicentric hegemony has enabled the development of phenomenal scientific, theoretical, and technological achievements, but this hegemony neglects, constrains, and discourages the contribution and participation of Third World people.
4. Communicentric hegemony leads to the distortion of the knowledge it seeks to produce.
5. The roots of this problem are not limited to factors external to Third World people. Members of these minority groups are themselves part of the problem (to paraphrase Brother Malcolm) because they have not actively become part of the solution. Uncritical complicity with the hegemonic culture and counter-hegemonic dogma are equally dysfunctional adaptations to communicentricity.

The social sciences are those disciplines primarily concerned with understanding the nature of, and the relationships between, human behavior and social systems by which it is expressed. Traditionally, these sciences have been characterized by the examination of the relationship between social experience and the development and manifestations of individual, group, and systemic characteristics. A tradition in these sciences is the incessant search for universal principles by which these relationships may be explained. Scientists working in this tradition look for principles or invest their notions in multicultural, multiethnic, non–gender specific, and multicontextual applications.

COMMUNICENTRIC BIAS

Although there are some common denominators across all human experiences and groups, there is reason to believe that an overemphasis on the search for universals has been, at the very least, premature, if not mistaken. Indeed, in some cases, the search for universals has inhibited rather than enhanced the encirclement of social science knowledge. Despite the historical concern with the relationships between experience, behavior, and social structures, insufficient attention has been given to the impact of unique cultural, ethnic, and/or gender experiences on the development of behavioral repertoires and the social systems by which behavior is expressed. This neglect is probably the result of androcentric, cultrocentric, and ethnocentric chauvinism in Euro-American and male-dominated production of social science knowledge. We refer to this chauvinism as communicentric bias—the tendency to make one's own community the center of the universe and the conceptual frame that constrains all thought. This communicentricity has sometimes resulted in knowledge production that has negative consequences for the life experiences of groups that have been inappropriately represented in the enterprise. Knowledge about African Americans and the treatment of this group in the social science knowledge base is a case in point. In his book *The Souls of Black Folk*, DuBois (1903/1965) poignantly wrote concerning this issue:

> It is a peculiar sensation, this double consciousness, this sense of always looking at one's self through the eyes of others, of measuring one's soul by the tape of the world that looks on in amused contempt and pity. One ever feels his twoness, an American, a Negro; two souls, two thoughts, two unreconciled strivings; two warring ideals in one dark body, whose dogged strength alone keeps it from being torn asunder. (p. 215)

Examination of the social and educational research knowledge bases relative to African-Americans indicates that these sciences have traditionally attempted to understand the life experiences of African-Americans from a narrow cultrocentric perspective and against equally narrow cultrocentric standards. Diversity has been viewed as deficit. Thus, the issue of cultural and ethnic diversity has been incompletely or inadequately assessed, and has insufficiently influenced knowledge production. These problems are compounded when we recognize that the traditionally dominant, communicentric bias frames not only the conceptual paradigms we use to study social phenomena, but the methodological paradigms as well. We tend to forget that many of the core propositions on which the sciences rest, such as objectivity, positivism, and empiricism, are cultural products and thus may be culture-bound. These hallmarks of sciences may be more limited in their explanatory usefulness than is generally presumed.

THE PARADOX OF THE SCIENTIFIC METHOD

However, before hastily dismissing the core propositions of the scientific method, we should remember that rationalism, positivism, and logical empiricism represent major advances in humans' pursuit of knowledge and understanding. These advances place, in the hands of educated people, the capacity to generate knowledge for themselves, thus freeing human thought from control by the political and religious nobility. Unfortunately, this democratization of knowledge production carries the potential for tyranny by the majority. The problems of consensus and majority rule consolidate and empower communicentric bias in knowledge production.

It may be that knowledge production cannot proceed without common frames of reference. Conceptual, descriptive, experimental, and taxonomic endeavors require consistency across observers and investigators. Common frames of reference provide for some such consistency. Yet such frames arrived at arbitrarily or through consensus can hardly avoid reflecting the context or community in which they are conceived. Thus, communicentricity may be a naturally occurring and essential phenomenon that enables, even while it constrains, knowledge production. Most of the "facts" of science are agreed on because when items are measured, different assessors come up with the same measurements; when experiments are replicated, similar findings result; and when conceptions are debated, the same conceptual terms and rules of logic are employed. The consistency provided by these common frames of reference has enabled great advances in humanity's understanding of the natural and social worlds.

This consistency has not been cheaply won. The common frames of reference are born of the achievement of communicentric hegemony over ways of thinking about and producing knowledge. Coming out of old-world cultures and technology, and dominating contemporary epistemology, positivism, and logical empiricism, are the foundation stones for scientific methodology. This communicentric hegemony in knowledge production has enabled the development of phenomenal scientific, technological, and theoretical achievements. However, we contend that this same hegemony in knowledge production is a constraining and distorting force, which compromises the contribution and participation of Third World people in knowledge production. Thus, the problem is not that the methods of science are dysfunctional for the research and scholarly efforts of ethnic minorities. The problem is cultural and methodological hegemony, which favors too narrow a range of perspectives and investigative techniques.

In the final analysis, all knowledge is relative to the context in which it is generated. We know a phenomenon by representing it to ourselves in a form that relates to existing affective and cognitive structures. Learning, understanding, and knowing are extensions or elaborations of one's real world and existential self. Thus, we individually and collectively perceive and eventually conceive of the world and its events in terms that either fit or are adjusted to the context that we know. This process of accommodation requires that we deal with the recognizable aspects of the phenomenon to be known, and that we reduce and distort it until it is manageable. Thus, we perceive what our lenses enable us to see and know that which the context permits.

As available knowledge expands, and our technology for generating and processing this knowledge increases and becomes more intricate, we gain in our appreciation of its complexities and infinite nature. In various ways, critics of the social sciences have reminded us that knowledge is not only the product of socially validated consensus, and may be problematic, since many frequently observed relationships are not necessarily universal. Specifically, such critics have called into question the traditional epistemologies, theories, and methods of the various social sciences in such a way as to challenge naturalistic, a priori assumptions about knowledge development and knowledge application. Thus, these critics claim social science knowledge is often imprecise and of questionable validity (Berger & Luckmann, 1966; Sullivan, 1984).

On this general level of criticism, there has been little discussion as to how the social sciences, as cultural products, shape the cognitive parameters of issues such as concept formation, the election of methods, and the development of distorted, unconfirmed paradigms with truncated theories. Little effort has been made to explore how the cultural and ethnic identities of the producers and consumers of social science knowledge may be implicated in the generation of fallacious explanatory constructs that wield considerable discursive power (Block, 1976; Gergen, 1973; Gouldner, 1970; Taylor, 1971). Yet these same paradigms inform the production of new social science knowledge.

Some researchers have begun to address the problem. For instance, Gilligan (1977) has found that sex-role socialization influences moral development in ways that call into question the universality of the widely accepted theory of moral development advanced by Kohlberg and Kramer (1969). Similarly, Banks and colleagues (1979) have suggested that socialization experiences that adhere to ethnocultural identity shape the sources of one's motivation and the conditions of gratification delay, and thus challenge traditional concepts of both. Scribner and Cole (1981) have suggested that the assumed functions of literacy in the development of intellect are based more on the cultural value assigned to literacy than on the actual functional impact of literacy on intellectual development. Scriven (1972) and Von Wright (1971) have examined, in a philosophical context, the manner in which the epistemological basis of current approaches to the social sciences has shaped the concern, methods, and products of those sciences. Implicit in these lines of work and thought is the notion that the relative magnitude or strength of a social variable may be more a function of the stimulus characteristics that are attributed or adhere to the variable than to the variable itself. Obviously, the attributional character of the stimulus is also a cultural product (Banks et al., 1979; Gilligan, 1977; Scribner & Cole, 1981; Scriven, 1972; Von Wright, 1971).

These formulations and other emerging notions grow out of social science research that challenges the traditional notions of situation and population universality concerning the relationships between independent and dependent variables. We are led to conclude that variables may have different characteristics, different meanings, and different impacts for persons whose life experiences are different, and whose attributions may be idiosyncratic to their positions in life. For example, gender, culture, ethnicity, and social class are increasingly understood to influence the mechanisms by which the behaviors are developed and consequently the theories by which they are explained.

We contend that the diversity in the characteristics and experiences of human populations makes the study of human behavior subject to explanations that are relevant to that behavior which is developed, expressed, and investigated, and the contexts in which the behavior occurs. Yet we find it understandable that those who produce knowledge, as well as those who utilize it, will seek paradigms and theories that are stable and as broadly generalizable as possible, because it is difficult to manage realities that are perceived as constantly changing and that have narrow reference points. We fully appreciate the fact that the manner in which social scientists approach the understanding of behavior is greatly influenced by the theoretical positions held by the researcher with respect to genesis of patterned behavior. That is, explanations of human behavior are dependent on the investigator's interpretation of the origins of the behavior, the values placed on the behavior and the behaving persons, and the interpretation of the behavior itself. The questions and problems of interest to the investigator generally reflect the theoretical bias of the investigator. However, given that human populations are diverse, problems arise when universalist conceptions are married to communicentric hegemony. It is then that the search for universals within the context of the investigator's chauvinist paradigms may lead to the distortion of the knowledge produced.

Many of us have devoted substantial effort to criticizing and complaining about the social science and educational research establishment. We have argued that human behavior is largely shaped by social/cultural experiences; that the Euro-American cultural hegemony has made the social sciences biased to favor the values and world view of White, male, middle-class persons; that this androcentric, cultrocentric, and ethnocentric bias may have distorted and limited the social science knowledge base. We are concerned about the impact of these factors, not only on the knowledge base, but also on the careers and work of minority social scientists.

THE ROLE OF MINORITY SCHOLARS

Minority scholars are confronted with problems of distortion in the utilization and foci of their efforts. As a result, much of the minority scholar's time is consumed in efforts to refute or neutralize fallacious findings, questionable theories, and inappropriate interpretations. Even worse, many minority scholars find themselves in the schizophrenic bind of using ethnocentric paradigms that are generally accepted as scientific truisms, but are lacking validation in the minority scholar's experiences and/or intuitions.

This counterestablishment work is frustrating and often unrewarding. It can even lead to counterrewards and attack. Yet, as Gould (1981) has reminded us, correction, perspective broadening, even debunking are positive aspects of science. Criticism is an essential and necessary role. Gould writes: "Scientists do not debunk only to change and purge. They refute older ideas in the light of a different view about the nature of things" (p. 322). We contend that this different view may be born of cultural-, ethnic-, or gender-related experience and that knowledge in the social sciences is greatly influenced by experiences of a hegemonic culture, which is insufficiently sensitive to cultural, ethnic, and general diversity.

Thus, we are on target when we critique this knowledge and the methodologies by which it is produced, but critique and refutation are insufficient. We find ourselves in a reactive mode when a proactive stance is indicated. There are not enough of us doing the conceptual homework that is necessary to generate alternative paradigms. We must do the systematic observations and ethnographic analysis, which are the foundation for the development of alternative or parallel taxonomies more appropriate to the classification and investigation of our life conditions. Too many of us have been co-opted by the Euro-American male establishment traditions, which render us insensitive to perspectives born of our own cultural traditions.

We, along with many establishment social scientists, are insufficiently educated. DuBois (1973) has said that no society can advance if it fails to nurture the talented one-tenth of its population. We are not providing adequate nurturance of the intellect that resides in the ablest of our members. We lose too many even before the completion of high school. Minority numbers are declining in the pool of college graduates. We are grossly underrepresented in graduate and professional schools. In addition, as we examine the quality and character of the education of even the best of those who succeed, it is too often found to be vocational or professional and insufficiently academic. Even those few who emerge as scholars tend to have mastered the traditional content of their disciplines. Rare are the renaissance scholars among us, and rarer still are those who are capable of critical analysis and critical interpretation of the consensus and phenomenological knowledge bases. We are victims of Euro-American cultural bias, but we are also victims of our own complicity in this bias and underdevelopment. What can we do about both?

We argue that it is in the best interest of knowledge production that the knowledge producers represent, in the experiences they bring to research, diversity comparable to the experiences of the populations that must be studied in order to answer the research questions posed. In many cases, this would mean that investigative teams include persons who are members of, or intimately familiar with, the groups under investigation. This argument should not be confused with the outsider-versus-insider debate (Merton, 1972). We believe that both insiders and outsiders have respective advantages and disadvantages when they function as researchers. In general, it would be wise to ensure that both participate in most studies. In the absence of either, however, it is essential that the impact of the limitations imposed by the absence of one be seriously considered by the other.

UNDERSTANDING RESEARCHERS AND SUBJECTS

We assert that the question posed for research investigation, the methodologies selected, and the interpretations of findings are often influenced by the perspectives with which the investigator approaches his or her work. Likewise, this perspective is born of the special experiences of the investigator. We wish that experience could render research scientists pristinely objective or universally subjective with respect to perspective. Either condition would, however, be handicapping. In the absence of both, we argue that the perspective of the investigated and the perspective of the investigator must be accorded the same seriousness of attention in the design, conduct, and interpretation of research investigations. This assertion, however, does not argue for equal representation in design, conduct, or interpretation because scholarly analysis and formal education sometimes do inform perspective more accurately than personal experience. We do argue, though, that the indigenous perspective be recognized and considered and that the design, conduct, and interpretation of research be informed by it.

We recognize the dynamic, dialectical, and reciprocal nature of knowledge production in the social sciences. Clearly, there is a need for greater symmetry in our understanding of those investigating, as well as those being investigated; both of our concerns for implications relative to staffing of research projects and identification of research perspectives speak to this need. We argue that the subjects of studies are influenced by those who conduct these studies. Moreover, those who investigate should be, and often are, influenced by the process and because there is so much diversity, as well as similarity, within and between them both, effective knowledge production requires greater symmetry in our understanding of both sides, rather than greater distance and pseudo-objectivity. Due to the abstract quantification and institutionalization of most social science research, this transactional aspect of such work is increasingly being neglected and is usually discouraged.

The state of much of our comparative knowledge in the social sciences is a labile one. Furthermore, we lack adequate data and understanding of the behaviors of the groups we wish to compare, given the tendency for social science to originate in studies by and of the male European-American. Therefore, we think that it would be in the best interest of knowledge production for greater emphasis to be given to intragroup studies, rather than to comparisons between groups, until these inadequacies are remedied. In particular, we need to know more about subgroups within Black, Hispanic, and Native-American populations. It may well be that the differences within any one group are greater than the differences between any two. In contrast, the mechanisms and meanings of a group's behaviors may be so different as to make comparisons meaningless and easily subject to distortion. Accepted canons of knowledge production require that this idiographic knowledge be generated and that more appropriate taxonomies be developed before we move ahead with further comparisons.

We recognize that the traditional assumption of homogeneity in populations, which has been the focus of social science research, often camouflages the realities of heterogeneity in human populations. This self-imposed blindness distorts our findings and our thinking. As a result of the limited attention accorded the issue, there is a lack of understanding of the mechanisms by which some of the behaviors of minorities—Blacks in particular—can be explained. Furthermore, there is an even greater lack of knowledge concerning the meaning of much of this behavior. All of this ignorance underscores the importance of the need for intragroup studies. Moreover, it emphasizes the need to examine the differential validity of many extant constructs when they are applied to diverse populations.

The work of Hill (1972), Billingsley (1968), and others demonstrates some of the problems encountered when we apply the construct *family* to Black collectivities of relatives. The Cole et al. (1971) work at least broadens our use of the construct *intelligence* when used to refer to the adaptive capacities of any group of children. The construct *illegitimate*, in its use to refer to children born out of wedlock, simply does not have the same meaning in many cultures that are not influenced by European and American Judeo-Christian values. Nonetheless, we recognize that assumption of population homogeneity can be useful in pursuing some questions. We argue that it can also be a source of distortion. In knowledge production there is some utility in most assumptions, even if they are used as strawpersons to illustrate a fallacy. Problems arise when purpose is not specified and assumptive validity is generalized. We must remember that when we decide to look at a phenomenon in a particular way, we greatly increase the likelihood that certain features will be revealed and others will be concealed.

Finally, our considerations lead us to recognize a need for additional good descriptive investigations of the behaviors, contexts, and development of Blacks and other ethnic minorities. Although this work need not be atheoretical, it should be sufficiently naturalistic and unstructured to be sensitive to factors and relationships that have as their intent the development of such broad and new taxonomies as the realities of the these groups' experiences may dictate.

This may not be enough. We have argued that hegemonic cultures, existing knowledge structures, and social experience not only shape but also constrain thought and knowledge production. How do people oppressed by this circumstance rise above and seek some liberation from it? It is the function of hegemony to regularize and control. We have seen that there are gains to be made from such systematization and consistency. Yet new knowledge and changed perspectives are not born simply by seeing and doing things in an orderly manner. We also know that new or better insight, and often discovery, is likely to come from atypical and nonconformist ways of viewing and thinking. To achieve such perspective, given the constraints of the real and existential worlds in which we live, the creative thinker and the renaissance scholar must utilize multiple ways of knowing.

ART, SCIENCE, AND KNOWLEDGE PRODUCTION

In another context, we have argued for a marriage between the arts, humanities, and social sciences to create distinct but related ways of knowing. If we are to understand the behavior and experiences of Blacks, Latinos, and Native Americans, we may need to turn to the arts and humanities. This is because the meanings of our behavior are often better explicated in our artistic and fictional work than they are explained by social science research, whether done by us or by others. How much more rich are the depictions of Black men in the works of fiction by Ellison, Wright, and Baldwin than in the social science works of Gary, Staples, and Wilson. As insightful as are the works of Steiner in his treatment of the life conditions of Native Americans, to understand the spirits and to capture the meanings of the lives of our Native-American brothers and sisters, we turn to *Black Elk Speaks* (Neihardt, 1959) or *Bury my Heart at Wounded Knee* (Brown, 1970). We have not adequately explored how these multiple ways of knowing can contribute to knowledge production. Counter hegemonic research will require that we work harder to integrate these several ways of knowing.

In addition to the arts, humanities, and sciences, there are still other ways of knowing. Philosophy and religion are among them, but probably least familiar and most neglected is the theory of critical interpretation, that is, the critical use of analytic, synthetic, and synergistic capacities of the human brain as the source of generative research. Mills (1959), writing of the conceptual needs of the general populace in a modern world, asserts: "What they need, and what they feel they need, is a quality of mind that will help them to use information and develop reason in order to achieve lucid summations of what is going on in the world and of what may be happening within themselves" (p. 5). Mills argues for

> the capacity to shift from one perspective to another—from the political to the psychological; from examination of a single family to comparative assessment of the national budgets of the world; from the theological schools to the military; from the considerations of an oil industry to studies of contemporary poetry. It is the capacity to range from the most impersonal and remote transformations to the most intimate features of the human self—and see the relations between the two. Back of its use there is always the urge to know the social and historical meaning of the individual in the society and in the period in which he has quality and his being. (p. 7)

Now what is the epistemological context for the development of such capacity? Paradoxically, for many of us who have complained about the domination of world scholarship by European and Euro-American scholarship, it is from the Frankfurt School, for which Habermas (1972) is a major spokesperson, that the concept of critical theory has emerged. It is from the critical theory movement that models for critical interpretation have been advanced. Habermas has identified three types of knowledge interests: prediction and control as reflected in empirical/analytical disciplines; understanding, exemplified by historical/hermeneutic disciplines; and emancipation, which is the manifested interest of critical theory.

To serve the interest of emancipation, Sullivan (1984) argues that critical interpretation must "elucidate and criticize those features of human situation that frustrate intentional agency (the deliberate actions of agents on their own behalf)" (p. 123). Fay (1975) argues for the importance of "intentions and desires of actors . . . as well as the rules and constitutive meaning of their social order" (p. 97). Fay asserts further that "a critical social theory is meant to inform and guide the activities of a class of dissatisfied actors—revealing how the irrationalities of social life which are causing dissatisfaction can be eliminated by taking some specific action which the theory calls for" (p. 98). Of special concern within the context of this discussion is Sullivan's (1984) conclusion that "what is important in a critical psychology [interpretation] is to make some linkages between the structural dynamics of class, race [and gender-based communicentricism] and the projects of human agents embedded in these historically constituted structures" (p. 124). Thus, a critical interpretation is not objective, not apolitical, but is clearly normative; that is, prescriptive of what ought to be, based on the critical analysis of what is and the varied special interests of the forces involved.

Sullivan (1984), recognizing that knowledge production is not and cannot be value-free, argues that scientists must make their values explicit and try to understand how such values shape their work. We argue further that just as establishment scientists have values, which are implicit if not explicit in their work, minority scientists must also clarify their values and, with equal deliberateness, use them, and even make them explicit in their work. Enough of the claims to pseudo-objectivity. If we cannot be objective let us at least strive to be honest.

Critical theorists openly assert human emancipation as a guiding value. DuBois (1973) refers to the liberating effects of the knowledge of arts, humanities, and sciences. Liberation is a value worthy of science. That should be the perspective from which minority scientists seek to advance multiple perspectives, and methodological rigor: not for the purpose of simply predicting, controlling, and understanding, but for the purpose of emancipating (liberating) the bodies, minds, communities, and spirits of oppressed humankind. We join them in doing so, and invite you to do the same.

References

Acton Society Trust. (1953). *Size and morale.* London: The Society.

Anastasi, A. (1980). Abilities and the measurement of achievement. In W. B. Schroder (Ed.), *Measuring achievement: Progress over a decade. New Directions for testing and measurement* (pp. 1–10). San Francisco: Jossey-Bass.

Appiah, A. (1992). *In my father's house: Africa in the philosophy of culture.* Oxford: Oxford University Press.

Banks, W. C., McQuarter, G., & Hubbard, J. (1979). Toward a reconceptualization of the social-cognitive bases of achievement in Blacks. In A. W. Boykin, A. J. Franklin, & J. F. Yates (Eds.), *Research directions of Black psychologists* (pp. 381–397). New York: Russell Sage Foundation.

Barker, R. (1968). *Ecological psychology.* Stanford, CA: Stanford University Press.

Barker, R., & Wright, H. F. (1949). Psychological ecology and the problem of psychosocial development. *Child Development, 20,* 131–143.

Baumrind, D. (1991). To nurture nature. *Behavioral and Brain Sciences, 14*(3), 386–387.

Berg, I. 1971. *Education and jobs: The great training robbery.* Boston: Beacon.

Berger, P. L., & Luckmann, T. (1966). *The social construction of reality: A treatise in the sociology of knowledge.* New York: Doubleday.

Billingsley, A. (1968). *Black families in white America.* New York: Prentice Hall.

Birch, H. G. (1966). (Ed.) Research needs and opportunities in Latin America for studying deprivation in psychobiological development. In *Deprivation in psychobiological development* (Scientific Publication No. 134). Washington, DC: Pan American Health Organization (WHO).

Birch, H. G., & Gussow, J. D. (1970). *Disadvantaged children: Health, nutrition and school failure.* New York: Harcourt, Brace & World.

Block, J. H. (1976). Issues, problems and pitfalls in assessing sex differences: A critical review of the psychology of sex differences. *Merrill Palmer Quarterly, 22,* 282–308.

Bloom, B. S. (1968). *Human characteristics and school learning.* New York: McGraw-Hill.

Bloom, B. S. (1969). Letter to the editor. *Harvard Educational Review, 39,* 419–421.

Bloom, B. S., Davis, A., & Hess, R. (1965). *Compensatory education for cultural deprivation.* New York: Holt, Rinehart, and Winston.

Bourdieu, P. (1986). The forms of capital. In J. Richardson (Ed.), *Handbook of theory and research for the sociology of education* (pp. 241–258). Westport, CT: Greenwood.

Bowles, S., & Gintis, H. (1976). *Schooling in capitalist America.* New York: Basic Books.

Brown, D. (1970). *Bury my heart at Wounded Knee: An Indian history of the American West.* New York: Holt, Rinehart, and Winston.

Bruner, J. (1966). *Toward a theory of instruction.* Cambridge, MA: Belknap Press of Harvard University.

Carroll, J. B. (1963). A model of school learning. *Teachers College Record, 723–733.*

Coch, L., & French, J., Jr. (1948). Overcoming resistance to change. *Human Relations, 1,* 512–532.

Cole, M., Gay, J., Glick, J., & Sharp, D. W. (1971). *The cultural context of learning and thinking.* New York: Basic Books.

Coleman, J. S., Campbell, E. Q., Hobson, C. J., McPartland, J., Mood, A. M., Weinfeld, R. D., & York, R. L. (1966). *Equality of educational opportunity.* Washington, DC: Government Printing Office.

Coleman, J. S., & Hoffer, T. (1987). *Public and private high schools: The impact of communities.* New York: Basic Books.

Collins, R. A., & Hanson, M. K. (1991). *Summative evaluation report: School-based management/shared decision-making project 1987–88 through 1989–90.* Miami: Dade County Public Schools Office of Educational Accountability.

Cremin, L. (1989). *Education and its discontents.* Cambridge, MA: Harvard University Press.

Cronbach, L. J. (1957). The two disciplines of scientific psychology. *The American Psychologist, 12,* 671–684.

Cronbach, L. J., & Snow, R. E. (1977). *Aptitudes and instructional methods.* New York: Wiley.

Darling-Hammond, L. (1992). *Standards of practice for learner-centered schools.* Unpublished manuscript prepared for New York State's Standards for Excellence Project, NCREST at Teacher's College.

DeParle, J. (1994, October 9). Daring research or "social science pornography?" *New York Times Magazine,* pp. 48–53, 62, 70–71, 74, 78, 80.

Dollard, J. (1935). *Criteria for a life history analysis.* New Haven: Yale University Press.

Drake, S., & Cayton, H. R. (1945). *Black metropolis.* New York: Harper and Row.

DuBois, W. E. B. (1899). *The Philadelphia Negro.* New York: Schocken Books.

DuBois, W. E. B. (1965). *The souls of Black folk.* In J. H. Franklin (Ed.), *Three Negro classics: Up from slavery, The souls of Black folk, and The autobiography of an ex-colored man* (pp. 207–389). New York: Avon Books. (Original work published 1903)

DuBois, W. E. B. (1973). *The education of Black people.* New York: Monthly Review Press.

Dumke, C. (1985). Epilogue. In W. Johnston (Ed.), *Education on trial: Strategies for the future* (pp. 257–269). San Francisco: Institute for Contemporary Studies.

Edmonds, R. R. (1979). Effective schools for the urban poor. *Educational Leadership, 37,* 15–27.

Endler, N. S., & Magnusson, D. (Eds.) (1976). *Interactional psychology and personality.* New York: Wiley.

Esposito, D. (1971). *Homogeneous and heterogeneous groupings: Principal findings and implications of a research of the literature.* New York: Teachers College, Columbia University. (ERIC Document Reproduction Service No. ED 056 150)

Fay, B. (1975). *Social theory and political practice.* London: G. Allen.

Flanagan, J. C. (1973). The first fifteen years of Project TALENT: Implications for career guidance. *Vocational Guidance Quarterly, 22,* 8–14.

Flanagan, J. C., Shanner, W. M., Brudner, H. J., & Marker, R. W. (1975). An individualized instruction system: PLAN. In H. Talmadge (Ed.), *Systems of individualized education.* Berkeley: McCutchan.

Flexner, A. S. (1910). *Medical education in the United States and Canada.* New York: Carnegie Foundation.

Franklin, J. H. (1967). *From slavery to freedom.* New York: Knopf.

Franklin, J. H. (1989). *Race and history: Selected essays 1938–1988.* Baton Rouge: Louisiana State Press.

French, J., Jr., Israel, M., & As, A. (1960). An experiment in participation in a Norwegian factory. *Human Relations, 13,* 3–19.

Fried, M. H. (1968). The need to end the pseudoscientific investigation of race. In M. Mead, T. Dobzhansky, E. Tobach, & R. E. Light (Eds.), *Science and the concept of race* (pp. 122–131). New York: Columbia University Press.

Fuller, J. L. & Thompson, W. R. (1960). *Behavior genetics.* New York: Wiley.

Gagné, R. M. (1974). *Essentials of learning for instruction.* Hinsdale, IL: Dryden Press.

Gardner, H. (1983). *Frames of mind: The theory of multiple intelligences.* New York: Basic Books.

Gardner, H. (1993). *Multiple intelligences: The theory in practice.* New York: Basic Books.

Gardner, H. (1994). *Brinkmanship on three fronts.* New York: Free Press.

Geertz, C. (1973). *Interpretation of cultures.* New York: Basic Books.

Gergen, K. (1973). Social psychology as history. *Journal of Personality and Social Psychology, 26,* 309–320.

Gergen, K. (1990). Social understanding and the inscription of self. In J. W. Stigler, R. A. Shweder, & G. Herdt (Eds.), *Cultural psychology* (pp. 470–606). New York: Cambridge University Press.

Gilligan, C. (1977). *In a different voice.* Cambridge, MA: Harvard University Press.

Glaser, R. (1977a). Adapting to individual difference. *Social Policy,* 27–33.

Glaser, R. (1977b). *Adaptive education: Individual diversity and learning.* New York: Holt, Rinehart, and Winston.

Glass, B., & Li, C. (1953). The dynamics of racial intermixture: An analysis based on the American Negro. *American Journal of Human Genetics, 5,* 1–20.

Goffman, E. (1963). *Stigma: Notes on the management of spoiled identity.* New York: Simon & Schuster.

Gordon, E. T. (1992, March). *Subaltern culture and assessment.* Paper presented at the African American Adolescent Males Seminar, San Diego, CA.

Gordon, E. W. (1967). Equalizing educational opportunity in the public school. *Bulletin of the Information Retrieval Center of the Disadvantaged, 3*(5), 1.

Gordon, E. W. (1977). Diverse human populations and problems in educational program evaluation via achievement testing. In M. J. Wargo & D. R. Green (Eds.), *Achievement testing of disadvantaged and minority students for educational program evaluation* (pp. 29–40). New York: CTB/McGraw-Hill.

Gordon, E. W. (1979). New perspectives on old issues: Educating the poor in the USA. In Doxey Wilkerson (Ed.), *Educating all our children* (pp. 52–73). Westport, CT: Mediax, Inc.

Gordon, E. W. (1985). Social science knowledge production and the Afro-American experience. *Journal of Negro Education, 54,* 117–133.

Gordon, E. W. (1986). *Foundations for academic excellence.* Brooklyn, NY: NYC Chancellor's Commission on Minimum Standards, New York City Board of Education.

Gordon, E. W. (Ed.). (1988). *Human diversity and pedagogy.* New Haven: Center in Research on Education, Culture and Ethnicity, Institution for Social and Policy Studies, Yale University.

Gordon, E. W. (1991a). Human diversity and pluralism. *Educational Psychologist, 26*(2), 99–108.

Gordon, E. W. (1991b). *A new compact for learning.* Albany: New York State Education Department.

Gordon, E. W. (1991c). *Report of consultant panel: Mid-course review of Project Canal, Chicago Public Schools.* Pomona, NY: Gordon and Gordon Associates.

Gordon, E. W., & Armour-Thomas, E. (1991). Culture and cognitive development. In L. Okagaki & R. Sternberg (Eds.), *Directors of development: Influences on the development of children's thinking* (pp. 83–100). Hillsdale, NJ: Erlbaum & Associates.

Gordon, E. W., & DeStefano, L. (1984). Individual differences in development and learning. In J. E. Ysseldyke (Ed.), *School psychology: The state of the art* (pp. 81–96). Minneapolis: National School Psychology Inservice Training Network.

Gordon, E. W., & Nembhard, J. G. (1993). *Reflections on the goals of education in a modern democratic society.* Unpublished manuscript.

Gordon, E. W., & Roberts, F. (1991). *One nation many peoples: A declaration of cultural interdependence.* Albany, NY: New York State Department of Education.

Gordon, E. W., Rollock, D., & Miller, F. (1990). Coping with communicentric bias in knowledge production in the social sciences. *Educational Researcher, 19*(3), 113–116.

Gordon, E. W., & Shipman, S. (1979). Human diversity, pedagogy, and educational equity. *American Psychologist, 34,* 1030–1036.

Gordon, E. W., & Song, D. L. (1992, January 30–31). *Variations in the experience of resilience.* Paper presented at the Conference on Resilience, Temple University Center for Research on Human Development and Education, Philadelphia, PA.

Gordon, E. W., & Thomas, K. (1990). Reading and other forms of literacy: Implications for teaching and learning. *Journal of Negro Education, 59*(1), 70–76.

Gordon, E. W., Wang, M. C., & DeStefano, L. (1982). *Temperament characteristics and learning.* Pittsburgh, PA: Learning Research and Development Center, University of Pittsburgh.

Gould, S. J. (1981). *The mismeasure of man.* New York: Norton Press.

Gouldner, A. W. (1970). *The coming crisis of Western sociology.* New York: Basic Books.

Greenough, W. T., Black, J. E., & Wallace, C. S. (1987). Experience and brain development. *Child Development, 58,* 539–559.

Gruenwald, H. (1963). *Facilitating reading achievement in the developmentally handicapped.* Unpublished student paper. Yeshiva University, Graduate School of Education.

Guess, R. (1981). *The idea of a critical theory.* Cambridge: Cambridge University Press.

Habermas, J. (1972). *Knowledge and human interests.* Boston: Beacon Press.

Haeckel, E. (1866). *General morphology.* Oxford: Oxford University Press.

Haeckel, E. (1892). *History of creation.* Oxford: Oxford University Press.

Hale-Benson, J. E. (1986). *Black children: Their roots, culture, and learning styles* (rev. ed.). Baltimore, MD: The Johns Hopkins University Press.

Hatcher, R. (1973). W. E. B. Du Bois Centennial Address. *Freedom Ways, 8,* 3–9.

Harrington, C. (1988). Culture as a manifestation of human diversity. In E. W. Gordon & Associates (Eds.), *Human diversity and pedagogy* (pp. 6.1–6.51). New Haven, CT: Institute for Social and Policy Studies, Yale University.

Haussermann, E. (1957). *Evaluation of educational potential in children with cerebral damage.* New York: Grune and Stratton.

Hebb, D. (1949). *The organization of behavior: A neuropsychological theory.* New York: Wiley.

Hebb, D. (1975). What is psychology about? *The American Psychologist, 30,* 635–669.

Herrnstein, R., & Murray, C. (1994). *The bell curve: Intelligence and class structure in American life.* New York: Free Press.

Hiernaux, J. (1975). *The people of Africa.* New York: Scribner's.

Hill, R. (1972). *The strengths of Black families.* New York: Emerson-Hall.

Hirsch, E. D., Jr. (1987). *Cultural literacy: What every American needs to know.* Boston: Houghton Mifflin.

Hirsch, J. (1969). Behavior genetic analysis and its biosocial consequences. *Bulletin of Information Retrieval Center of the Disadvantaged, 5,* 4, 16–20.

Hunt, D. E. (1975). Person-environment interaction: A challenge found wanting before it was tried. *Review of Educational Research, 45,* 209–230.

Illich, I. (1971) *Deschooling society.* New York: Harper & Row.

Illich, I. (Ed.). (1973). *After deschooling, what?* New York: Harper & Row.

Jackson, M. (1989*). Paths toward a clearing: Radical empiricism and ethnographic inquiry.* Bloomington: Indiana University Press.

Jaynes, G. D., & Williams, R. M. (Eds.). (1989). *A common destiny.* Washington, DC: National Academy Press.

Jencks, C. (1972). *Inequality.* New York: Basic Books.

Jensen, A. (1967). Varieties of individual differences in learning. In R. M. Gagné (Ed.), *Learning and individual differences* (pp. 165–187). Columbus, OH: Charles E. Merrill.

Jones, H. E. (1954). The environment and mental development. In L. Carmichael (Ed.), *Manual of child psychology* (pp. 631–696). New York: Wiley.

Kagan, D. (1990). E pluribus unum: All roads lead to Rome: Address to class of 1994. *Yale Daily News, 113,* 2.

Katz, I. (1967). *Desegregation or integration in public schools?* Washington, DC: U.S. Commission on Civil Rights.

Keil, F. (1990). Constraints on constraints: Surveying the epigenetic landscape. *Cognitive Science, 14,* 135–168.

Kerner, O. (1968). *The report of the National Advisory Commission on Civil Disorders.* New York: Bantam Books.

Klausmeier, H. J. (1976). Individually guided education. *Journal of Teacher Education, 27,* 199–205.

Kohlberg, L., & Kramer, R. (1969). Continuities and discontinuities in child and adult moral development. *Human Development, 12,* 93–120.

Kuhn, T. (1970). *The structure of scientific revolutions.* Chicago: University of Chicago Press.

Labov, W. (1972). *Language in the inner city: Studies in the Black English vernacular.* Philadelphia: University of Pennsylvania Press.

Lashley, K. S. (1963). *Brain mechanisms and intelligence.* New York: Dover Publications.

Lashof, J. (1965). Unpublished report to the Department of Public Health, City of Chicago.

Lau vs. Nichols (1974). U.S. Federal Court. San Francisco.

Lewin, K. (1935). *A dynamic theory of personality.* New York: McGraw-Hill.

Lightfoot, S. L., & Franklin, J. H. (1989). *Vision of a better way: A Black appraisal of public schooling.* Washington, DC: Joint Center for Political Studies Press.

Maurant, A. E. (1983). *Blood relations: Blood groups in anthropology.* New York: Oxford University Press.

Mayr, E. (1982). *The growth of biological thought.* Cambridge, MA: Belknap Press, Harvard University.

McGuire, W. J. (1983). A contextualist theory of knowledge: Its implications for innovation and reform in psychological research. In L. Berkowitz (Ed.), *Advances in experimental social psychology* (Vol. 16, pp. 1–47). New York: Academic Press.

McGuire, W. J. (1989). A perspectivist approach to the strategical planning of programmatic scientific research. In B. Golson et al. (Eds.), *The psychology of science: Contributions to metascience* (pp. 214–245). New York: Cambridge University Press.

Mead, M., Dobzhansky, T., Tobach, E., & Light, R. (Eds.) (1968). *Science and the concept of race.* New York: Columbia University Press.

Mercer, J. R. (1973). *Labeling the mentally retarded: Clinical and social system perspectives on mental retardation.* Berkeley: University of California Press.

Merton, R. K. (1972). Insiders and outsiders: A chapter in the sociology of knowledge. In H. S. Becker (Ed.), *Varieties of political expression in sociology* (pp. 9–47). Chicago: University of Chicago Press.

Messick, S. (1976). *Individuality and learning.* San Francisco: Jossey-Bass.

Messick, S. (1982). *Cognitive styles in educational practice.* Paper presented at the annual meeting of the American Educational Research Association, New York.

Miller, L. S. (1995). *An American imperative: Accelerating minority educational advancement.* New Haven: Yale University Press.

Mills, C. W. (1959). *The sociological imagination.* New York: Oxford University Press.

Murray, H. A. (1938). *Explorations in personality.* New York: Oxford University Press.

Myrdal, G. (1944). *An American dilemma: The Negro problem and modern democracy, Volumes I & II.* New York: Harper and Brothers.

Neihardt, J. G. (1959). *Black Elk speaks.* New York: Washington Square Press.

Nojan, M., Strom, C. D., & Wang, M. C. (1982, March). *Measures of degree implementation and program evaluation research.* Paper presented at the annual meeting of the American Educational Research Association, New York.

Ogbu, J. U. (1978). *Minority education and caste: The American system in cross cultural perspective* (Carnegie Council on Children Monograph). New York: Academic Press.

Pasamanick, B., & Knobloch, H. (1958). The contribution of some organic factors to school retardation in Negro children. *Journal of Negro Education, 27,* 4–9.

Pettigrew, T. F. (1968). Race and equal educational opportunity. *Harvard Educational Review, 38,* 67–78.

Piaget, J. (1973). *The psychology of intelligence.* Totawa: Littlefield and Adams.

Pliven, F., & Cloward, R. (1993). *Regulating the poor: The functions of public welfare.* New York: Dale.

Plomin, R., Defries, J., & Fulkner, D. (1988). *Nature and nurture during infancy and childhood.* New York: Cambridge University Press.

Rawls, J. (1971). *A theory of justice.* London: Oxford University Press.

Resnick, L. B. (1987). Learning in and out of school. *Educational Researcher, 16(9),* 13–20.

Rose, F., & Kamin, L. (1984). *Not in our genes: Biology, ideology and human nature.* New York: Pantheon.

Rosehan, D. L. (1967). Cultural deprivation and learning: An examination for learning. In H. L. Miller (Ed.), *Education for the disadvantaged* (pp. 38–42). New York: Free Press.

Rothkopf, E. Z. (1978). The sound of one hand plowing. *Contemporary Psychology, 123,* 707–708.

Schlesinger, A. M., Jr. (1991). *The disuniting of America.* Knoxville, TN: Whittle Direct Books.

Schulman, L. (1987). Knowledge and teaching: Foundations of the new reform. *Harvard Educational Review, 57* (1), 1–22.

Scribner, S., & Cole, M. (1981). *The psychology of literacy.* Cambridge, MA: Harvard University Press.

Scriven, M. (1972). Objectivity and subjectivity in educational research. In H. Thomas (Ed.), *Philosophical redirection of educational research* (pp. 94–142). Chicago: University of Chicago Press.

Sexton, P. (1964). *Education and income.* New York: Viking.

Shipman, S., & Shipman, V. (1988). Cognitive styles: Some conceptual, methodological and applied issues. In E. Gordon (Ed.), *Human diversity and pedagogy* (pp. 12.1–12.80). New Haven: Center in Research on Education, Culture and Ethnicity, Institution for Social and Policy Studies, Yale University.

Shuey, A. (1966). *The testing of Negro intelligence.* New York: Social Science Press.

Shweder, R. (1990). Cultural psychology—what is it? In J. W. Stigler, R. A. Shweder, & G. Herdt (Eds.), *Cultural psychology* (pp. 1–46). New York: Cambridge University Press.

Sirotnik, K. A., & Goodlad, J. (1985). The quest for reason amidst the rhetoric of reform: Improving instead of testing our schools. In W. Johnston (Ed.), *Education on trial: Strategies for the future* (pp. 277–300). San Francisco: Institute for Contemporary Studies Press.

Sizer, T. (1984). *Horace's compromise: The dilemma of the American high school.* Boston: Houghton Mifflin.

Skinner, B. F. (1954). The science of learning and the art of teaching. *Harvard Educational Review, 24,* 86–97.

Stanfield, J. (1985). The ethnocentric bias of social science knowledge production. In E. W. Gordon (Ed.), *Review of research in education* (Vol. 12, pp. 387–415). Washington, DC: American Educational Research Association.

Sternberg, R. (Ed.) (1994). *The encyclopedia of human intelligence.* New York: Macmillan.

Stewart, W. A. (1972). Black dialect. *Florida Reporter, 10, 61.*

Stigler, J., Shweder, R., & Herdt, G. (1990). *Cultural psychology: Essays on comparative human development.* New York: Cambridge University Press.

Sullivan, E. (1984). A *critical psychology.* New York: Plenum Press.

Talmage, H. (1975). *Systems of individualized education.* Berkeley, CA: McCutchan.

Taylor, C. (1971). Interpretation and the science of man. *Review of Metaphysics, 25,* 3–51.

Thomas, A., & Chess, S. (1977). *Temperament and development.* New York: Brunner/Mazel.

Tyler, R., & Wolf, R. (1974). *Crucial issues in testing.* Berkeley, CA: McCutchan.

Tyler, L. E. (1978). *Individuality: Human possibilities and personal choice in the psychological development of men and women.* San Francisco: Jossey-Bass.

Tylor, E. B. (1958). *The origins of culture.* New York: Harper Torch Books.

Von Wright, D. H. (1971). *Explanation and understanding.* Ithaca, NY: Cornell University Press.

Vygotsky, L. S. (1978). *Mind in society.* Cambridge, MA: Harvard University Press.

Wallace, A. (1961). Schools in revolutionary and conservative societies. In F. Gruber (Ed.), *Anthropology and education* (pp. 29–54). Philadelphia: University of Pennsylvania Press.

Wang, M., & Walberg, H. (Eds.). (1985). *Adapting instruction to individual differences.* Berkeley, CA: McCutchan.

Waxman, H. C., de Felix, J. W., Anderson, J. E., & Baptiste, H. P., Jr. (Eds.). (1992). *Students at risk in at-risk schools: Improving environments for learning.* Newbury Park, CA: Corwin Press.

Webster's New Collegiate Dictionary. Springfield: G&C Merriam Company, 1977.

Webster's Third New International Dictionary and Seven Language Dictionary (unabridged). Chicago: William Benton, 1966.

Weinberg, R. (1989). Intelligence and IQ: Landmark issues and great debates. *American Psychologist, 44*(2), 98–104.

Wolf, R. (1966). The measurement of environments. In A. Anastasi (Ed.), *Testing problems in perspective* (pp. 491–503). Washington, DC: American Council in Education.

Zigler, E. (1966). Mental retardation: Current research and approaches. In A. Hoffman & F. Hoffman (Eds.) *Review of child development research* (Vol. 11). New York: Russell Sage Foundation.

Index

About the Author

Edmund W. Gordon is the John M. Musser Professor of Psychology, Emeritus, at Yale University, where he also served as professor of African and African-American Studies. Professor Gordon began his career as a parish minister and later served for 5 years as the Assistant Dean of Men at Howard University. He has served as Chief Psychologist in the Department of Pediatric Psychiatry at the Jewish Hospital of Brooklyn, Research Director for the national project Head Start in the U.S. Office of Economic Opportunity, and co-founder, with his wife, of the Harriet Tubman Clinic for Children in New York City. In addition Professor Gordon has held numerous academic positions at several universities, including the Richard March Hoe Professorship in Psychology and Education at Columbia's Teachers College. He is also former director of the Center for Urban and Minority Education at the Educational Testing Service and Columbia's Teachers College. Currently he is Senior Advisor to the President of the College Board.

Professor Gordon's publications include *Compensatory Education: Preschool Through College; Educational Resilience in Inner-City America; Human Diversity & Pedagogy;* and *Equality of Educational Opportunity.* Currently he is working on *Defiers of Negative Prediction: Success Against the Odds.* He also served for 3 years as editor of the *Review of Research in Education* and 5 years as editor of the *American Journal of Orthopsychiatry.*

DATE DUE